"Richard Kyte's *An Ethical Life: A Practical Guide to Ethical Reasoning* is first-rate. It is wonderfully accessible, deeply informed, and genuinely constructive. The text's integrating theme is that the influential and contending theories arising out of Mill's utilitarianism, Kant's categorical imperative, and an Aristotelian account of the virtues can converge—creatively—in one's personal moral vision, in our shared problem-solving, and in fashioning good public policy. This creative convergence, Kyte emphasizes, depends on a healthy regard for the framework of facts that at every level are the context of moral inquiry.

A key to the text's success is the wealth of examples Kyte explores. He shows a keen awareness of particular challenges in securing a sustainable ecological balance. He is on good terms with contemporary research in moral psychology. At the same time, he is at home with both the shining lights of American philosophy and the enduring wisdom of the Greek classics, and he does not hesitate to build bridges between the insights of philosophers and the wisdom of theologians.

I warmly recommend this fresh and engaging book to anyone looking for a balanced and student-friendly introductory text in ethics."

—James G. Hanink, professor of philosophy
Loyola Marymount University

An
Ethical
Life

A PRACTICAL
GUIDE TO
ETHICAL
REASONING

Richard Kyte

Created by the publishing team of Anselm Academic.

Cover image royalty free from istockphoto.com.

Printed in the United States of America

7040

ISBN 978-1-59982-074-3

To Ian and Evan

Author Acknowledgments

My deepest gratitude goes to my wife Cindi, first reader and daily conversation partner, and to Robert Schreur, friend, poet, and critic. Many colleagues helped substantially with suggestions on improving chapters or by talking through difficult ideas: Pete Gathje of Memphis Theological Seminary; Eric Kraemer of University of Wisconsin-La Crosse; Tom Thibodeau, Jason Howard, and Matthew Bersagel-Braley of Viterbo University. Kathleen Walsh provided invaluable advice regarding chapter structure and copyediting. Deb Kappmeyer cheerfully designed the diagrams in this book. Many of the ideas presented here were first expressed in a series of columns published in the *La Crosse Tribune*, and I'm grateful to the publisher, Rusty Cunningham, and editors Chris Hardie and Scott Rada, for their kind encouragement and patience. Jerry Ruff of Anselm Academic has been a delight to work with. Finally, I would like to acknowledge my indebtedness to students over the years and to former teachers, especially Joseph Norio Uemura, Duane Cady, David Sachs, and Susan Wolf.

Publisher Acknowledgments

Thank you to the following individual who reviewed this work in progress:

Nancy Rourke
Canisius College, Buffalo, New York

Contents

Preface

WHY STUDY ETHICS? The obvious answer is to become a better person, that is, to become a better citizen, neighbor, parent, coworker, leader, teacher, or friend. How does studying ethics help one to accomplish that goal? How, in particular, does reading a textbook or taking a course in ethics help one become a better person?

In the summer of 2002, after a series of high-profile corporate scandals that shook national confidence, not to mention the financial markets, then-president George W. Bush gave a speech on Wall Street in which he declared that "our schools of business must be principled teachers of right and wrong, and not surrender to moral confusion and relativism."[1] Bush certainly was right that schools of business should not "surrender to moral confusion and relativism," but could improved courses in ethics really have prevented the failures of corporations such as Enron, WorldCom, and Tyco?

In response to the president's speech, journalist Dan Seligman wrote in *Forbes* magazine: "The sleazeball population is far less malleable than is assumed in all the talk about business schools as restorers of confidence." He added, "The 'discipline,' if ethics teaching can even be called a discipline, is hollow."[2]

Seligman is right about one thing: ethics teaching rings hollow (at least in the way it is often taught) whenever it promises to provide a quick fix to pervasive societal failings. In such a case, it is expected to do something it cannot possibly do. Imagine a college

---

1. Dan Seligman, "Oxymoron 101," *Forbes*, October 28, 2002, *http://www.forbes.com/global/2002/1028/114_print.html*.
2. Ibid.

graduate, with the benefit of the best ethics instruction money can buy. Imagine, as the poet Samuel Butler put it, that

> He was in LOGIC a great critic,
> Profoundly skill'd in analytic;
> He could distinguish, and divide
> A hair 'twixt south, and south-west side.[3]

Then imagine the graduate finds a job in a large corporate office in which favoritism, sexual harassment, conflicts of interest, and dishonesty pervade. Is it more likely that he or she manages to change the corporate culture or that the corporate culture eventually changes the employee?

So what can we expect from an ethics textbook or a course in ethics? First of all, that it does not "surrender to ethical confusion and relativism." In other words, ethics should be presented in a way that is understandable and leads to an understanding of what is true. Second, it should provide students not with the skills to "win" arguments and a determination to "fix" unethical behavior but rather with the ability and confidence to engage others in meaningful conversation about what is good and right. It should also prepare students to participate in such conversation for a lifetime, as part of the soul's journey toward the good.

This book is structured in three parts: chapter 1 addresses common misconceptions about ethics to prepare the reader for a discussion of ethical reasoning; chapter 2 introduces four ways of ethical thinking and provides a method for ethical decision making; chapters 3 through 6 analyze and illustrate the four ways of ethical thinking. In addition, an appendix discusses how to use the method in different practical contexts and provides examples of applying the method to cases and issues.

In short, this book is intended to help people think more thoroughly and consistently about ethics. It is not aimed at teaching people how to engage in debates with professional philosophers but rather how to engage in productive discussions with friends, neighbors, coworkers, family members, and fellow citizens. That requires

---

3. Samuel Butler, *Hudibras*, lines 65–69, *http://www.exclassics.com/hudibras/hudibras.txt*.

the introduction of some new concepts, and perhaps some new ways of thinking about familiar concepts, but it will not require the acquisition of an entirely new and specialized vocabulary. Indeed, a specialized vocabulary makes communicating effectively more difficult in those situations where most ethical problems arise, are discussed, and are ultimately resolved. So although this book introduces some new terms, it does so mainly to make clear the connections between what is being discussed here and what is discussed in other books and articles. The goal is always to see how far one can get in making sense of difficult problems using everyday language.

A Note to Instructors

DOZENS OF INTRODUCTORY TEXTBOOKS in ethics exist. Many of them begin with a description of various ethical theories and then show how to apply the theories to practical situations. The problems with using such a textbook are well known to instructors of ethics courses. Their use tends to (1) decrease students' confidence in their native abilities to think clearly about complex issues, (2) inculcate a distrust of deliberative processes as a means to reach agreement, and (3) create an appearance of moral relativism, either by using a misguided attempt to give "balanced" arguments on two sides of every controversial issue or by presenting overly complicated arguments that lead the reader to think that very smart people who have studied ethics for years cannot agree on what is right and wrong, so perhaps there is no definitive answer.

This textbook addresses all three of these concerns. It aims to enhance readers' confidence in their natural abilities by helping them see how moral reasoning is already embedded in the language they use every day. It also helps readers see how moral reasoning works and therefore allows them to be more effective and intentional participants in group discussions. Finally, it helps readers understand the various causes of moral disagreements so they will not be inclined to dismiss serious moral disputes as "just matters of opinion."

The emphasis on everyday moral language has another purpose, as well. Jean Piaget's groundbreaking work in the area of cognitive development[1] established, and Lawrence Kohlberg's later work on

---

1. For Piaget's research on moral development, see Jean Piaget, *The Moral Judgment of the Child* (New York: The Free Press, 1965).

moral development confirmed, that individuals are more likely to progress to higher stages of reasoning when participating in regular active discourse with people who reason at a stage just slightly above their current level of reasoning.[2] Movement from one stage to another is prompted by cognitive dissonance, or a felt dissatisfaction with one's inability to resolve problems. This dissatisfaction tends to arise when someone is faced with ethical reasoning slightly advanced from one's current stage but not when faced with ethical reasoning far beyond one's current stage. Encounters with ways of reasoning that are far beyond one's own level of reasoning tend to be reinterpreted into terms that fit a lower stage.[3]

This explains why instructors who use typical ethics textbooks may succeed in "teaching theories" while often failing to help students make progress in their own moral reasoning. The theories that are introduced and then applied to cases often represent an advanced stage of moral reasoning, well beyond the current reasoning level of many of the students in the classroom. The result is that students learn the terminology of the theories but do not actually make significant cognitive moral progress.

The key to this book is its presentation of four ways of thinking in language already familiar to readers who speak everyday English. (It also describes the relationship of these ways of thinking to the main ethical theories, but that is chiefly for the benefit of the instructor and students who will go on to study ethics in more advanced classes.) This allows students to talk confidently with one another about how to resolve complex issues, and it allows them to be in regular conversation with people who reason at, below, and above their own level of reasoning, thus providing opportunities for cognitive dissonance and subsequent moral progress.

---

2. In other words, a person reasoning at stage three on Kohlberg's scale is more likely to advance to stage four through regular conversation with people who reason at stage four than through conversation with people who reason at stage five or stage six. Lawrence Kohlberg, *Essays on Moral Development, Vol. 1: The Philosophy of Moral Development* (San Francisco: Harper and Row, 1981).

3. See James Rest, "The Hierarchical Nature of Moral Judgment: A Study of Patterns of Comprehension and Preference of Moral Stages," *Journal of Personality* 41 (1973): 86–109.

Concepts and Misconceptions

TO ENGAGE IN ETHICS is to engage in a particular type of human activity, one that involves thinking and talking about how we should act—what we should do, say, think, or even feel in certain situations. Like many kinds of activities, ethics is not a simple, straightforward matter. Various ways of thinking and talking constitute "doing ethics," just as many different sorts of actions constitute doing science; for example, hypothesizing, gathering evidence, evaluating, and measuring. Just as it is essential to know the difference between forming a hypothesis and gathering evidence in the scientific realm, it is important to know the difference between the diverse types of thinking that constitute ethics. Examining these—learning how to use them better and to recognize when others are using them—is the chief focus of this book.

Thinking more clearly and consistently about ethical issues requires having a shared understanding of what ethics is. Part of developing a shared understanding consists of finding out what terms mean in order to use them in ways that enhance rather than detract from productive discussion. When the terms we are interested in learning about are already widely used in our society and are used in many different ways by different people, it is necessary first to address common misconceptions before examining how to use ethical language more constructively. Addressing common misconceptions in ethics will remove some potentially serious obstacles at the outset.

MISCONCEPTION 1:
ETHICS AND MORALITY ARE DISTINCT

The terms *ethics* and *morality* both originally referred to the same thing. The Latin term *mores* was a translation of the Greek term *ethike*, and they both meant something like "custom" or "habit." The closest contemporary equivalent would probably be what sociologists call a norm, a social standard or expectation of appropriate behavior. The meanings of words change over time, though, and during the past one hundred years or so the terms *ethics* and *morality* have begun to drift apart. Most people now tend to use the term *ethics* when referring to the study of appropriate behavior in public or professional contexts and to use the term *morality* when the behavior referred to is relatively personal or private. Because we as a society have also come to think of religion as belonging primarily to the private rather than to the public sphere, we have come to use the term *morality* in connection with religion. Hence, we refer to legal ethics, health care ethics, and business ethics, because these are regarded as areas of public accountability. One rarely hears someone speak of legal morality or health care morality, but people will refer to Christian morality or to an individual's personal morality.

Despite the different senses that the terms *ethics* and *morality* have acquired, in many contexts the terms may be used interchangeably because there is little benefit in making a hard and fast distinction between the two terms. Indeed, such a distinction, as we shall see later, cannot be philosophically defended, since ethical (or moral) decisions arise primarily in the context of relationships. Even actions normally considered personal or private often have public implications. For example, my decision to stay up late last night watching television has made me irritable this morning and affected how I interact with my coworkers. Is the question of whether I should have stayed up late last night a matter of ethics or morality? In a case such as this, using one term or the other matters little in helping answer the question of what I should have done. This is not to say that there is no difference between private actions and public actions. There is significant difference, which is important to observe when discussing, for example, what kinds of behavior governments may legitimately regulate or what kinds of rules an employer may impose upon an employee.

In the remainder of this book, the terms *ethics* and *morality* will be used, for the most part, interchangeably, with no great significance attached to slight differences in meaning between the two.

MISCONCEPTION 2:
ETHICS IS "NOTHING BUT WORDS"

A fairly frequent objection to the study of ethics—actually, to the study of philosophy in general—is that it consists of "nothing but words." Although the study of ethics, like the study of most things, is done primarily in words, assuming that words amount to nothing is a mistake. Words matter immensely.

The laws that shape our society are made up of words. Oaths and vows, which mark the most significant passages in our lives, are composed of words. Wars are begun with a declaration and ended with a treaty built from words. Long-standing relationships are broken up by an insult and repaired with an apology. Without words we would not have a recognizably human life at all.

No one would think of saying to an engineer, "What you do is nothing but numbers." If an engineer gets his calculations wrong, terrible things may happen: bridges may fail, buildings may collapse, or oil rigs may blow up. What happens if we get crucial words wrong? What if a jury misunderstands instructions from a judge? What if a pharmacist misreads a prescription from a physician? What if a college student studies the wrong material for an exam?

One person who fully appreciated the importance of words for human life was the Greek philosopher Socrates (469–399 BCE). Of all the memorable expressions attributed to him, the best known is this: "The unexamined life is not worth living." The way in which one examines one's life is with words—by reading, and writing, and, most importantly, talking. The rest of the sentence reads: ". . . I say that it is the greatest good for a man to discuss virtue every day . . . for the unexamined life is not worth living. . . ."[1] Socrates put his life on the line for words and for what they can do to shape human life

---

1. Plato, *Apology*, in *The Trial and Death of Socrates*, trans. G.M.A. Grube (Indianapolis, IN: Hackett, 1975), 38a, 39.

in society. He uttered these particular words while on trial, charged with corrupting the youth and believing in false gods. At the end of the trial he was found guilty by a jury of about five hundred citizens and executed a short time later.

SOCRATES (469–399 BCE)

Socrates

© Nick Pavlakis/Shutterstock

More has been written about Socrates than perhaps any other philosopher in history, yet we actually know very little about him. He wrote nothing himself, and most of the stories and legends passed down about him came from dialogues written after his death by his student Plato. From those dialogues, and a few other sources from the same era, historians have pieced together a compelling portrait of an original, courageous, and controversial thinker who has continued to inspire people for over two thousand years.

Socrates was a citizen of Athens, Greece, during the height of that city's cultural achievements, but it was also a time of war with Sparta and Persia, internal political turbulence, and revolution. He was a polarizing figure, spending most days in the agora (or marketplace) having conversations with leading figures in the city about how best to live one's life. Those conversations attracted a great deal of attention, especially from young men who would gather to listen to the dialogues and then try to emulate his method.

Socrates developed a method of question-and-answer dialogue (called *dialectic* or "the Socratic method") in which he would ask for a definition of some key term, and when the definition was provided would point out difficulties or inconsistencies in the answer, which would then call forth a new definition, to which he would point out additional problems,

Continued

Socrates *Continued*

and so on. His purpose in such dialogues was to help people see for themselves what is true and false.

Although Socrates was a citizen, he was poor and lived a simple, some would even say ascetic, lifestyle. He was probably a stonecutter by trade, though he seems never to have practiced it, preferring to spend his days talking. He wore the same cloak year round and went about barefoot, even in the winter. The only times he ventured beyond the city walls were when he went on military campaigns, serving as a citizen soldier. He served with distinction on those occasions, even saving the lives of fellow soldiers during a retreat.

In 399 Socrates was charged with the capital crimes of believing in false gods and corrupting the youth. He was tried and convicted by a jury of about five hundred citizens and executed a short time later by being compelled to drink a cup of poison hemlock.

Socrates' enduring influence is chiefly due to three things: (1) his question-and-answer method of inquiry; (2) his insistence that all wrongdoing is the result of ignorance; and (3) the calmness and courage with which he faced death.

Most would perhaps agree that the greatest good is to be virtuous every day. But to discuss virtue? Did Socrates really mean that discussing virtue is more important than being virtuous, that words are more important than actions?

Let us assume that he chose his words carefully.[2] First, he said that discussing virtue is the "greatest good." Such a claim would not make sense if one already possessed a clear understanding of how one ought to act. But suppose one doesn't already have such clear understanding. One could then make sense of Socrates' claim as meaning

---

2. This is known as a "charitable" interpretation of a text. An interpretation is charitable when credit is given to the author for the intentional use of her or his words. An interpretation is uncharitable when the reader assumes that the author didn't choose the words carefully or didn't understand what the words meant. As a general rule, it is a good idea to give the benefit of the doubt to authors for understanding and intending their own words, unless one has some good reason for thinking otherwise.

something like: as long as we don't already *know* how we ought to act, the most important thing to do is to *find out* how we ought to act. Second, by "discuss virtue," Socrates most likely means we don't discover what is good simply by observing or imitating others, nor simply by meditating or reflecting on what we should do. We find out how we should live by talking to others. Finally, we must engage in such talk "every day." We shouldn't wait until we have a problem in urgent need of resolution, nor should we think just reading a book or taking an ethics course will give us sufficient knowledge of ethics. On the contrary, ethics is a matter of gradually acquiring an understanding of how one should live through daily discussions with others throughout one's lifetime.

MISCONCEPTION 3:
ETHICS IS JUST A MATTER OF OPINION

Who decides what counts as ethical? Who decides what is right or wrong, good or bad, when a dispute arises among people about what to do?

The difficulty in answering this question is one of the reasons people sometimes give up on ethics and declare it is "all just a matter of opinion." In a sense, that is correct: ethics is a matter of opinion. Then again, not all opinions are equal. Some opinions are true and some are false, and it is important to know the difference. It may be my opinion, for example, that it is raining outside right now, but that is not *just* an opinion; it is also a statement about something that is either true or false independently of what I happen to think. It is a statement of fact.

Ethical statements are both like and unlike factual statements. One interesting characteristic of ethical statements is that they almost always indicate the speaker's attitude about the topic under discussion. For example, if I say, "lying is wrong," you can be fairly confident that I disapprove of lying. That is not the case with most factual claims a person makes during the course of a day. If I say, "It is raining outside," you would not be able to tell (apart from tone of voice or facial expression) whether I was delighted or disappointed by the rain.

In this respect moral statements are similar to expressions of personal opinion. If I were to say, for instance, "Broccoli is delicious," or "Bob Dylan is a fantastic songwriter," you would be justified in believing that I like to eat broccoli and listen to Bob Dylan's music.

This similarity may lead some people to equate moral statements with statements of opinion, but there is a significant difference between the two. When I make a personal statement, I am really just telling you something about myself (my attitude toward something), whereas when I make a moral statement, I am telling you something both about myself (my attitude toward something) and about something external to myself (the thing I'm talking about). That explains why people can have a meaningful disagreement about moral statements but not about personal statements. If you objected to my claim that broccoli is delicious, we would just have to conclude that our tastes differ: I like broccoli and you don't. The fact that you do not find it delicious does not mean I was wrong to say it is. Both of us are just trying to make clear to the other what we ourselves like to eat. We are not making an objective (that is, independently verifiable) claim about the nature of broccoli.

Disagreement about moral statements results in a very different situation. If I say "lying is wrong" and you say "lying is permissible," we are doing more than merely insisting that we have different *feelings* about lying. I am saying both that *I* dislike lying and that *you* (among others) should not tell lies. Whereas you are saying that *you* do not dislike lying and that it would be okay if *I* (among others) occasionally tell lies. Because we are making claims about what would be appropriate for others to do, it would be reasonable for me to ask you to give *reasons* for thinking that lying is permissible or for you to ask me for reasons why I think lying is wrong. In other words it is perfectly normal to have rational arguments about whether certain actions are right or wrong, good or bad, in the same way that it is perfectly normal to have rational arguments over a variety of factual claims, like whether it is raining outside, whether there was once life on Mars, or whether the Cubs will ever win the World Series. We could not have a rational argument over whether broccoli tastes good. In matters of personal opinion, once we make clear our different preferences, the discussion is over. There is no room for meaningful disagreement.

This demonstrates that moral statements are not merely statements of personal opinion. They resemble personal opinion in that they typically reveal our attitudes about something, but they are also like factual statements in that they assert something about the world outside us, something that may be either true or false.

Another reason why some people think of ethics as just a matter of opinion is that it seems like so little progress is made in settling ethical disputes. Some controversies in our society, like abortion and capital punishment, seem to go on and on without resolution. Moreover, very good people take up positions on both sides of the controversies. Because ethics textbooks and courses tend to focus mainly on the difficult controversies, it may appear that ethical agreement is a rare thing and that the arguments on each side of a controversy have roughly equal merit. That is a deceptive appearance. There is near universal agreement across cultures about fundamental ethical behavior.[3]

Ethicists find most disagreement in those cases where it is difficult to agree on what kind of behavior a certain action is. For example, nearly everyone agrees that people should not tell lies, but when it comes to whether someone should tell a lie to save another person from harm, we do not find such universal agreement. This does not mean that the permissibility of lying is a matter of opinion; it just means that people do not share a thorough and consistent understanding of what constitutes a lie in every instance.[4] Likewise, nearly everyone agrees that it is wrong to commit murder, but they may disagree about what falls under the description of murder. Is it murder to kill a fetus? Is it murder to kill a murderer? These questions are admittedly difficult and finding answers that result in widespread agreement even more so. But consider all the actions a typical person performs in the course of a day that are morally unproblematic, and then compare that to the number of actions per day society would consider to be deeply controversial. To insist that all of ethics is just

3. See, for example, the discussion in chapter 5 of the "Golden Rule," many versions of which are found throughout the world.

4. There is a long history of attempts by philosophers to define lying. For a recent effort, see Thomas L. Carson, "Lying, Deception, and Related Concepts" in *The Philosophy of Deception*, ed. Clancy Martin (New York: Oxford University Press, 2009), 153–187.

a matter of opinion because of difficulties resolving the (relatively few) controversial cases, would be like insisting that the difference between night and day is a matter of opinion because we cannot agree on the precise times of sunrise and sunset.

Why should ethics be different from any other area of academic study? Every discipline has its points of agreement and disagreement. Economists, for example, nearly all agree that spending stimulates the economy, but they disagree about how much debt should be encouraged to increase spending. The fact that sincere and competent economists disagree does not reduce economics to a matter of opinion. It means that economies are extremely complex and difficult to understand. The same goes for ethics.[5] The world is complex, and so the study of how human beings should act in the world is a difficult subject. This does not mean ethics is just a matter of opinion; it does, however, call for a certain amount of caution, especially in areas where there is significant disagreement. Claims of moral certainty should not extend beyond one's understanding of the issues.

MISCONCEPTION 4:
ETHICS CONSISTS OF A SET OF VALUES

It has become commonplace to talk about people's ethical beliefs as "values": we speak of "personal values," "shared values," "value statements," and "corporate values." Yet, what does it mean to say that I (or we) value something?

Houses, cars, books, coffeemakers, and bicycles have value. How much? Whatever someone is willing to pay for them. Some items may also have personal or sentimental value, things like family photographs or heirlooms. We might say such things are "priceless"; in other words, we wouldn't take any amount of money for them. But the underlying assumption about anything we value is that it has a certain amount of worth. The relevant question is always, "How much worth does it have?"

---

5. It could be argued that there is a great deal more subjectivity in ethics than in other fields of study. The point of this section of the book is simply to insist that such a claim must be argued for and supported with good reasons; it cannot simply be assumed on the basis of disagreements within the field.

In that context, what does it mean to say, for example, that I value honesty? Does it mean I think it is important? How important? What if I would be greatly embarrassed by admitting I had done something, so I decided to tell a lie? Would that mean I do not value honesty, or would it mean merely that I value it less than avoiding embarrassment? Could it perhaps mean that I did value honesty in the past, but now, in this circumstance, I don't? However, that would not rule out the possibility that I may value it again in the future—say, right after I finish telling a lie.

Such questions indicate one of the problems with value terminology: it is hopelessly vague. Saying one values something doesn't commit one to any particular behavior. It expresses little more than a positive attitude toward something, and ethics, as we will see, is a great deal more than positive attitude.

This does not mean that the term *value* has no place in the discussion of ethics. Many daily ethical decisions consist of choices among competing values. For instance, if I value my friendship with Tom, and I haven't spent much time with him recently, I may decide to go have coffee with him instead of going fishing, an activity I value. From the time we wake up in the morning until we go to sleep at night we are making choices about things we value. But merely noting that we value a number of things doesn't help us choose as we should. Nor does the activity of clarifying our values, insofar as that is even possible, help us ensure the goodness or appropriateness of our choices, for the question always remains whether we *ought* to value various things to the extent we do.

Values language misleads when it replaces the language of ethics. It suggests something stronger than personal preference while not actually committing the person to anything more than personal preference. For example, people will frequently defend their position with regard to the abortion controversy by referring to their values. Those who generally oppose laws that would permit abortions are called "pro-life," and those who generally favor laws that would loosen restrictions on abortion procedures are called "pro-choice." The problem is this: nearly everyone on both sides of the controversy values both life and choice. Few rational people will argue that human life or freedom is unimportant. So the terms *life* and *choice*, which in this context refer to what people value, do not provide any substantial reason for why people take the positions they do on the abortion issue.

Values language remains popular because it allows one to enjoy the illusion of having reasons for one's choices without having to do the hard work of figuring out and then expressing those reasons in ways that make sense to others. That's comforting because, in many cases, our reasons are inadequate to fully support our actions. When engaging in serious ethical disputes or facing hard choices about how to live, we want to be able to do more than just express preferences. We want to be able to give reasons that will be persuasive or even compelling. We want to be able to explain why we think certain actions are good or right, and to do that well requires something more robust than the language of values.

MISCONCEPTION 5:
ETHICS CONSISTS OF MORAL ABSOLUTES

People often use the term *moral absolute* to claim that certain kinds of behavior, for example, lying or murder, are always and everywhere wrong and that there are no exceptions. The trouble with this thinking is that it just isn't helpful. The hard work of ethics is not determining whether, for example, it is wrong to lie: every culture in the world agrees it is. The difficult part is determining what counts as a lie. That's where cultures and individuals differ. Insisting that "lying is wrong" is a moral absolute does not help anyone determine whether a certain action—say, misleading one's friend about his surprise birthday party or failing to provide complete information about a car when trying to sell it—is or is not a lie.[6] The same goes for the idea of murder, which is universally acknowledged as morally prohibited. The problem is in defining what constitutes murder. Is all intentional killing murder, or only the killing of innocents? In a country at war, are all civilians innocent? What about children who

---

6. I would argue that the first example is not a lie and the second example is a lie, but that argument will have to wait for further explanation; the important point here is that the idea of moral absolutes is not helpful in deliberating about what is right or wrong. Fuller consideration of whether certain actions may be morally wrong in every instance is taken up in chapter 5.

are being used to transport ammunition to combatants? Is it murder to execute a justly convicted criminal? Is it murder to destroy a human embryo? These are all examples of important questions that are not settled by declaring that the prohibition against murder is a moral absolute.

Once we agree that moral statements may be either true or false and that reasons are required to support moral statements, nothing more is gained by insisting that moral claims are absolute. The difficult work of moral reasoning consists of figuring out, through careful deliberation, which claims are true and which are false and in what sense. This requires close attention to the meanings of words and their context. If asserting that moral claims are absolutes means that moral terms are somehow immune to the contextual ambiguity that affects all human language, then the assertion is false. If it simply means that some moral claims are true and others are false and that they are not merely a matter of opinion, then, yes, that is the case (see misconception 3).

MISCONCEPTION 6:
ETHICS CONSISTS OF A SET OF RULES

Many people assume ethics is about what one *has* to do, not about what one *wants* to do, that it is a matter of "following the rules."

The typical family has more than two hundred rules that apply to daily behavior inside the house—rules like, "Don't slam the door," "Turn off the light when you leave the bathroom," or "Put your dirty clothes in the laundry basket."[7] Hundreds more guide behavior outside the house—in the yard, in the car, at the grocery store, in a restaurant—and for special occasions, such as visiting relatives or going on a vacation or to a movie theater. Schools, of course, are notorious for the number of rules they impose, and most workplaces are equally demanding, with some large corporations having layers upon layers of rules issuing from various departments, agencies, and governing bodies.

---

7. Denis Wood and Robert J. Beck, *Home Rules* (Baltimore: Johns Hopkins University Press, 1994).

In the last thirty years or so, society has increasingly used the term *ethics* in the context of rules oversight and enforcement. Thus there are ethics compliance officers in many corporations; ethics commissions in federal, state, and local governments; health care ethics committees in hospitals; and professional ethics committees of the state bar associations. The list goes on and on. What they all have in common is the task of creating, implementing, and in some cases, enforcing rules and policies that, in effect, restrict people's freedom. Such restrictions are generally well intended. They aim to protect people from injury or abuse of power. There are laws prohibiting pollution, sexual harassment, bullying, and conflicts of interest: all are meant to protect people. Yet, ethics is more than just restrictions on behavior.

Thinking about ethics primarily in terms of rules for behavior is a relatively new development. For at least two thousand years, up until quite recently in our history, happiness was widely regarded as central to any robust understanding of the ethical life. This view goes back to the Greek philosopher Aristotle (384–322 BCE), who claimed that happiness was the highest good, that is, the thing everyone seeks and the ultimate reason we do everything we do. By happiness, he didn't mean a temporary state of amusement or pleasure (such as one might get from watching a funny TV show or getting a new car); he meant instead a lasting and deep-seated condition, something we might refer to as "satisfaction" or "fulfillment."

Somewhere along the way, the term *ethics* was applied to what used to be called, more simply and directly, rules, regulations, laws, policies, etiquette, or civility. A couple of dangers come along with this change in language.

The first danger is a tendency to think that the only way to create a more ethical society (or organization or family) is to put more rules in place. In fact the opposite is true. An overemphasis on rules corresponds to an underemphasis on character. Character, not rules, constitutes the heart of ethics.[8] As Plato observed, good people don't need rules to make them do what is right, and bad people will find ways around rules. Of those who try to stop people from acting irresponsibly through legislation, he says, "They always think they'll find

---

8. For a defense of this claim, see chapter 6 on "Character."

a way to put a stop to cheating on contracts and [so on], not realizing that they're really just cutting off a Hydra's head."[9]

The second danger consists of losing sight of the point of ethics and thinking that the various rules, regulations, and policies that authorities put in place are, in themselves, the determinants of right and wrong. But if we have no conception of ethics that goes beyond the rules, how do we know when the rules themselves are unethical? How do we find the words to express our sense that something we are required to do is not right?

As any child can attest, parents can have rules that are nonsensical, contradictory, or flat-out unfair. Bosses can implement rules that are counterproductive, self-serving, or even demeaning. And a common complaint about governmental bureaucracies is that they produce rules that at times appear designed to set up unnecessary obstacles. Ethics cannot consist of any particular set of rules because we need a standard against which to evaluate whether various activities—and the rules put in place to govern them—are genuinely good or merely arbitrary.

Ethics is what supplies the reasons for various rules (laws, policies, procedures). An action is never right or wrong just because there is a rule in place; rather, rules are put in place because someone wants to reinforce certain types of behavior. And if good (i.e., ethical) reasons support the rule, then (generally speaking) it is right to follow the rule. The important thing to note is that ethics determines whether a rule is right or wrong, not vice versa.

MISCONCEPTION 7:
EACH PERSON DECIDES WHAT IS ETHICAL

Occasionally one may hear someone say something like "What's right for you is different than what's right for me," or "Everybody has to decide for themselves what's right and wrong," or "You shouldn't impose your morality on someone else." Such sentiments express the

---

9. Plato, *Republic*, trans. G.M.A. Grube, rev. C.D.C. Reeve (Indianapolis: Hackett, 1992), 426e, 102. In Greek mythology the Hydra is a serpent with many heads. Every time one head is cut off, two grow back in its place.

notion that ethics is an individual choice. This is known as *egoism*, the doctrine that the scope of ethical statements is limited to the person who makes the statement. In other words, if I say it is wrong to lie, what I really mean is that it is wrong for *me* to lie.

There is an element of truth in this notion, namely, that we should be cautious about thinking we understand enough about another's situation to determine how that person should act. However, the idea that a person cannot make ethical judgments for and about others is contradicted by the ways in which people actually do make and employ ethical judgments. For example, Andrea believes people must decide right and wrong for themselves, and she also happens to think it is wrong to steal. According to the doctrine of egoism, her ethical statement merely means it is wrong for *her* to steal—other people must decide for themselves whether stealing is wrong for them. Then suppose Tim comes along and steals Andrea's bicycle. Would Andrea have to ask Tim whether he thinks stealing is wrong before she could object to what he did? If Tim said he didn't find anything wrong with stealing, would that mean Andrea would have to think it was okay for Tim to steal her bicycle? After all, he had to decide right and wrong for himself, and he decided that stealing was not wrong. Notice, however, that if Andrea wanted to get her bicycle back, she would have to ask Tim's permission to take it; she couldn't just take it back without asking. After all, that would be stealing, and by her own admission, Andrea believes stealing is wrong.

This is a preposterous situation. Few people actually limit their ethical judgments to themselves in practical situations. Calling ethics a matter of individual choice is equivalent to saying there is no such thing as ethics; it reduces all talk of right and wrong to questions of personal opinion (likes and dislikes). But, as shown earlier in this chapter, ethical statements are not just statements of personal opinion; they make claims about what *we ourselves and others* should or should not do. If Andrea really believes it is wrong to steal, then that implies, among other things, that she thinks people should not take other people's bicycles without permission. If she thinks that, then she does not really believe that all people must decide right and wrong for themselves. She cannot believe both things at the same time without being logically inconsistent.

MISCONCEPTION 8:
CONSCIENCE DECIDES WHAT IS ETHICAL

"You should always do what you think is right." This is generally good advice, except, however, when what a person thinks is right, isn't. How does one know when moral judgments are reliable?

The capacity for making moral judgments is sometimes referred to as conscience. One could call this a sense of right and wrong or moral sense. In most instances, it is probably best to follow our conscience when a situation arises that requires a quick decision. At other times, when the need for action is not immediate, it is more important to examine one's conscience, to figure out through critical conversation with others how one should act, because conscience is not an infallible guide.

In a famous passage from *The Adventures of Huckleberry Finn*, Huck is floating down the Mississippi River on a raft with Jim, a slave who has escaped from Miss Watson.[10] Huck likes Jim and considers him a friend, but he also considers Jim to be the property of another character in the book, and he believes that helping Jim escape is wrong because it is stealing. He wants to help Jim escape, but he thinks it wrong to do so.

> I tried to make out to myself that *I* warn't to blame, because *I* didn't run Jim off from his rightful owner; but it warn't no use, conscience up and says, every time, "But you knowed he was running for his freedom, and you could a paddled ashore and told somebody." That was so—I couldn't get around that, noway. . . . My conscience got to stirring me up hotter than ever, until at last I says to it, "Let up on me—it ain't too late, yet—I'll paddle ashore at the first light, and tell."[11]

A short time later, when Huck has an opportunity to turn Jim over to some men searching for him, he doesn't do it. He instead

---

10. For a well-known interpretation of this passage, see Jonathan Bennett, "The Conscience of Huckleberry Finn," in *Philosophy* 49 (1974): 123–134.

11. Mark Twain, *The Adventures of Huckleberry Finn*, 2nd ed., Sculley Bradley, Richmond Croom Beatty, E. Hudson Long, and Thomas Cooley (New York: W. W. Norton, 1977), 73–74.

makes up a tale about smallpox that causes the men to steer clear of the raft. But he doesn't feel good about it. He still thinks he did something wrong by saving Jim.

> They went off and I got aboard the raft, feeling bad and low, because I knowed very well I had done wrong, and I see it warn't no use for me to try to learn to do right; a body that don't get *started* right when he's little ain't got no show—when the pinch comes there ain't nothing to back him up and keep him to his work, and so he gets beat. Then I thought a minute, and says to myself, hold on,—s'pose you'd a done right and give Jim up; would you felt better than what you do now? No, says I, I'd feel bad—I'd feel just the same way I do now. Well, then, says I, what's the use you learning to do right when it's troublesome to do right and ain't no trouble to do wrong, and the wages is just the same? I was stuck. I couldn't answer that. So I reckoned I wouldn't bother no more about it, but after this always do whichever come handiest at the time.[12]

Huck feels inclined to give up on ethics altogether because he is convinced that doing what is right is the same as doing what his conscience tells him to do, and in this case conscience is telling him to do something that feels wrong. Huck's conscience is personified, so that it seems to him like an indisputable voice of authority on all matters of right and wrong conduct. That makes it harder for him to question it. He has no way of distinguishing the different sources of moral judgment, such as what he has learned through friendship, what he has been explicitly taught, and what he has acquired through the experience of growing up white in a racist culture. By acknowledging that conscience is really just a set of internal judgments about how to act and that such judgments are by no means infallible, we can take measures to avoid Huck's dilemma.

When somebody says, "You should always do what you think is right," the proper response is simply to say, "No, you should always do what *is* right, whether you think it is right or not." Of course, that is easier said than done, because how can one do what is right when

---

12. Ibid., 76.

one thinks it is wrong? But recalling what Socrates said in the *Apology* proves instructive: "It is the greatest good to discuss virtue every day. . . ." The study of ethics is important precisely because no one possesses an infallible guide (as Huck Finn imagines his conscience to be) to tell us how to live. Figuring out how to live well requires daily conversations with others, so when the time comes to act, we may do so on the basis of our considered judgments, which is the best we can do.

MISCONCEPTION 9:
EXPERTS DECIDE WHAT IS ETHICAL

If we cannot rely on conscience to provide guidance in difficult circumstances, and if the only way to determine right or wrong is by developing the capacity for moral judgment, what do we do in the meantime? Can we look to experts to guide us about what to do and how to live? Perhaps in some cases, but ethics is not a field that lends itself to expertise, unless by *ethics* we mean some narrowly defined context, such as biomedical ethics in a particular health care system or legal ethics in a particular state (where the state bar association has published a set of ethics rules or guidelines for attorneys licensed to practice in the state). In such contexts an ethics "expert" is somebody who knows the agreed-upon rules in the profession and has experience interpreting how those rules apply to particular cases. Seeking ethical advice from an expert (in such contexts) is similar to seeking advice on fishing from a fishing guide or seeking advice on building a house from an experienced contractor.

When talking about ethics in general, the person who studies ethics for a living generally does not possess the kind of knowledge or authority required for expertise. The world is just too large, and the variety of ways in which human beings interact with one another is too great, for a single person to be able to make repeatedly reliable judgments. That is not to say that some people don't know more than others about how to live well or that there is no benefit to studying ethics. It points out, instead, that the benefit of studying ethics is a better knowledge of how to use ethical language precisely and consistently, so the discussion of ethical issues is more fruitful than it would be otherwise.

In ancient Athens individuals called sophists claimed to be able to teach others how to win arguments. Their name came from the Greek term *sophia*, which means "wisdom," and they were widely regarded as knowing how to tell the true from the false and the good from the bad. Even more significantly, they were regarded as knowing how to teach others how to know those things as well, and wealthy citizens would pay the sophists a great deal of money to teach their male children[13] how to win arguments in public debates and become successful, honored citizens. In contrast to the sophists, Socrates described himself as a philosopher (from the Greek terms *philo*, or "love," and *sophia*, or "wisdom"). In other words, he described himself not as having wisdom, but as loving—or desiring—wisdom. Thus his favorite method of discussion consisted of asking questions, partly to learn more for himself, but primarily as a way of helping others learn.

Socrates understood that one of the problems with "experts" in ethics has to do with how words are interpreted, so he was always asking people to articulate and defend their ideas about how to act.[14] The most important part of learning to be a moral agent is learning to see the world (people, things, activities) in a certain way. If the moral perception of the listener does not fit well with the moral perception of the speaker, the listener cannot recognize the sense in which the words are spoken. Thus a great deal of ethics consists of talking with others in an attempt to reach a shared understanding of the meaning of words.

One kind of ethics "expert" is the professional philosopher who writes or teaches classes about ethics. People who do this for a living

---

13. In Athens at that time, girls were not given the same kind of education as boys, because only men were citizens, and women were not expected to play a public role in the life of the city.

14. A particularly good example of this method occurs in the *Euthyphro*, where Socrates questions Euthyphro about why he thinks it is right to charge his own father with murder. Readers of Plato's dialogues often express frustration at the way in which Socrates interrogates his subjects without offering his own judgment about how to act in the situation in question, but that is to miss the point that there is no advice Socrates could give that would be practically relevant to his subject. What Euthyphro—and the reader who identifies with Euthyphro—needs is not a moral rule to follow but rather the willingness to surrender his certainty so he will start paying attention to what is significant.

are sometimes expected to know something more than or different from what the average person does. Professional philosophers
(for the most part) know theories, which help people make sense
of things that go on in the world.[15] Theories provide explanations
and reveal patterns in events that might otherwise be confusing. By
understanding the theories, and the rich variety of concepts that go
along with them, the philosopher can help people reason clearly and
consistently about their actions. However, that kind of knowledge
does not necessarily make one better at figuring out how to act in a
particular situation, especially if the situation is complex and requires
specialized knowledge of the practical circumstances involved to
understand adequately. For example, the typical philosopher would
not be good at determining what military officers facing an ethical
dilemma in a battlefield situation should do; however, the philosopher may help the officers figure things out for themselves, by listening carefully to their reasoning, spotting inconsistencies or errors of
reasoning, suggesting they think about things in different ways, and
so on.

Understanding the nuances and complexities of what is going
on in a particular setting is one kind of skill; understanding how to
use ethical concepts clearly and consistently is another. Competent
ethical reasoning requires both. Sometimes (as discussed in chapter 2)
that means more than one person needs to be involved in the decision making for ethical reasoning to reach a satisfactory conclusion.

Another kind of ethics "expert" in our society is the advice col-
umnist. There have been several popular and respected ones over the
years, such as Ann Landers and Abigail van Buren. Currently, Amy
Dickinson writes a daily advice column titled "Ask Amy," which
appears online and in newspapers all over the United States. Sometimes the advice-seeker just wants some straightforward information,
and such advice is generally not problematic. Frequently, however,
the advice-seeker wants help interpreting the significance of certain
events in life, and in such cases it remains unclear whether the person
who needs the advice has the ability to understand and then follow
the kind of advice Dickinson is prepared to give.

---

15. There are many kinds of ethical theories. Some of the more prominent, such as
utilitarianism and *deontology*, will be discussed later in this book.

In a recent "Ask Amy" column, the writer "Baffled Bride" wanted to know whether she was justified in scheduling her wedding just two weeks before her cousin's wedding. Her mother was upset because two large weddings so close together would be stressful for the family, but Baffled thought her wedding should come first, because she had been engaged for eighteen months and her cousin had been engaged for only eleven months.

What kind of advice could possibly be useful in a situation like this? Dickinson tells Baffled she is being "petty and just a little hostile," and she should change her wedding date. It is good advice, but will it do any good? Will someone who thinks a wedding is a competition be able to understand why she should change the date?

Such situations occur regularly in most of our lives. Over the years they have made excellent material for novelists. In Jane Austen's *Pride and Prejudice*, Lydia is discovered to have run off with the disreputable Mr. Wickham. Her older sister, Elizabeth, reflecting on the lack of judgment that must have led to such a foolish action, observes that Lydia "has never been taught to think on serious subjects; and for the last half-year . . . has been given up to nothing but amusement and vanity. She has been allowed to dispose of her time in the most idle and frivolous manner, and to adopt any opinions that came in her way."[16] It turns out that even after Lydia's reputation has been saved by the timely intervention of her uncle and Mr. Darcy, she remains unable to appreciate her own foolishness. She refuses to listen to any conversation that calls her behavior into question.

Austen's novels consist mostly of dialogue. She seems to know that doing what is right requires understanding what is right and that understanding comes through discussion. Recall, once again, the statement by Socrates: "The greatest good is to discuss virtue every day . . . for the unexamined life is not worth living for human beings." Such a claim would not make sense for people who possess a clear and complete understanding of how they should act in the wide variety of circumstances that life presents, but nobody has such comprehensive understanding. The great virtue of Austen's novels is

---

16. Jane Austen, *Pride and Prejudice*, in *The Complete Novels* (New York: Penguin Classics, 2006), 363.

that the most admirable characters are not the ones who think themselves perfect but rather the ones who are troubled by their inability to know what to do, and who therefore persist in talking, questioning, and being questioned.

Like Austen and Plato, Amy Dickinson seems to understand that no set of rules will provide infallible guidance on how to live—no foolproof rules, that is, for how to run a company, how to raise children, or how to be a friend. Rules are only as reliable as the judgment of the person who comprehends them. Acquiring good judgment does not happen in a few hours or a few days. One can't go to the library and check out a copy of *Good Judgment for Dummies*. But one can talk about how to live. One can keep trying to figure things out, a little bit at a time.

It may be the case that advice is least useful for the person who needs it most. But a good advice column may help the reader for whom it constitutes a small part of her daily conversation about how to live well.

This alerts us to the real function of an "ethics expert" in a society. He or she does not solve particular ethical problems facing people, but rather helps people—whether readers of an advice column or students in a classroom—enhance their moral perception, gradually, by directing them to distinguish the morally significant from the morally insignificant, saying, "Pay attention to this" and "Pay attention to that."

MISCONCEPTION 10: SOCIETY DECIDES WHAT IS ETHICAL

An old and popular expression says, "When in Rome, do as the Romans do." Some use it to defend the idea that right and wrong are really just cultural conventions. This idea is known as *cultural relativism*. The earliest articulation of this notion occurs in *The Histories* by the Greek historian Herodotus (484?–425? BCE). He recounts a story about Darius I, the Persian king who reigned from about 522 to 486 BCE. Darius was interested in learning about the various cultural beliefs and practices of the people he encountered, and so he would question people from the lands bordering his kingdom.

During his reign Darius summoned the Hellenes [Greeks] at his court and asked them how much money they would accept for eating the bodies of their dead fathers. They answered that they would not do so for any amount of money. Later Darius summoned some Indians called Kallatiai, who do eat their dead parents. In the presence of the Hellenes, with an interpreter to inform them of what was said, he asked the Indians how much money they would accept to burn the bodies of their dead fathers, as the Hellenes did. The Kallatiai responded with an outcry, ordering him to shut his mouth lest he offend the gods.[17]

On the face of it, the Hellenes and the Kallatiai have very different and inconsistent moral beliefs: the Hellenes believe it is necessary to burn their dead relatives, and the Kallatiai believe it is necessary to eat them. Yet everything depends on how one describes the situation, for both the Hellenes and the Kallatiai have distinctive cultural rituals by which they express reverence for the dead. Ignoring those rituals, by doing something else with dead bodies, is regarded as an act of sacrilege. So one could say that both the Hellenes and the Kallatiai have the same ethical views, namely, that one should always express reverence toward dead relatives. To put it another way, they have different rules for proper treatment of the dead but base their respective rules on the same ethical principle.

In the time since Herodotus, historians, journalists, and anthropologists have recounted thousands of instances of cultural practices that appear to the observer from another culture as strange, abhorrent, or, occasionally, amusing. In many cases, the differences among cultures stem from particular ways of doing things that reveal an underlying commonality: different methods of punishment that reveal an underlying commitment to deterring theft or different ways of conducting oneself in battle that reveal an underlying commitment to courage. This is not to say there are no fundamental ethical disagreements among cultures, but they are not as common as they appear to be when one looks at only the surface description of behaviors. In fact an examination of basic ethical commitments

---

17. Herodotus, *The Histories*, trans. Andrea L. Purvis, in Robert B. Strassler, ed., *The Landmark Herodotus* (New York: Anchor Books, 2007), 3.38.3–4, 224.

shows widespread agreement across cultures regarding the importance of honesty, courage, generosity, hospitality, and respect. This becomes evident, however, only if one understands the broader significance of specific behaviors within particular cultural contexts.

Even when fundamental ethical differences among cultures exist, it is still misguided to think that ethical views simply proceed from cultural practices, and that accepted practices within a particular culture cannot be morally questioned. If that were so, residents of a pluralistic society would have no way of determining what is right and what is wrong. Take, for instance, someone like Barack Obama, the forty-fourth president of the United States. His mother was from Kansas, and his father was from Kenya. He was born in Hawaii and spent a portion of his childhood in Indonesia. He attended college in New York and law school in Boston, and he began his political career in Chicago. Which culture determines what is right or wrong for him? The answer is that several different cultures have most likely contributed to how Obama views ethical issues, but no single culture has the final say on how he should respond to the various choices that face him. The same holds true for anybody who is raised in or lives in a pluralistic society. We bring different ethical points of view to the discussion, based in part upon cultural influences, but those cultural influences are not decisive in determining how we should live.

Another difficulty with cultural relativism is that it paves the way for what the French writer Alexis de Tocqueville (1805–1859) termed the "tyranny of the majority."[18] This refers to the problem of not being able to challenge dominant practices or laws because they express the will of the majority. According to the notion of cultural relativism, dominant cultural practices determine what is right and wrong, leaving no conceivable basis for objecting that something with wide acceptance within a culture is wrong. Cultural relativism says that individuals could not morally object to practices such as slavery, female genital mutilation, and infanticide if they enjoyed widespread acceptance within a particular culture. Significant social reform, such as the civil rights movement in the United States in the 1960s, would have no moral basis, because it is an effort to change dominant cultural practices, and by definition, dominant cultural practices are

---

18. *Democracy in America*, vol. 1, ch. 16, *http://xroads.virginia.edu/~HYPER/DETOC/*.

always right. According to cultural relativism, such practices are not only right, they also determine what it means to be right.

Different cultures have different norms or standards, but it is not possible to reduce ethics to those cultural norms. One task of the student of ethics is to look carefully at cultural differences and neither dismiss as ethically wrong those practices that are unfamiliar nor superficially accept all practices as equally worthy of adoption. Instead, one must try to distinguish the surface expression of a norm from the underlying basis of that expression and then critically examine those norms using one's best reflective judgment.

MISCONCEPTION 11:
THE POWERFUL DECIDE WHAT IS ETHICAL

There is an old and widely used expression: "Might makes right." This means that those who hold power in a society determine what is right and what is wrong. Although it is certainly true that those who hold power in any society can use their influence to shape laws and the enforcement of those laws, it is not the case that such influence extends to determining whether those laws are actually good. For example, plantation owners in the southern United States held considerable power in the late eighteenth and early nineteenth centuries. They had the ability to influence the U.S. Constitution, state laws, court decisions, and law enforcement to establish and maintain an institution of slavery. That power, however, did not make slavery morally right. Their power allowed them to sustain a practice that was morally wrong, but it did not keep some people from recognizing the moral evil of slavery and resisting it. In fact, one of the chief limitations on the use of power in society is moral opposition to the abuse of power.

The Society of Friends (also known as Quakers) is known for the practice of "speaking truth to power," which comes from the determination to resist injustice by renouncing violence and using moral suasion to accomplish positive social reform.[19] Many social

---

19. Hans A. Schmitt, *Quakers and Nazis: Inner Light in Outer Darkness* (Columbia: University of Missouri Press, 1997).

reformers, such as Mohandas Gandhi, Martin Luther King Jr., and Nelson Mandela, have used public ethical criticism of laws that favored the interest of the powerful in society to overturn those laws.

Even though power does not determine right and wrong, it does have considerable persuasive effect on the perception of right and wrong, particularly on those who wield power. Lord Acton, the nineteenth-century British historian, famously said: "Power tends to corrupt, and absolute power corrupts absolutely. Great men are almost always bad men."[20]

The idea of power as a corrupting influence has a long history. Yet, in and of itself, power is a good thing. It consists of the ability to get things done. It can take many forms: strength, intelligence, persistence, wealth, cleverness, reputation, experience. It can do harm to the people subjected to the effects of power if it is used negligently or without their consent. It may also be harmful to the person who wields it, particularly if it allows one to evade the social consequences of bad behavior.

In the *Republic*, Plato tells the story of a shepherd named Gyges, who found a magic ring:

> There was a violent thunderstorm, and an earthquake broke open the ground and created a chasm at the place where he was tending his sheep. Seeing this, he was filled with amazement and went down into it. And there, in addition to many other wonders of which we're told, he saw a hollow bronze horse. There were windowlike openings in it, and, peeping in, he saw a corpse, which seemed to be of more than human size, wearing nothing but a gold ring on its finger. He took the ring and came out of the chasm. He wore the ring at the usual monthly meeting that reported to the king on the state of the flocks. And as he was sitting among the others, he happened to turn the setting of the ring towards himself to the inside of his hand. When he did this, he became invisible to those sitting near him, and they went on talking as if he had gone. He wondered at this, and, fingering the ring, he turned the setting outwards again and

---

20. *Letter to Mandell Creighton* (April 1887), quoted in John Emerich Edward Dalberg-Acton, *Essays on Freedom and Power* (Boston: Beacon Press, 1949), 364.

became visible. So he experimented with the ring to test whether it indeed had this power—and it did. If he turned the setting inward, he became invisible; if he turned it outward, he became visible again. When he realized this, he at once arranged to become one of the messengers sent to report to the king. And when he arrived there, he seduced the king's wife, attacked the king with her help, killed him, and took over the kingdom.[21]

PLATO (429–347 BCE)

Plato

Aristocles Platon ("Plato") was a member of the aristocratic elite in the city of Athens. At some point in his youth he encountered Socrates and joined the group of young men who regularly followed him to the agora to witness his public conversations. After Socrates died Plato began writing dialogues, most of which included Socrates as the central figure. He wrote about thirty-five dialogues and several letters.

© Nick Pavlakis/Shutterstock

Around 387 he opened a school called the "Academy," but unlike other schools of that time, he did not charge tuition. Instead, he accepted donations of whatever students could afford to pay. Students lived in community, sharing everything in common, and were encouraged to challenge their teachers. It was a school based on the search for ideas, not obedience to authority.

The twentieth-century philosopher Alfred North Whitehead said famously that philosophy "consists of a series of footnotes

Continued

---

21. Plato, *Republic*, trans. G.M.A. Grube, rev. C.D.C. Reeve (Indianapolis: Hackett, 1992), 359d–360b, 35–36.

Plato *Continued*

to Plato." And, in fact, it is hard to find any topic that Plato didn't deal with in some fashion. Goodness, truth, beauty, evil, politics, war, poverty, evolution, love, hatred, dreams, death, poetry, music, mythology, mathematics: you name it, you can probably find it somewhere in one of the dialogues.

Plato is best known for developing what is referred to as the Theory of Forms. Though just what that theory is, or whether Plato even believed it himself, is difficult to tell, because all of his theories are presented by various characters in his dialogues, never in his own voice. But at least this much is clear: Plato held that the world we know through the intellect (the world of *eidos*, "forms" or "ideas") is at least as real or even more real than the world we apprehend through the senses. The only way we can tell that somebody's action is good, that somebody's claim is true, or that somebody's poem is beautiful, is because we have some notion of goodness, or truth, or beauty, against which to compare the particular instances. It is the business of philosophy to help us think more clearly and consistently about such ideas, by engaging in thorough discussion and argumentation.

Though Plato's dialogues deal with many topics, his most frequent themes are ethics and politics, which for Plato, like most Greeks of that time, were intertwined, for he believed that a good life must of necessity be a public life as well.

Then Plato posed this question: If two people, one who is just and the other who is unjust, each found magic rings, would they both end up acting in the same way?

That's a hard question to answer. We don't have any magic rings lying around to do an experiment. But we do have examples of many people—movie stars, athletes, politicians, entrepreneurs—who have risen from humble origins to positions of wealth and prestige. Many of them have acted despicably. The news media are replete with stories of powerful people behaving irresponsibly, but we could probably name just as many powerful people who lead decent or even exemplary lives. Chapter 6 in this book looks more closely at how various circumstances and character traits influence people's perception of right and wrong. For now, it is enough to recognize that even though might may influence the perception of right, might does not "make" right. Even if everyone would act just as Gyges did if they came into possession of great power, it would not prove that right and wrong are determined by the possession of power. It would just show that people who want to maintain their ethical sense must be cautious when it comes to acquiring and wielding power over others.

MISCONCEPTION 12:
ETHICS IS SEPARATE FROM RELIGION

When considering the relationship between ethics and religion, one confronts two different questions. The first concerns the conceptual relationship between the two areas of study; philosophers and theologians tend to be most engaged with this question. The second question concerns the practical connection between ethics and religion; it is the question at issue in most popular discussions of the topic. For example, when someone says, "You don't have to be a Christian to be a good person," they are responding to the second question, but when someone says, "The *Analects* of Confucius are philosophical and not religious," or "Ethics should be based on an impartial, objective system of values informed by natural science instead of religious prejudice," they are addressing the first question. Let's consider this question first.

Is there a conceptual connection between ethics and religion such that thinking about one necessarily involves thinking about the other? Because ethics concerns potentially anything we say or do in our lifetimes, it is difficult to draw a line in the sand and say, "Everything on this side of the line is a matter of ethics, and everything on that side is not." That is not because everything actually is a matter of ethics but rather because anything we study is potentially relevant to ethics and therefore may be included in our deliberations when trying to figure out what to do. Take, for example, the study of science. Science and ethics are different subjects with different methodologies, yet much of what science does is relevant to ethics—in fact, one could even say indispensable. If a person does not accept or understand certain basic things about the world as revealed by the scientific method, then she or he will not be able to make good, responsible choices about how to live in the world. The person who dismisses all evidence regarding global climate change or who refuses to consider sociological and economic studies of the effects of the death penalty will be unable to deliberate responsibly on the topics of pollution or capital punishment. In the same way, the person who declares that religion has no relevance for ethics discounts in advance the significance of many beliefs and motivations of believers from across the religious spectrum. So in this way, ethics and religion are interdependent, just as ethics and science are interdependent: to make coherent, responsible judgments about how to act, one must be familiar with the basic orientations toward the world by means of which human beings understand themselves and their relationships. Because a majority of people in the world consider themselves to be followers of some particular religion, religion must be considered fundamental to how people perceive themselves and the world.[22]

Religion and ethics have an even stronger connection than this. A religion is composed, in part, of a worldview—a picture of the universe and the place of humans and other beings within the universe that gives coherence and meaning to life. The ethical judgments of adherents of any particular religion tend to make sense (if they make sense at all) within the context of their religious worldview. A significant part of the Christian worldview, for example, is the belief that human beings are created by a good God. Certain ethical implications about how to live follow from this picture of human existence, implications that may not make sense in the context of some other worldview. Thus, in Catholicism for example, Pope John Paul II writes:

> It is not wrong to want to live better; what is wrong is a style
> of life which is presumed to be better when it is directed

---

22. According to the Gallup International Millennium Survey, 87 percent of respondents claimed to belong to some religious group. Sixty-three percent of respondents claimed that God was very important in their lives. Results of the Gallup International Millennium Survey are available online at *http://www.gallup-international.com/ContentFiles/millennium15.asp.*

towards "having" rather than "being," and which wants to have more, not in order to be more but in order to spend life in enjoyment as an end in itself. It is therefore necessary to create lifestyles in which the quest for truth, beauty, goodness and communion with others for the sake of common growth are the factors which determine consumer choices, savings and investments. In this regard, it is not a matter of the duty of charity alone, that is, the duty to give from one's "abundance," and sometimes even out of one's needs, in order to provide what is essential for the life of a poor person. I am referring to the fact that even the decision to invest in one place rather than another, in one productive sector rather than another, is always a moral and cultural choice.[23]

In passages such as this, it is important to note not only that the reason for doing something good ties in conceptually to a religious picture of human existence but also that what it *means* to do something good is conceptually tied to that picture. The claim that it is morally wrong to spend one's life in "enjoyment as an end in itself" is put forth in the context of human life as created—as opposed to accidental—and as intended for "communion with others." Thus Pope John Paul II proposes an ethical way of life based upon a religious understanding of human nature. One cannot take the religious understanding of human nature out of the picture and still have a coherent expression of *that kind* of ethical obligation.

However, some people claim that religious beliefs are simply false and that, therefore, religion is either detrimental or irrelevant to ethics.[24] That's perfectly understandable. Most people would agree that any false beliefs, regardless of whether they are religious in nature, are detrimental or irrelevant to ethics. The key thing to remember is that when people disagree about the relevance of religion to ethics,

---

23. *Centesimus Annus* 36, *http://www.vatican.va/holy_father/john_paul_ii/encyclicals/documents/hf_jp–ii_enc_01051991_centesimus-annus_en.html*.

24. Of the many recent books arguing for that claim, perhaps the best is Walter Sinnott-Armstrong's *Morality without God* (New York: Oxford University Press, 2009). There are also many popular, but less reasonably argued, books advancing similar ideas, such as Richard Dawkins, *The God Delusion* (Boston: Houghton Mifflin, 2006), and Christopher Hitchens, *God Is Not Great: How Religion Poisons Everything* (New York: Twelve Books, 2007).

the basis of their disagreement rests on whether they think religious beliefs are true or false.[25]

Sincere followers of any of the world's major religions must believe in a conceptual tie between religion and ethics. If truly sincere, they will think that their religiously informed understanding of the world is true (or more or less true) and that their judgments about how to live (i.e., what's right and wrong, good and bad) follow in some sense from that understanding of the world. People who don't subscribe to one of the world's religions will, of course, think differently, but they will do so not just because they think ethics and religion are different subject matters but also because they think any particular religiously informed understanding of the world is, for the most part anyway, false.[26] It is reasonable for adherents of a religion to think that ethics and religion are conceptually linked. It is also reasonable for critics of religion to think that ethics and religion are independent of each other. The only way to settle that disagreement is to address the truth or falsity of religious beliefs.

Is there a practical connection between certain kinds of religious beliefs and practices and being able to live a good (i.e., ethical) life? A church in my neighborhood regularly sends a team of people to Haiti to staff a temporary health care clinic. Some go in response to Jesus' command to "love your neighbor as yourself" (Mark 12:31). One could say, many of the people who go on the mission trip do it for religious reasons. But could they have done it instead for entirely secular reasons? Yes, they could have done it for other reasons, just as most of our actions could be done for reasons other than those for which we actually do them. It matters little what other reasons could be given for going on the mission trip; the reasons people actually give are what count. If people actually do good things for religious reasons—and the things do not just happen to be good, but

---

25. There is another kind of argument one can give for the relevance of religion to ethics, namely, that without God, morality lacks authority. This is the kind of argument given by John Hare in *Why Bother Being Good? The Place of God in the Moral Life* (Downers Grove, IL: InterVarsity Press, 2002).

26. The only way to settle this disagreement between believers and unbelievers is by addressing the question of whether religious belief is (or can be) true, and that goes beyond the scope of this book.

their purpose in doing them is to accomplish something good (for example, to save lives)— then ethics does depend upon religion *in the lives of those people.*

This is not to deny that people also do good things for secular (or nonreligious) reasons. Of course they do. Nor does it deny that people may also do bad things for religious reasons. People have started wars, tortured, cheated, lied, and committed all sorts of foul deeds for religious reasons. But that those things have happened (and do happen) doesn't affect the claim that religious beliefs and practices often supply crucial motivation for ethical behavior.

Suppose someone were to ask whether health depends on diet and exercise. Everyone would agree it does. Some people, through fortunate genetic circumstances, may remain healthy while eating mostly junk food and exercising very little, but such people are the exception. There are other people who injure their health through diet and exercise, for example, by going on some extreme diet that deprives them of essential nutrients or by participating in some form of exercise that causes injury. Such examples, however, don't mitigate the claim that health depends on diet and exercise, because what one means by such a claim is that proper diet and exercise are significant factors in the health of most people.

This example can help one understand how to interpret the claim of a practical connection between religion and ethics. It means that proper religious practices tend to lead to a better (i.e., more ethical) life. To determine whether such a claim is true we would have to ask a number of specific questions. For example, does the practice of praying regularly help one live a better (i.e., more ethical) life? Or does the practice of daily meditation help one to live a better life? Or is forgiveness crucial for happiness? Possible answers to some of these questions will be considered in chapter 6, in the context of a discussion of virtue ethics. For now, it is important simply to keep in mind that different religions emphasize the significance of different kinds of practices for living a good life, and so the only way of responsibly answering the question of the practical connection between ethics and religion is to look at how such practices manifest themselves in the lives of people who embrace them. It is the same approach one would take to discover whether any sort of activity in which people regularly engage supplies practical motivation for ethical behavior.

MISCONCEPTION 13:
HUMAN BEINGS KEEP GETTING MORALLY WORSE

My grandfather's favorite complaint was the moral degeneration of society, and he had a long list of examples to illustrate the downward path: hippies with long hair, rock music, drug use, illegitimate children, disrespect of elders, women driving pickup trucks, TV shows (except *Bonanza* and *Hee Haw*), cities, politicians, movie stars (except John Wayne), littering, the failure to remove one's hat when the flag passed by during parades, and graffiti (especially the graffiti on the town's water tower and on the back of his garage).

Being an impressionable youth, and curious to know what things were like before my generation had come along to mess them up, I would sometimes ask him to tell me what it was like when he was growing up. Then I would hear stories of his early adventures: tipping outhouses on Halloween, stealing watermelons, disassembling a neighbor's wagon and reassembling it on top of his barn, hustling pool, making plugged nickels. The stories went on and on. One of his favorites was about how he and other kids in his North Dakota town would go up to an aging Civil War veteran who had been a soldier in the Confederate Army. They would stand in the street and sing "Marching through Georgia" until the old man would grab his cane and chase them down the street. "He'd get so angry he couldn't even speak," my grandfather would say. Then after a reflective pause, "Oh, we were a terrible bunch of kids."

We find worries about the moral character of the succeeding generation expressed in all cultures at all times in history. We find them in Plato's *Dialogues* from 350 BCE. Socrates, remember, was executed after being convicted on the charge of corrupting the youth, a pretty fair indication that the people of Athens thought their youth had, in fact, been corrupted. We find similar worries about the youth expressed in the writings of Roman historians Sallust and Livy during the height of the Roman Empire about the time of Jesus. We find them in newspapers from Victorian England and in early American diaries.

It is easy to find evidence that certain things in society are getting worse, because society is large and complex. There will always be someone ready to point out the latest survey showing that dishonesty in the workplace has increased by 5 percent over the past three years or that the high school graduation rate in some large city has reached an alarming new low.

In response one could point out that although some aspects of our society are getting worse, other aspects are getting better. Studies show steadily increasing numbers of young people volunteering in their communities and crime rates that have been steadily dropping.[27]

Despite the tendency of people to say that society is getting worse, there's no way of backing up that claim with reliable evidence. Every generation seems worse than the previous one in some respects and better than the previous generation in others. Moreover, as society changes and new types of ethical problems arise, people's actions have implications and consequences they did not previously carry, and so it may appear that more and more ethical problems are arising. But until we decide on consistent criteria for measuring "better" and "worse," all we can bring to bear on the argument is anecdotal or partial evidence. In the meantime we can ask ourselves the question: Which is more likely, that every generation in the history of the world was morally worse than the previous generation, or that the observers tend to be biased?

CONCLUSION: ETHICS AS COMMON SENSE

There is an old joke about a drunken man pacing back and forth under a streetlamp and looking down at his feet. A passerby stops and asks what he's doing. "I'm looking for my car keys," the drunken man says. So the passerby begins pacing under the streetlamp as well, looking earnestly for the keys. After about fifteen minutes, he stops and says, "I don't see your keys anywhere. Are you sure this is where you lost them?" "Oh no," replies the drunken man, "I dropped them way over there in front of the bar. But it's no use looking over there; it's so dark you can't see a thing."

---

27. For a summary of trends on youth volunteering, see Mark Hugo Lopez, "Volunteering among Young People," a report by the Center for Information and Research on Civic Learning on Engagement, February 2004, available at *http://civicyouth.org/PopUps/FactSheets/FS_Volunteering2.pdf*. For crime rates see the Uniform Crime Reporting Statistics from the FBI and the U.S. Department of Justice, available at *http://www.ucrdatatool.gov/Search/Crime/State/RunCrimeStatebyState.cfm*.

Most of the widespread misconceptions about ethics share a common feature: they attempt to reduce ethics to something less than it is, something that may be compartmentalized into a more easily managed area of life or academic study. But looking for answers only in well-defined and comprehensible areas doesn't mean the answers to ethical questions can be found there. Those who insist that ethics is just a matter of cultural practice, for example, tend to think that ethics can be confined to the study of sociology or anthropology. Those who think ethics is not related to religion sometimes claim that ethics really is just a branch of psychology or evolutionary biology. But ethics has always resisted efforts to reduce its scope.

Questions about how to live come up in every aspect of life, and so every area of study is potentially relevant in the attempt to answer ethical questions. Every profession has questions that come up regularly about how to engage in that profession honestly, responsibly, in ways that are fair and that benefit—or at least do not harm—others. Questions of ethics come up outside the professions, as well, in areas of life that everyone shares, questions about how to be a good parent, friend, neighbor, or citizen. Different aspects of our lives generate questions about how to live, but they also provide knowledge and insights about how to answer those questions, none of which can be ruled out in advance as irrelevant. This makes the study of ethics complex, confusing, and, often, frustrating. We want to know: Where are the answers found, and how do we know when we have found them?

We find the answers in conversation with others, that is, in discussion or dialogue. Some people might say we find the answers in books, or in some books in particular, say the Bible, the Koran, or Aristotle's *Nicomachean Ethics*. But a book is just conversation with someone who is absent, or, we might say, someone whose presence is mediated by the printed word. Finding the answers in a book always depends on the ability of the reader to converse (from a Latin term meaning to "turn together") with the author and participate in the making of meaning. In the same way, learning from a speaker requires an ability to listen and speak in return, to discover meaning in shared words. All of this is to say that ethics comes from common sense, that is, from the ability to find shared meaning in the words we use together to make sense of our lives.[28] In making sense of our lives together, we also give shape to them, by creating rules, policies, laws, conditions of praise and blame, standards of excellence and of failure.

Perhaps we never do know when we have found the answers. At least, one never can be sure of having found the final answers to questions of what is right and wrong or good and bad, for those answers are inextricably bound up in descriptions of the world, and our comprehension of the world is partial (to say the least). Claiming to have the final word in ethics is tantamount to claiming to know everything.

So what do we do if we want to know how to live good lives? We keep learning, we keep listening and talking, we keep taking part in the attempt to reach some sort of shared understanding. Then we test that understanding, seeing what becomes of a life lived with such an understanding, making our very lives part of the conversation. That is the best we can do, and it is a great deal.

However, we don't start with a clean slate, attempting to discover everything for ourselves for the first time. We start with where we find ourselves, and we find ourselves in a culture with a rich inheritance, in the middle of an ongoing conversation about how to live that has been taking place for centuries.

We turn next to consideration of the key terms of that conversation so we can become meaningful participants in it, knowing better how to read, how to listen, and how to speak to one another.

---

28. This idea of common sense (i.e., making sense of things in common) is nearly opposite in meaning to the way in which people often use the phrase *common sense* to mean something like relying only upon what one already thinks.

Four Ways of Ethical Thinking

SOME PEOPLE LIKE TO REDUCE ALL OF ETHICS to a simple principle like, "Don't do anything you wouldn't want to see printed in the newspaper" or "Always follow your gut instinct." Although such principles are not bad as rules of thumb in certain situations, they hardly serve as reliable guides for everyone in every circumstance. After all, some people have a high tolerance for embarrassment and wouldn't mind anything being printed in the newspaper about them, as long as it didn't cost them money. Some people also have poor instincts; following their "gut" could lead to all sorts of trouble.

If some people make ethics too simple, others make it entirely too complicated. Ethics instructors, in particular, are sometimes inclined to introduce a new set of terms, concepts, and principles before students begin deliberating the relative merits of controversial issues.

In fact, ethics is no more, nor less, complicated than grammar. We begin engaging in ethical reasoning almost as soon as we begin to talk, and it is not long before that ability extends to fairly complex patterns of ethical decision making. Whenever we use words to try to convince others that something is right or wrong, good or bad, praiseworthy or blameworthy, we are using ethical thinking. We learn how to do this almost as soon as we learn to speak in sentences. We learn at an early age how to put words together to represent the world and our place in it, how to ask for something, or how to demand it, how to blame, praise, express gratitude, express our desires and frustrations. Most significantly, we learn how to give reasons to sway people to give us what we want, to justify and explain ourselves, or to get people to see things from our point of view.

We don't know at an early age that we are using ethical thinking, of course, much less that we are engaging in different and sometimes quite sophisticated ways of ethical thinking. But that's what we are in fact doing. By the time we have become competent speakers of a language, we have also become quite skilled at using sophisticated methods of reasoning to make ethical decisions.

This shouldn't be surprising. After all, most of us become competent and reliable users of grammatical structures like the pluperfect subjunctive at a young age, even though most adult speakers of the English language could no more define *pluperfect subjunctive* than they could the *special theory of relativity*.

Learning how to think about the ways we think comes after we have become proficient at doing it. We typically learn how to think about sentence structure in elementary school, a few years after becoming competent users of those structures. People typically learn how to think about ethical reasoning many years after becoming competent in its use, sometimes in high school but more often in college or even later.[1]

Knowing how to do something and knowing how to describe what one is doing are two different things. Knowing how to hit a golf ball, for example, is not the same as knowing how to describe what happens when one hits a golf ball. We learn one thing from a golf instructor and the other from a physics teacher. In the same way, most people learn how to make ethical decisions from their parents or friends, but they learn how to describe what happens when they use ethical reasoning by taking a course in ethics.

Knowing a great deal about physics won't necessarily make someone a better golfer, and knowing a great deal about ethics won't necessarily make a person more ethical. But understanding something about the process of ethical reasoning may incline one

---

1. See Miles Burnyeat, "Aristotle on Learning to Be Good," in *Essays on Aristotle's Ethics*, ed. Amelie Oksenberg Rorty (Berkeley: University of California Press, 1980), 69–92.

toward greater patience and civility when taking sides on hotly disputed issues. It may also give one more confidence to find solutions to difficult problems.

FOUR WAYS OF ETHICAL THINKING

We live in an historical and pluralistic society, a result of thousands of years of cultural development, much of it known and recorded. Our society is the product of languages, practices, and customs derived from many different cultures. This makes our society fascinating to live in, but it also makes certain things about our lives complex. This is especially true of ethics.

A pluralistic society provides its members with different, distinctive ways of thinking about ethical problems. There are general terms, such as *good*, *bad*, *right*, and *wrong*, as well as broad but more specific terms like *duty*, *obligation*, *value*, and *virtue*. Society has terms it tends to use mainly in the ethical deliberations of certain professions like health care, terms such as *beneficence* (from the Latin for "doing good") and *nonmaleficence* (from the Latin for "doing no harm"). Finally, some terms come from the philosophical study of ethics and are used almost exclusively in academic contexts, such as *deontology* and *utilitarianism.*

All of these different terms have a history and an original cultural context. They represent not only different ideas but also different ways of thinking about ethical problems. This can make ethical discussions confusing.

When two or more people disagree about what should be done, how can they better understand what they are saying to one another? How can they determine who is right and who is wrong? How can they reach agreement, or at least not go away angry with each other?

When people focus too quickly on the details of their disagreements, they tend to get mired in conflict. Ethical thinking is complex, just as grammar is complex. So the best way to study it is to set forth a framework to gain a general understanding of the subject. Then we can move on to examine some of the complexities.

This book employs a framework that relies on four basic types of ethical thinking and also suggests a method for discussing ethical problems that helps clear up some common confusions and misunderstandings.[2]

Whenever one makes an ethical claim and supports that claim with reasons, one uses one of four general ways of thinking, as follows:

Truth: *Thinking in terms of the facts of the situation*
What's really going on? What laws or policies apply? What is the overall context of the situation? What is the history of the situation?

Consequences: *Thinking in terms of the results of an action*
Who is going to be affected? How will they be affected? What positive things could happen? What negative things could happen?

Fairness: *Thinking in terms of equality and consistency*
How would you feel if someone were doing this to you? Would the action under consideration be fair or just? Would it be treating people[3] equally or with respect? What would happen if everyone did that?

Character: *Thinking in terms of people's motivations, character traits, or both*
Why are they doing this? What's in it for them? Are the people involved in this situation being generous, lazy, courageous,

---

2. The method for ethical decision making presented here is influenced by the "Four Topics Method" described in Albert R. Jonsen, Mark Siegler, and William J. Winslade, *Clinical Ethics*, 5th ed. (New York: McGraw-Hill, 2002). The expression *four ways of thinking* alludes to the Four-Way Test written by Herbert Taylor in 1932 and later adopted by Rotary International as one of its guiding principles. The Four-Way Test consists of four questions: "Is it the truth? Is it fair to all concerned? Will it build goodwill and better friendships? Will it be beneficial to all concerned?" In Paul Engleman, "Is It the Truth?" *The Rotarian,* August 2009, *http://www.rotary.org/en/MediaAndNews/TheRotarian/Pages/Taylor0908.aspx.*

3. The question of whether ethical reasoning applies directly only to people or whether it also applies to others, such as animals, living things, or natural objects, is interesting and worthy of more discussion than it typically receives. We will not settle this question here but will return to a fuller consideration of it in subsequent chapters.

self-serving, spiteful, considerate, and so on? Are they acting out of anger or resentment or some other negative motivation? Are they acting out of some positive motivation, like gratitude? How will their character be influenced by acting in this way?

These are not different theories of ethical reasoning; they are merely different ways of thinking about ethical problems or situations. Ways of thinking simply describe how ethical reasoning is done. Ethical theories propose and defend a certain way of thinking as the best way to solve ethical problems. Some of them, namely, *consequentialism, deontology,* and *virtue ethics,* correspond to three of these ways of thinking. *Consequentialism* proposes that ethical problems are best resolved by thinking in terms of consequences. *Deontology* proposes that ethical problems are best resolved by thinking in terms of certain types of action, often characterized by fairness. *Virtue ethics* proposes that ethical problems are best resolved by thinking in terms of character. The theory proposed in this book is that none of the well-established ethical theories proves sufficient on its own. Instead, all four ways of thinking must be used together.

All four types of thinking have merit. They have survived and persisted in our society because people find them useful. They help us think through situations for ourselves and persuade others to go along with us. Because people in everyday situations regularly use all four ways of thinking when talking about what is right or wrong, good or bad, praiseworthy or blameworthy, no single way of thinking can be used exclusively to reach widely acceptable conclusions. To argue that everyone should solve every ethical dispute by thinking only in one way (for example, by thinking in terms of consequences only) would be like saying a grocery store should conduct all its transactions only with cash. Even though there might be good reasons for making all purchases with cash, it is not in fact how people do things. People also make purchases by credit card, checks, and barter. Similarly, engaging in the give-and-take of ethical conversation in society requires fluency in the different ways people actually think and talk. After all, ethics is not a private matter; it is a matter of how we live in relation to others.

Just using a way of ethical thinking does not guarantee that one's reasoning about a given situation is correct. Each way of thinking may be used correctly or incorrectly. For example, one could argue that donating to a certain charity would have better consequences than using the same money elsewhere, not knowing that the charity in question has little positive effect on the people it serves. In such a case one would be appealing to good consequences—a legitimate way of ethical reasoning—but doing it in a way that leads to a poor conclusion. To think in terms of consequences correctly requires one to do more than simply guess at the effects one's donations could have. As another example, one could think ethically in terms of character, praising a person for acting generously but not knowing that the underlying motive for the behavior is to make a profit. Reasoning about character in such an instance won't produce a justified conclusion unless one knows what the person's real motives are. In short, just using a way of ethical thinking doesn't guarantee a sound argument. Each way of thinking must be used appropriately.

Sometimes when two people disagree with each other about the right thing to do, both are using the same kind of thinking but disagree about the course of action to take. This is generally a straightforward disagreement about what ought to be done, and both parties know why they disagree. However, sometimes when people disagree about an ethical issue, they simply talk past one another. Each uses a different type of reasoning—let's say one is concerned with consequences, the other with personal character—without recognizing the difference in their reasoning. This can cause considerable confusion and misunderstanding.

Let's consider an example. Roy, Tonya, Arthur, and Bertha serve on a committee of the city council that is debating whether to recommend a new recycling policy for the city. Roy supports the recycling policy. He says recycling is good for the environment, saves energy and resources, reduces waste, and will lower the city's landfill fees. Tonya, however, has reservations. She thinks city residents should be given the opportunity to recycle, but she doesn't support a policy that would require all residents to recycle. She thinks residents should have a choice. Then Arthur enters the discussion. The only reason Tonya doesn't support the recycling policy, he says, is because her brother-in-law owns the company that has the contract for trash removal, and his company probably would not win the bid for the city's recycling. Tonya takes offense at Arthur's statement. She angrily defends herself, insisting she has never allowed her personal relationships to influence her public duties. Roy tries to bring everyone back to the main issue. The thing they have to decide, he says, is whether the current method of handling the city's trash is responsible to the taxpayers and to future generations. The question before them, he insists, is one of economic and environmental impact. Bertha, who has remained quiet until this point, raises a different question. She says she has recently read that it takes more energy to recycle a plastic bottle than to produce one from raw materials. So maybe, she suggests, they should revise the policy to exclude the recycling of plastics.

In a situation like this, each person is using just one way of thinking. Roy focuses on the *consequences* of recycling. Tonya does not think the proposed policy is *fair* to the city's residents. Arthur challenges Tonya's *character*. Bertha questions the *truth* of Roy's assumption that all forms of recycling are good for the environment. The reasons they give to support their positions do not practically address the reasons given by the other parties to the dispute.

When something like this takes place, the people engaged in the dispute tend to believe that the reasons they put forth in support of their positions are "ethical" reasons. That is, they believe the reasons they are giving demonstrate that the action they support is good or right. Because of this, they may think those who disagree with them are being ignorant or stubborn. They may think the others are ignorant if they are unable to comprehend the reasons being put forth. They may think the others are being stubborn if they refuse to acknowledge those reasons. The longer they go on talking without addressing the types of reasons the others are using, the more angry and frustrated they will become. After all, each person thinks he or she is thinking ethically and the others, by refusing to address their reasons, are not thinking ethically at all. This is why many ethical disputes have as much to do with the type of reasoning used as with the content of the issues.

Consider, for example, the contemporary debate over embryonic stem cell research. The debate as usually expressed consists of two sides using different types of reasoning, often without realizing it.

Proponents: Embryonic stem cell research may result in many positive *consequences* for people suffering from presently untreatable injuries or diseases. Because the stem cells are taken from already-existing frozen embryos, no new negative consequences are caused by using the embryos for research.

Opponents: Using embryonic stem cells for research involves killing the embryos. Such a practice violates a basic principle of *fairness* by killing people who cannot speak for themselves. It shows a basic lack of respect for human beings.

When participants in the debate use different ways of thinking about the ethics of embryonic stem cell research, advancing toward some kind of resolution of their differences becomes more difficult. Not only that, but each side is likely to suspect that their opponents in the debate are either unable or unwilling to engage in ethical reasoning. Thus they will suspect that their opponents are motivated by something other than what is good or right, such as financial gain, religious prejudice, or fear.

Another example is the debate over capital punishment.

Proponents: Murderers deserve to be killed. By taking an innocent human life, they have given up their humanity and are beyond redemption. Their *character* is such that they can no longer be part of civilized society. They have become monsters.

Opponents: Capital punishment is *unfair,* because it is biased against the poor and against racial minorities. That it isn't proven to reduce crime means there are no positive *consequences* to outweigh the considerable financial costs of administering it.

Most of the persistent, divisive issues in our society are characterized not only by the different conclusions that people support but by the different types of reasoning used to defend those conclusions. Abortion, euthanasia, immigration, gun control, free speech, torture: the two sides in each instance predominantly use one or two different ways of ethical thinking.

This does not mean that every ethical dispute is characterized by different ways of thinking. Things are more complicated than that. For example, it is common for people who disagree on an issue to employ multiple ways of thinking to defend their relative positions. A proponent of capital punishment may argue in terms of consequences (e.g., that executing a murderer costs less than life imprisonment), or she might argue in terms of truth or fairness. Frequently, however, in long-standing disputes over ethical issues, the majority of people on each side favors one way of thinking over the others. This makes resolution of the dispute difficult, at best.

Interestingly, most people do not tend to favor one way of thinking over another for all the issues they support. A group or individual tends to use whatever type of reasoning gives some kind of rhetorical advantage in the argument at hand. This is done subconsciously, without thinking about it first. Just as one changes tone of voice and the choice of words depending on the person to whom one is talking—whether a small child, a teacher, or a close friend—in the same way one changes the kinds of reasons used in making an ethical argument, depending on which way of thinking serves one's purposes at the time.[4]

Conservatives, for example, tend to speak in terms of fairness when defending their position on issues such as abortion and gun control but often use consequences to defend their position on euthanasia and immigration. Liberals tend to use consequences as their primary way of speaking about abortion and gun control but use fairness in defending their position on euthanasia and immigration. These are just general tendencies, something one may observe in listening to arguments as presented in the newspapers or on television. Over time, a group's favored way of thinking about a particular issue may change.

Not attending to the ways in which we think is the source of frequent misunderstandings. When people engage in an argument, their attention is focused predominantly on the content of what they are saying, not so much on how they are thinking. Given the four different ways of thinking about ethical issues, we may get

---

4. The tendency subconsciously to alter one's thinking to make things seem more reasonable is known as rationalization. For a study of how rationalization works in the context of ethical reasoning, see C. G. Lord, L. Ross, and M. R. Lepper, "Biased Assimilation and Attitude Polarization: The Effects of Prior Theories on Subsequently Considered Evidence," in *Journal of Personality and Social Psychology* 37 (1979) 2098–2109.

frustrated when our way of talking about something doesn't line up with the way someone else is talking about the same thing. We know the person we are arguing with doesn't agree with us; we know the reasons presented do not persuade us; and we know the reasons we present do not persuade them. But we are not sure why the disagreement persists.

However, if we know that we think about an issue in terms of fairness, for example, and the person we are talking to approaches the issue in terms of consequences, then we can make the conversation more constructive by responding to the other person's concern about the consequences and asking that the other person address our concerns about fairness. This does not guarantee agreement on the issue. Serious disagreements may persist, but at least we will be talking to each other and not past each other. That is the first step toward reasonableness and civility in relationships.

Recognizing the four ways of ethical thinking thus proves crucial. It is important for one's own self-understanding—being able to think clearly, consistently, and reasonably about ethical issues—and for one's ongoing relationship with others. One is often unable to reach complete agreement with friends, family members, coworkers, or neighbors. But complete agreement is not the goal of the ethical life; rather the goal is to live well, and that requires knowing how to get along even in the face of disagreement.

A CASE STUDY IN ETHICAL DISAGREEMENT

In 2003, Mathy Construction, a road construction company located in western Wisconsin, purchased some farmland on which to build a new asphalt-production plant. Business had increased over the years, and the old plant could no longer supply enough asphalt for all the road construction projects it had to supply during the summer months. The company considered expanding the existing plant, which was located in the city of La Crosse, but much of the equipment was old and outdated, and the property where the plant was located had little room for expansion. But the proposed new location had problems also. It was situated just across a two-lane road from several lakefront homes on Lake Onalaska. The people who lived along the lake didn't want an asphalt plant in the midst of their charming rural setting.

The controversy over the proposed plant divided the community for more than a year. It was a bitter controversy, and the longer the dispute went on, the stronger the language and the divisions became.

Two conflicting sets of interests were at stake: on the one hand were the homeowners who did not want an asphalt plant in their neighborhood; on the other hand were the employees of the construction company who wanted job security. Interestingly, neither party mentioned personal interest as the reason for taking the side it did. Instead, both parties used a variety of ethical arguments to justify their own position and to win additional supporters to their cause. As the dispute went on, it became clear that not only were the parties using ethical arguments to support their positions but each also seemed to believe that only its own side possessed ethical merit.

The homeowners gave several reasons for opposing the plant. (1) Groundwater runoff from the plant would pollute the lake. (2) Emissions from the plant would pollute the air and contribute to respiratory disease for the residents of the area. (3) The proximity of the plant to lakefront homes would drive down property values. (4) Truck traffic on the road leading to the plant would increase significantly, posing a safety hazard for cars, cyclists, and pedestrians.

Employees of the plant had many reasons to support the new plant. (1) If the construction company couldn't expand, it would have to turn down new business, resulting in fewer jobs in the region. (2) If the company were forced to relocate to another community, even more jobs would be lost in the region. (3) The property had been zoned for industrial use, so any attempt to change the regulations would be unfair. (4) Mathy Construction had been a good employer, paying good wages, treating employees well, and contributing significantly to charitable causes in the region. (5) The community should do whatever it could to encourage companies like Mathy Construction to stay in the area, because they raised the standard for other employers.

Both sides had solid ethical claims supporting their positions. However, just because two sides have solid ethical support does not mean both have equal merit. The key to good ethical decision making is figuring out which possible solution to a problem has the most merit while acknowledging the extent of the merit of other possible solutions.

A town hall meeting was held to allow people on both sides of the dispute to learn more about the proposed plant and to discuss their concerns. The event turned into a shouting match and ended up driving the existing divisions even deeper.

In a situation like this, would it help to bring in an expert on ethics to help negotiate a reasonable solution between the two sides? Perhaps it would, but only if the people on both sides were willing to listen attentively and perhaps even change their minds about the positions they had taken. Sometimes, especially in cases like this, that is too much to expect. For one thing, the dispute was caused by competing personal interests, and those interests had only an indirect tie to the reasons the two groups gave for their positions. So even if someone were able to address each side's reasons adequately, it is not clear that doing so would change anyone's mind. Second, by the time of the town hall meeting, so many people were involved and they had been debating the issue for so long that it would have been difficult to have a constructive discussion.

However, what if the principal people involved from the very beginning had known how to use ethical reasoning in public discussion effectively, that is, how to deliberate about, communicate, and facilitate discussion of controversial issues? Such an approach may have been helpful, not necessarily in changing people's positions, but in toning down the negative rhetoric and allowing people in the community to continue living and conversing with one another in good faith.

Sometimes one uses ethical reasoning to help make difficult decisions (either as individuals or as groups of people). Sometimes one uses ethical reasoning to communicate decisions so other people understand what one is doing and why. Sometimes one uses ethical reasoning simply to make differences clear, so parties may proceed on a basis of mutual respect even when agreement is not possible. When ethical reasoning is used just to score political points, for example, to convince observers that the other side in a debate should be forced to back down or to improve one's own public profile, the use of ethical reasoning may actually increase the level of disrespect among people by contributing to misunderstandings of fact and suspicions of motive.

In the controversy over the proposed asphalt plant, the discussion tended to be civil at the beginning, with people saying things like, "I would vote for it because it was zoned for industrial use. The property owner and Mr. Mathy do have the right to do it," or "There are many problems and questions that should be looked at, like effects on the environment, traffic, and the health and safety of the residents."[5] But as the dispute extended over weeks and months, the tone became harsh, and personal attacks became more common. People began to lose patience with one another. Each side sincerely believed that it alone was on the side of what was good and right.

Situations like this take place every day in communities throughout the world. Somebody does something. Some people like what is happening; others do not. Sides are chosen. Each side tries to win more members to its cause. Conversations are had at the dinner table or over a cup of coffee; letters are written; speeches are made. Over time the divisions, which were mere cracks at first, become gaping fissures. Ethical reasoning, which could be used to bridge the gap, becomes instead a means of widening it.

For human beings, ethical reasoning is our primary means of persuasion. Over the course of a lifetime, we may become accomplished at using ethical reasoning to persuade others, but we can also use it just to reassure ourselves and the people who are already inclined to agree with us. This can happen because, even though we may be skilled at using ethical reasoning, we may also be unable to describe clearly what we are doing when we use those skills, and this may make our efforts counterproductive.

THE FOUR-WAY METHOD
FOR ETHICAL DECISION MAKING

A good way to make progress in ethical disputes is to be aware of the type of reasoning everybody is using and then do one's best to address one another's points using the same type of reasoning. This doesn't mean people should always agree. Rather, they should make disagreements clear. They may not resolve the dispute right away,

---

5. Linda McAlpine, "Asphalt Plant at Heart of Forum Missed by Two Incumbents," *La Crosse Tribune*, March 26, 2003.

Four-Way Method for Ethical Decision Making

CONSEQUENCES

For each proposed solution:
- Who are those most likely to be affected?
- How are they likely to be affected?
- Which solution will be most beneficial and/or least harmful to those affected?

FAIRNESS

- Do the proposed solutions treat others the way you would want to be treated?
- Do the proposed solutions treat all involved with respect and dignity?
- Are the proposed solutions motivated by goodwill?
- Do the proposed solutions enhance or diminish the autonomy of all involved?

TRUTH

- What are the facts?
- What are the relevant laws?
- What is the institutional/company policy?
- What are the relevant professional standards?
- What are the possible solutions to the problem?

CHARACTER

- Can the proposed solutions be enacted virtuously (i.e., compassionately, wisely, courageously, etc.)?
- Will doing the proposed actions tend to make the agent(s) more or less virtuous?
- Can the proposed solutions be implemented in a way that builds trusting relationships?

but at least they can then engage in real conversation and make some progress.

Doing this requires having a method that everyone participating in the discussion agrees to use. Agreeing on a method for discussion is not the same as agreeing on its outcome. It doesn't even mean favoring one type of outcome over another. It simply helps ensure that everyone participating in the discussion is productively engaged in contributing toward some kind of resolution (even if that resolution is never reached).

The Four-Way Method provides a way of participating constructively in discussions about controversial and complicated issues or cases.

Establishing a Shared Understanding of Truth

The first step consists of trying to come up with a shared understanding of the case or issue under consideration. This is the most difficult step of the process, in part because people tend to want to argue for or against their favored position right away. It can be a challenge to step back and look dispassionately at the facts and context of the issue at hand. It is also difficult because people rarely have access to all of the relevant information. Or it may be that they have too much information and can't determine which information is reliable.

In early 2010, during the final weeks of debate over passage of health care reform legislation, the United States Conference of Catholic Bishops released a statement saying the bishops could not support the proposed reform because it would permit the federal funding of abortion.[6] The Catholic Health Association also released a statement saying the proposed reform would not permit the federal funding of abortion and that the association therefore supported the bill.[7] One might think it would be easy to determine who is right

---

6. Office of the General Counsel of the United States Conference of Catholic Bishops, "Legal Analysis of the Provisions of the Patient Protection and Affordable Care Act and Corresponding Executive Order Regarding Abortion Funding and Conscience Protection," *http://usccb.org/healthcare/03-25-10Memo-re-Executive-Order-Final.pdf.*

7. Catholic Health Association, "Catholic Health Association Congratulates Nation's Leaders for Enacting Historic Health Reform," *http://www.chausa.org/newsdetail. aspx?id=2147484842.*

and who is wrong in a case like this: just read the bill and see what it says. In fact, it was extremely difficult to know just what the legislation would or would not allow; it depended on how various funding mechanisms would operate, whether executive orders function like statutes, and what would be considered relevant by courts that might hear challenges to the law.[8] For those who believed it would be ethically wrong to support a bill that would fund abortions, it was difficult to know whether they should or should not support health care reform. Their difficulty was not due to any confusion about their values or principles; it was due to confusion about the facts of the case.

Many "ethical disagreements" have at their root differences of perception about the facts of a situation. So the first step toward a productive discussion is to get as close as possible to a shared understanding of what is really going on: what is happening or has happened, who is involved, what their roles are, what laws or professional standards apply, and so on. Often questions will remain: things we would like to know but cannot, or things about which we can't agree. The important thing is to have, at least, a shared understanding of the facts upon which we do agree, so that we can move on to the next step.

Examining the Consequences

The second step is examining the consequences of proposed actions, for although there are four ways of ethical thinking, the dominant type of reasoning in public matters is consequences. Political debates use this mode of reasoning most of the time. For example, policy disputes over taxes, health care, education, and trade, focus almost exclusively on the consequences—with good reason. When talking about complex issues that affect large numbers or groups of people in different ways, we want to know what effect a proposed action will have on various people. Also many public policy issues come up for discussion precisely because certain negative effects of current policies have been identified, and a proposal is being made to correct them.

---

8. Kathleen Parker, "Federally Funded Abortions Are in Our Future," *The Washington Post*, March 28, 2010. Bart Stupak, "Executive Order Has Full Force and Effect of Law," *http://www.house.gov/list/speech/mi01_stupak/morenews/20100323eo.html*.

Individuals making personal decisions think about consequences all the time. If I have a toothache, I think about what my options are. I could take some pain medication, but that tends to upset my stomach. Is the pain worse than the upset stomach will be? I could go to the dentist, but that's expensive, and sometimes a toothache goes away after a day or two. Or if I'm thinking about buying a new car, I might consider how much it will cost to maintain my old car for another year versus the payments required for a new car. I would think about what kind of car to get, whether I want a car that gets better gas mileage or one that has more space for taking long trips.

We normally don't consider decisions like these to be ethical decisions, because they only take into account personal consequences. They easily could be ethical decisions, however, if we would widen the scope of our thinking to take into account the effects on others. In that case, I would be taking into account the effects on myself *and on others*, and this would move the deliberation into the realm of ethical decision making.[9]

It can be difficult to be thorough and consistent when assessing the effects of our actions on others, in part because of the tendency to focus first and foremost on how we ourselves are affected. In order to use consequences as a way of thinking ethically, it is helpful to think through situations in a step-by-step fashion.

Step One: Define the problem.

Step Two: Identify the most likely (i.e., plausible, reasonable) solutions to the problem.

Step Three: List everyone who could be affected by the various solutions.

Step Four: Describe how those people could be affected (i.e., positively or negatively) by the solutions.

Step Five: Identify the solution that has the greatest overall positive effects or the least overall negative effects.

---

9. It's not that thinking about effects on others is the defining factor in ethics; rather, whenever one uses consequences as the principal way of ethical thinking, it is essential to take into account how others are affected and not only the effects on oneself.

Identifying possible solutions and taking into account the effects on everyone does not always lead to a clear-cut solution, but it forces one out of a narrow self-centered focus on the issue at hand.

Considering Fairness to Others

The third step in ethical decision making is considering whether proposed actions are fair to everyone who may be affected by them. Considerations of fairness apply most readily in situations of inter-personal relations. Fairness is not concerned chiefly about the actual outcome of actions; it is concerned mostly about the process by which the outcome is reached. One way of expressing this is in terms of the Golden Rule: "Always treat others the way you would want to be treated." Fairness requires looking at situations from the other person's point of view. Parents and teachers regularly teach this to children. "How would you feel if someone did that to you?" When we place ourselves imaginatively in another person's situation, we apply a standard of equality to our behavior. If I would not like to be lied to when buying something, then I should not lie to others when I am selling something.

Think of a situation in which two people make a bargain: Mike agrees to pay Tom $200 for his bicycle. If we have concerns about the consequences of the sale, we might ask questions like: Could Tom have received more money from another buyer? Will Mike use the bicycle as much as he intends? What will Tom do with the money he gets from the sale? Such questions don't really apply when looking at the fairness of the transaction. Instead, we want to look at the conditions under which the transaction takes place. So, concerns about fairness might prompt different kinds of questions, like: Does Mike know the true condition of the bicycle, or did Tom tell him that it is in better condition than it actually is? Does Mike actually have $200, or is he hoping to get the bicycle from Tom before paying the whole amount and never pay the balance?

Another way to think about fairness is by asking the question: "What if everybody did that?" This takes consideration beyond the realm of interpersonal relations into more universal territory. For example, if I take my boat out to the lake and discover a gallon of deteriorated gasoline in the tank left over from last season, the easiest way to dispose of it may be simply to dump it in the lake. I might think to myself: "This lake has millions of gallons of water in it. One gallon of gasoline won't have any significant effect. Why not just dump it overboard?" But what if everybody disposed of their unusable gasoline that way? I wouldn't want tens of thousands of people dumping gasoline into the lake every summer. Why should I allow myself to do something that I wouldn't want others to do? Do I think I am better or more privileged than everyone else? In a case like this, I consider my proposed action (dumping a gallon of gasoline into a lake) to be wrong, not because it would actually lead to thousands of other people doing the same thing, but because there is no good reason to justify allowing myself to do it and not allowing everyone else to do it also. It wouldn't be fair.

Certain types of behavior are almost always ruled out when we think of them in terms of fairness: lying, stealing, cheating, manipulating, bullying, torturing, killing. Such behaviors are generally considered unethical because we can think of few, if any, situations in which we would agree that they should be done to us. None of us would like to live in a world in which those behaviors were standard practice.

Evaluating People's Character

The final step is taking into account the character of the people whose actions are in question. Character reasoning can be the most difficult type of reasoning for people to become proficient at because no general principle describes how to do it. Character reasoning places the person first. It looks at how a person does something rather than at the action in itself. This is generally not a preferred way of reasoning because people tend to evaluate actions on their own, apart from the person doing the action. We like to ask, "Is this the right thing to do?" or, "Is this action good or bad?" But using character reasoning raises questions such as: Why is he doing this? What kind of person is she?

For example, Arnie asks Arlene if she would like a ride to the shopping mall. Arlene says she would and thinks it is really thoughtful of Arnie to ask her. She had the impression he did not care about others, but now her opinion of him is changing. They get into his car, and when they reach the Interstate, Arnie says, "I'm really glad you came along. I always like to find someone to go on this trip with me so I can use the commuter lane. I hate driving in the slow lanes." Arlene thinks to herself, "So, he isn't being nice to me after all. I guess he really is just as self-centered as I always thought he was." Is there anything wrong with Arnie's action? Well, not when you look at it from the perspectives of consequences or fairness. The ride has positive benefits for both of them, and it's something they both freely agreed to do. At the same time, there is nothing praiseworthy or admirable about what he is doing. He did it for purely selfish reasons.

When evaluating situations from the perspective of character, one looks at what motivates a person's behavior. Does the action proceed from traits that tend to build good relationships among people? Is it done out of generosity or gratitude or hospitality? Or does the action proceed from character traits that tend to corrode relationships, such as vengeance, greed, spite, or selfishness?

CONCLUSION

Using the four ways of ethical thinking does not guarantee that one will not have serious disagreements with others, nor does it guarantee that one will always reach good, responsible conclusions. But it does make it more likely that one will appreciate the legitimate merits of the views of those with whom one has a conflict. It also proves useful as a way of making sure one does not take too narrow an approach in thinking through difficult cases or issues.

Of course, using the Four-Way Method competently requires a good grasp of each of the four ways of thinking. Despite learning how to engage in each of the four ways of thinking since early childhood, we can continue to learn how to use them better throughout our lives. It is to that end—learning to use each of the four ways of thinking more consistently and intentionally—that the following chapters turn.

Truth

EARLY IN PLATO'S *APOLOGY,* when Socrates is explaining to the jurors how he came to be disliked by so many people in the city of Athens, he tells the story of his friend, Chairephon, who made a trip to the oracle at Delphi to ask whether any man was wiser than Socrates.[1] The oracle answered, "No one is wiser." When Socrates heard this, he was suspicious. After all, the oracle had a reputation for giving notoriously ambiguous answers to straightforward questions. So he began to question his fellow citizens, especially those who had a reputation for wisdom, and he discovered that the people he questioned generally thought they knew much more than they did. In fact, he noticed that those who thought they knew what they were talking about were more likely to be ignorant than the people who didn't think they knew much. He said to himself: "I am wiser than this man; it is likely that neither of us knows anything worthwhile, but he thinks he knows something when he does not, whereas when I do not know neither do I think I know; so I am likely to be wiser than he to this small extent, that I do not think I know what

---

1. Delphi was thought to be located at the center of the world, and people from all over Greece would travel there to ask the oracle questions. The god Apollo was believed to speak through his priestess (called "Pythia"); her pronouncements would be translated by the priests attending the shrine and delivered to the supplicant. See Joseph Fontenrose, *Delphic Oracle: Its Responses and Operations, with a Catalogue of Responses* (Berkeley: University of California Press, 1978).

I do not know."[2] This has come to be known as "Socratic wisdom," namely, that wisdom consists in not thinking one knows what one does not know.

It is important to keep this story in mind when thinking about ethical issues because, just as in ancient Athens, people often assume too quickly that they know what is right or wrong in a given situation and are therefore inclined to act on what they want to be true rather than what actually is true.[3] Socrates teaches us that the first and most important task in ethical deliberation is not taking a position but rather asking questions.

Finding the truth is hard work. It proves difficult sometimes just to gather relevant information, but it may also be hard to prepare ourselves to acknowledge the truth of information we don't want to hear. Consider an example.

Ray loves to eat fish, and his favorite fish is salmon. He not only enjoys cooking and eating salmon, he also feels good about it because he imagines that salmon is pure and plentiful—neither raised in factory farms like most poultry nor a scarce resource like some other kinds of ocean fish, such as cod or snapper.

One evening Ray prepares a salmon dinner for his girlfriend, Penny. She asks him if it is Atlantic salmon or wild Alaskan salmon. He isn't sure. Is there a difference? Yes, Penny assures him, a big difference. Someone told her recently that Atlantic salmon is farm-raised and has high levels of toxins, whereas wild Alaskan salmon is much healthier. Anyway, she is pretty sure that's what she heard, though she cannot remember who told her.

The next time Ray goes to the grocery store, he asks the person at the fish counter what kind of salmon they sell and is told it comes from Chile. Does that mean it is farm-raised or wild? The person at the counter doesn't know.

Ray searches the Internet and finds lots of information about salmon, but much of it, especially about health benefits, is contradictory. He checks other grocery stores in town and finds only one that sells wild Alaskan salmon, but it costs twice as much as the salmon

---

2. Plato, *Apology*, in *The Trial and Death of Socrates* trans. G.M.A. Grube, rev. C.D.C. Reeve (Indianapolis, IN: Hackett, 1975), 21d.

3. Evidence for this claim will be examined later in the section on bias.

he has been buying for the past two years. He's not sure if the salmon he has been eating is good for him; he's not sure if fish farming is an industry he wants to support; and he's not sure if he wants to know, because he can't afford to buy wild Alaskan salmon regularly and doesn't want to give up his favorite meal.[4]

Think of all the things a person buys over the course of a year—food, beverages, clothing, computers, cars, and so on. Every purchase is an ethical act. But how can one possibly get enough information to make purchases responsibly? Where do the products come from? What is their environmental impact? How do they affect people's health? Were the people who made them paid a fair wage? How is the profit being used?

We live in what is sometimes called the information age, but more information is available than any person could discover, much less comprehend, in a lifetime. Much of the readily available information is unreliable, produced as part of marketing campaigns for products and services. Even when one's work requires a great deal of knowledge about certain kinds of things, it proves difficult to know enough to make consistently sound judgments. Medical doctors, for example, know relatively little about most of the drugs they can prescribe.[5] Judges tend to know little in advance about the relevant laws in the cases that come before them. Many professors have read only a small percentage of the published literature in the subject areas they teach. That's not to say that most doctors, judges, and professors are incompetent; it's just that there is too much information even in specialized professional fields for individuals to know most of it. What characterizes professional competence is not the ability to know everything in a particular field but rather the ability to sort out and comprehend the relevant information required to do one's job in a satisfactory manner.

The latter ability is not only time-consuming, it also requires a willingness to learn new things, which is sometimes uncomfortable, especially if what we learn forces us to change how we live and work. Determining the truth requires three things:

---

4. For information on the health and economic effects of wild vs. farm-raised salmon, see "Why Eat Wild?" *Trout* (Winter 2007), *http://online.qmags.com/TU0807S/*.

5. The *Physician's Desk Reference* contains thirty-five hundred pages of information on more than twenty-four hundred prescription drugs.

- **Responsibility**—taking ownership of one's beliefs
- **Acknowledgment**—being aware of the conditions that prevent one from recognizing the truth when faced with it
- **Discernment**—knowing where to look and how to sort through information to distinguish the relevant from the irrelevant

RESPONSIBILITY

People sometimes say, "Everyone is entitled to their own beliefs," as if people can have any beliefs they want and should never be criticized for them. That is not really the case. We actually do hold people accountable for their beliefs, especially when those beliefs result in actions that have good or bad effects on others. If a bicycle thief defends himself in court by saying, "I don't believe in the doctrine of private property," the judge's response is apt to be, "Well, that's too bad for you; what you did based on that belief will earn you time in prison." In other words, moral responsibility does not begin with the decisions that lead to one's actions. It begins with the beliefs one forms, which then shape one's decisions. In fact, one could even say that one's perceptions, which lead to belief, are part of the context of moral responsibility.

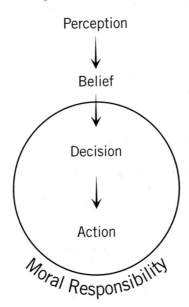

One can picture moral responsibility as a circle that encompasses certain aspects of a person's life. It is natural to think that the circle should encompass only intentional decisions and the actions that follow from them. After all, one "makes decisions" and "performs actions." We normally say that one "has" certain perceptions and "holds" certain beliefs, as if perception and belief are not something one does. However, a more accurate picture would place perception, belief, decision, and action all within the sphere of moral responsibility, for human beings are continually, actively shaping their beliefs, and even their perceptions result in large part from what they want to pay attention to.

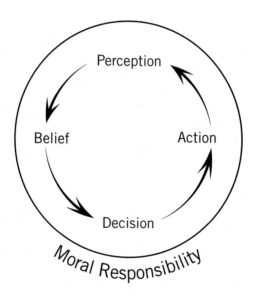

The complex relationship among perception, belief, decision, and action may be illustrated by looking at cases of disputed moral responsibility. For example, one of the probable factors in the April 20, 2010, explosion on the oil rig *Deepwater Horizon* was that the British Petroleum (BP) executives in charge of oil operations didn't believe a more expensive type of casing design was necessary. There were also a number of other possible factors in the blowout: deciding not to perform a crucial test of the stability of cement in the plug;

using seawater instead of drilling mud during a pressure test; installing a test valve in place of a variable bore ram that could stop oil flow in the event of a blowout; using only six centralizers to stabilize the pipe during a pressure test rather than twenty-one centralizers as recommended by a contractor for Halliburton, a large energy services company that helped erect the rig.[6] Having the wrong beliefs in that case was blameworthy. The BP executives should have known that the design carried great risk. Other key decision makers working for Halliburton and Transocean, the owner of the *Deepwater Horizon*, opted to take steps that in hindsight appear negligent. At the time of their decisions, they were likely acting appropriately based on their perception of the situation.

In many circumstances, we bear moral responsibility for what we believe because our actions follow directly from those beliefs. If we don't take care to ensure that we base our beliefs on what is really happening, our actions will fail to achieve what we intend. It is likely that none of the major decision makers intended for a blowout to occur on the *Deepwater Horizon;* nevertheless, a blowout resulted from decision makers' acting on their beliefs, and in at least some instances, they should have believed differently.

For the most part, people are held morally responsible for their actions only when those actions are intentional, and for actions to be intentional, one must know what one is doing. For example, if I step on someone's foot while carrying a bag of groceries, it is just an accident—painful, perhaps, for the person whose foot I just stepped on, and I might feel bad about it, but it's not a morally blameworthy action. I didn't mean to do it, and I couldn't be expected to see the person's foot while carrying the groceries. But if I back into my neighbor's car because I'm running late for an appointment, and I didn't take time to look behind me, I am morally responsible because I should have looked, and if I had looked I would have known that

---

6. For an overview of possible causes of the *Deepwater Horizon* blowout, see the following articles: Steve Mufson, "Pressure to Save Time, Money May Have Contributed to Oil Disaster," *The Washington Post*, May 25, 2010; Ramit Plushnick-Masti, "Gulf Oil-rig Explosion Preceded by Days of Worries, Arguments and Still-Unanswered Questions," *Orlando Sentinel*, September 9, 2010; David S. Hilzenrath, "BP Internal Investigation Report Leaves Some Things Unsaid," *The Washington Post*, September 12, 2010.

a car was parked there. As the *Deepwater Horizon* case illustrates, sometimes the most important thing for someone to do is to know. Acting out of ignorance is no excuse from moral culpability where one has a responsibility to know in the first place.

We cannot be held morally responsible to know everything. There are many things we cannot know, and sometimes we hold beliefs in the absence of knowledge. For example, I may believe it won't rain in the next hour. The consequence of that belief may be that, if I am wrong, I will get wet while walking back from the grocery store. It doesn't matter much in that case whether my belief is true or false, because the consequences are fairly minor and affect only me. But if I am a second-grade teacher planning a field trip to the zoo, much more depends on whether my belief about the potential for rain is accurate. I am responsible for forming that belief, and if I don't bother to check the weather prediction, I could be responsible for twenty-five seven-year-old children getting wet. In such a case I should be criticized not only for taking the children out into the rain but also for forming the belief, in the absence of any supporting evidence, that it would not rain.

Sometimes morally irresponsible beliefs are widely shared. According to a 2009 survey conducted by the Pew Research Center for the People and the Press, only 57 percent of Americans believe there is solid evidence of global warming.[7] That is so despite the near universal agreement among scientists who study global temperatures that Earth's temperatures have been increasing steadily for the past several decades.[8] In a situation like this, where the evidence supporting global warming is apparent and readily available to anyone who chooses to look for it, it is morally irresponsible to discount the evidence.

Americans may be reluctant to attribute moral responsibility to one's beliefs because of the high value put on freedom of speech. After all, aren't people free to express any beliefs they want? The answer is yes, within limits. Every society, including ours, imposes limits upon acceptable speech. People are not legally free, for example, to threaten

---

7. "Fewer Americans See Solid Evidence of Global Warming," Pew Research Center for the People and the Press, October 22, 2009, *http://people-press.org/reports/pdf/556.pdf*.

8. See "Climate Change: How Do We Know?" National Aeronautics and Space Administration (NASA), *http://climate.nasa.gov/evidence/*.

to harm another person, to discuss plans to commit a crime, or to incite people to violence, and so on. People do have the legal right to express most kinds of ideas, however. That means they cannot be charged and convicted of breaking a law for saying, for example, that global climate change is a conspiracy dreamed up by Al Gore, or that the Earth is flat, or that John F. Kennedy was assassinated by Rastafarians. That people cannot be legally charged for holding and expressing such ideas, though, does not mean they cannot be morally criticized for them. People believe all sorts of irresponsible things. Although they are, for the most part, legally free to express those beliefs, others are legally free to criticize them on moral grounds for expressing those beliefs. In the United States, it is legally permissible to deny publicly that the Holocaust took place, but it is morally impermissible to do so. Given the amount of historical evidence, there is no excuse for a reasonably educated person to believe the Holocaust did not happen.[9]

We bear moral responsibility not only for our own beliefs but also, in certain contexts, for the beliefs of others, especially in situations where we have access to information that is important for others or where we hold a position of authority. Parents are responsible for many (but not all) of their young children's beliefs. A father, for example, may tell his children, through words or behavior, that they do not have to wash their hands when they are sick. As a result the children may not believe in the importance of hand-washing, and they may spread germs to other children at school. In similar fashion a supervisor may be responsible for some of the beliefs of the people she supervises, especially regarding safety issues at work. A doctor has responsibility for some of the beliefs of his patients—for example, about whether one should take all of the antibiotics prescribed or just enough to make one feel better.

One of the underappreciated aspects of a democracy is that citizens are—to a certain extent—morally responsible for one another's beliefs. This is not to say that I, for example, am personally responsible for what the person across the street from me believes but rather that we have a general responsibility for our conversations

9. See Deborah E. Lipstadt, *Denying the Holocaust: The Growing Assault on Truth and Memory* (New York: Macmillan, 1995).

with one another, for participating in public discourse about laws and policies that affect our common life. In short sometimes a person is responsible both for knowing certain things and for passing that knowledge on to others.[10]

ACKNOWLEDGMENT

How does it happen that people sometimes believe things in the absence of any evidence or even in the face of evidence that should overturn their beliefs? There are several explanations for why this happens. This section will examine three: (1) self-deception, which is the human propensity for keeping the truth hidden from oneself; (2) power, which affects one's capacity for empathy and how one views events; and (3) bias, which is an unjustified selectivity in how one perceives things.

Self-Deception

E. M. Forster's novel *A Passage to India* depicts British colonialists as woefully ignorant of the lives and character of the native Indians. However, their ignorance is caused not by a lack of readily available information but rather by a determination not to know. The colonialists' political power, their social status, their wealth—all depend on a system of racial inequality they see as justified. The more evidence they can find to assist them in justifying the inequality, the better they feel about themselves and the advantages they enjoy.

> A little group of Indian ladies had been gathering in a third quarter of the grounds, near a rustic summer-house in which the more timid of them had already taken refuge. The rest stood with their backs to the company and their faces pressed into a bank of shrubs. . . .
> "They ought never to have been allowed to drive in; it's so bad for them," said Mrs. Turton, who had at last begun

---

10. A good example of this can be read in FBI agent Colleen Crowley's memo (dated May 21, 2002) to former FBI director Robert Mueller regarding lapses in communication that led to the 9-11 terrorist attacks on New York City and Washington, DC, "The Bombshell Memo," *Time*, *http://www.time.com/time/covers/1101020603/memo.html*.

her progress to the summer-house, accompanied by Mrs. Moore, Miss Quested, and a terrier. "Why they come at all I don't know. They hate it as much as we do. . . ."

"Do kindly tell us who these ladies are," asked Mrs. Moore.

"You're superior to them, anyway. Don't forget that. You're superior to everyone in India except for one or two of the Ranis, and they're on an equality."

Advancing, she shook hands with the group and said a few words of welcome in Urdu. . . .

"Please tell these ladies that I wish we could speak their language, but we have only just come to their country."

"Perhaps we speak yours a little," one of the ladies said.

"Why fancy, she understands!" said Mrs. Turton.

"Eastbourne, Piccadilly, High Park Corner," said another of the ladies. . . .

"She knows Paris also," called one of the onlookers.

"They pass Paris on the way, no doubt," said Mrs. Turton, as if she was describing the movements of migratory birds. Her manner had grown more distant since she had discovered that some of the group was Westernized, and might apply her own standards to her.[11]

This excerpt exemplifies the idea of self-deception—a kind of willful ignorance, a way of keeping certain facts hidden from oneself, so one can avoid facing uncomfortable truths about oneself or others. Sometimes self-deception is individual, and other times, as in the case of the British colonialists in the passage above, it is assisted by a community of people.

Imagine a restaurant that has operated successfully for many years. The owner, the chef, and the various employees are all satisfied with the business, and they haven't made any significant changes in either menu or décor since the restaurant opened. Business has been consistent over the years, but recently the number of customers has decreased. Those involved in the restaurant talk to one another about the situation, but just informally. The consensus seems to be that this is a normal cycle, and soon things will start to pick up again. Maybe people aren't eating

---

11. E. M. Forster, *A Passage to India* (New York: Harcourt, 1942), 41–43.

out as much anymore, someone suggests. The waitstaff reports that they haven't noticed any change in the level of satisfaction among the diners. They get occasional complaints, but no more than usual. Most customers seem satisfied with their dining experience. They all reassure one another. "We're doing everything we can," they say. "We just have to be patient. Business will pick up." Nobody proposes contacting some of the formerly regular customers who haven't patronized the restaurant recently. Nobody suggests dining at a competitor's restaurant to compare menus and the overall dining experience. Nobody even suggests researching data to find out whether business is down to the same extent at other restaurants in the region. In short, nobody does anything to find the real cause of the slowdown. Why? Because everyone has something to lose by the answers. The owner may have to invest in a remodeling project. The chef may have to come up with some creative new entrées. The business manager may have to develop new marketing strategies. The waitstaff may have to improve the level of customer service. So they not only avoid finding out the real cause of what's going on in their business, they actively discourage one another from asking the hard questions that might lead to changes.

This happens frequently in small businesses, churches, service organizations, and even families. The tendency to engage in self-deception is pervasive. Even in large corporations, which one might suppose have systems in place to ensure everybody squarely faces the facts, the human incentive to avoid facts remains powerful. Consider what Lee Iacocca, former CEO of Chrysler, said in August 2007 during an interview with Steve Inskeep on National Public Radio:

> **Inskeep:** What comes to your mind when you hear that Toyota is in the process of passing General Motors as the largest car company?
>
> **Iacocca:** We must have done something wrong. The Big Three is not the big three anymore as we used to know it.
>
> **Inskeep:** Any idea what might have gone wrong?
>
> **Iacocca:** Didn't adapt quickly enough to the energy problem in this country, and gas getting to $3.50 a gallon. Not ready with the right kind of cars. Japanese always had smaller fuel-efficient cars. We got to learn to build more small cars, good fuel-efficient cars.

Inskeep: Would you take me through time a little bit. When people were talking about energy efficiency in, say, the early 1980s, what was your view of all that?

Iacocca: Probably I wasn't very conscious of it. We were on a joyride on free oil almost. And we always made energy cheap. And we did it for too long.[12]

It was common knowledge at the time that the world was nearing peak oil (the point at which the world's oil production reaches maximum capacity and thereafter begins to decline). U.S. domestic oil production had already peaked in the 1970s. Economists were predicting the rise of oil prices as a result of increasing global demand and diminishing supplies. So it remains hard to understand why a large corporation like Chrysler did not foresee the future demand for more fuel-efficient automobiles, unless they simply did not want to acknowledge it.

Chrysler was not the only automobile manufacturer at the time engaged in self-deception. During the 1980s General Motors was the largest automobile producer in the world, and yet it was beset by labor problems and lack of quality control at many of its manufacturing plants. The worst of those was a plant in Fremont, California, known as NUMMI. Billy Haggerty, an assembly-line worker, recalled that if managers didn't have enough people to run the lines, they would "go right across the street to the bar, grab people out of there and bring them in." Once the assembly line started up, workers were not allowed to stop it, regardless of what problems they encountered; as a result numerous defects were simply overlooked. "So we had Monte Carlos with Regal front ends and vice versa," said Haggerty.[13] GM closed the plant in 1982 and then reopened it in 1984, using plant management techniques adopted from Toyota. Despite having nearly the same workforce they had had two years earlier, the quality of the automobiles produced immediately ranked among the

---

12. National Public Radio, "Iacocca Says Detroit Is Living in the Past," *Morning Edition*, aired April 26, 2007, *http://www.npr.org/templates/transcript/transcript. php?storyId=9839029.*

13. Frank Langfitt, "The End of the Line for GM-Toyota Joint Venture," National Public Radio, March 26, 2010, *http://www.npr.org/templates/story/story. php?storyId=125229157.*

highest in the United States. Steve Bera, one of the sixteen so-called NUMMI Commandos responsible for the remarkable resurrection of the Fremont plant, expected that they would be asked to share what they had learned about quality improvement with other GM plants across the nation. But there seemed to be little interest in improving the other plants. "Instead of coming back to the sixteen of us and saying, 'There's some secret sauce here, what is it? How can we use it to our advantage?' No one ever asked us that question."[14] Another of the NUMMI Commandos, Larry Spiegel, noted, "The lack of receptiveness to change was so deep. There were too many people convinced they didn't need to change."[15]

In large organizations, where people in different roles have different types of interests and, frequently, incompatible motivations for adopting changes, strategies of self-deception can become mutually supportive. The strategies are effective only because individuals within the organizations are already disposed to be deceived.

Power

One factor that both encourages and enables self-deception is power. It encourages self-deception because people are more likely to flatter, or at least remain silent in the presence of, the person who has power over them. Power also enables self-deception by making it easier to control one's experiences. For example, a person in a position of power generally has a greater ability to control whom she talks to, and when, and under what conditions. A CEO of a large corporation will typically have several people—and several doors—one has to go through to have a conversation. This makes it more likely she will not be corrected by others if she does not wish to be.

The Hebrew Scriptures contain a well-known story illustrating the relationship between self-deception and power. David, the king of the Israelites, happened to see a beautiful woman bathing. He asked about her and discovered that she was Bathsheba, the wife of Uriah, one of his soldiers who was gone fighting a campaign. David sent a servant to bring Bathsheba to him, had sex with her, and Bathsheba became pregnant. Wishing to avoid the scandal that would

---

14. Ibid.
15. Ibid.

ensue if Uriah learned of this, David ordered one of his officers to send Uriah into battle where the fighting was thickest. A few days later David received a report that Uriah had been killed. Then David brought Bathsheba to his palace and married her. After Bathsheba gave birth to their son, Nathan the prophet came to see David. He told the following story:

> "There were two men in a certain city, one rich and the other poor. The rich man had very many flocks and herds; but the poor man had nothing but one little ewe lamb, which he had bought. He brought it up, and it grew up with him and with his children; it used to eat of his meager fare, and drink from his cup, and lie in his bosom, and it was like a daughter to him. Now there came a traveler to the rich man, and he was loath to take one of his own flock or herd to prepare for the wayfarer who had come to him, but he took the poor man's lamb, and prepared that for the guest who had come to him." Then David's anger was greatly kindled against the man. He said to Nathan, "As the Lord lives, the man who has done this deserves to die; he shall restore the lamb fourfold, because he did this thing, and because he had no pity." Nathan said to David, "You are the man!" (2 Samuel 12:1–7)

Like other Hebrew prophets, Nathan had the ability to speak to the king in ways ordinary subjects did not. But prophets still had to find creative ways of getting kings to pay attention. Nathan accomplished this by getting David to pronounce judgment on the character in his story, thus piercing the veil of self-deception by self-condemnation.

One does not have to be a king to experience how power may lead to self-deception. Everyone has power to some extent. We all have the ability to influence others, to get certain things done, to change events for better or worse. Power is not in itself either good or bad; it can be used in many ways. But understanding how it affects our ability to perceive what is going on in our surroundings accurately proves crucial. Generally speaking, the more power one has within a social setting, the harder it is to perceive truthfully what is going on within that setting—both because of one's own tendency toward self-deception and because one's experiences are filtered. In most everyday situations, the power we have relative to others is offset by the corresponding power others have over us. Certain situations, such as war, upset that delicate balance, so some people have complete power over others. Simone Weil (1909–1943), in her essay *The Iliad, or The Poem of Force*, notes what occurs to people's perceptions of one another in such situations:

> Anybody who is in our vicinity exercises a certain power over us by his very presence, and a power that belongs to him alone, that is, the power of halting, repressing, modifying each movement that our body sketches out. If we step aside for a passer-by on the road, it is not the same as stepping aside to avoid a billboard; alone in our rooms, we get up, walk about, sit down again quite differently from the way we do when we have a visitor. But this indefinable influence that the presence of another human being has on us is not exercised by men whom a moment of impatience can deprive of life, who can die before even thought has a chance to pass sentence on them. In their presence, people move about as if they were not there; they, on their side, running the risk of being reduced to nothing in a single instant, imitate nothingness in their own persons. Pushed, they fall. Fallen, they lie where they are, unless chance gives somebody the idea of raising them up again.[16]

Conditions similar to this, though perhaps not so extreme, exist in any setting where one finds a significant imbalance of power: in many corporations, for example, or sometimes families, factories, or universities. Possession of great power tends to make other people less visible. So the ability to perceive accurately may, at times, require that one voluntarily surrender power or place oneself in situations where power cannot be easily exercised.[17]

---

16. Simone Weil, *The Iliad, or The Poem of Force* (Wallingford, PA: Pendle Hill, 1956), 7.

17. For some interesting studies of the effects of power in social settings see Deborah H. Gruenfeld, M. Ena Inesi, Joe C. Magee, and Adam D. Galinsky, "Power and the Objectification of Social Targets," *Journal of Personality and Social Psychology*, vol. 95, no. 1 (2008): 111–127; and Deborah H. Gruenfeld, M. Ena Inesi, Joe C. Magee, and Adam D. Galinsky, "Power and Perspectives Not Taken," *Psychological Science*, vol. 17, no. 12 (2009): 1068–1074.

Bias

Bias is a function of partiality. Human perception of events is nearly always partial, that is, more weight or prominence is given to certain features of things because of one's affections, fears, geographic location, experience, loyalties, and so on. Complete impartiality is impossible to attain, and yet one can learn to get closer to truth in one's perceptions and judgments by knowing how certain common types of bias tend to exert undue, and often unacknowledged, influence.

The idea that people are selective in their perceptions is not new. Francis Bacon (1561–1626), an English scientist and philosopher, observed long ago that people tend to favor evidence that supports their existing opinions:

> The human understanding when it has once adopted an opinion (either as being the received opinion or as being agreeable to itself) draws all things else to support and agree with it. And though there be a greater number and weight of instances to be found on the other side, yet these it either neglects and despises, or else by some distinction sets aside and rejects; in order that by this great and pernicious predetermination the authority of its former conclusions may remain inviolate.[18]

Known as "confirmation bias,"[19] it is the tendency to select evidence that confirms favored beliefs and to reject evidence that runs counter to them. People select evidence by paying attention to some sources more than others (for example, getting all of one's news from a single newspaper or Web site), by adopting critical or uncritical attitudes toward certain sources, by remembering certain kinds of information and forgetting others, and so on.

Confirmation bias may explain why people believe so many things that cannot be supported by evidence, even when the evidence

---

18. Francis Bacon, "Novum Organum," in *The English Philosophers from Bacon to Mill*, ed. E. A. Burtt (New York: Random House, 1932), 36. Cited in Raymond S. Nickerson, "Confirmation Bias: A Ubiquitous Phenomenon in Many Guises," *Review of General Psychology*, vol. 2, no. 2 (1998).

19. Raymond S. Nickerson, "Confirmation Bias: A Ubiquitous Phenomenon in Many Guises," *Review of General Psychology*, vol. 2, no. 2 (1998): 175–220.

is pointed out or readily available. Horoscopes have been popular for centuries, despite the lack of any evidence indicating a correlation between their predictions and the outcome of actual events. Roughly half of new businesses fail within five years,[20] yet no one starts a business thinking it will not succeed. People all over the nation regularly buy lottery tickets, believing the odds of winning a jackpot are much greater than they actually are. Many businesses even base their marketing on the likelihood that people will allow wishful thinking to convince them they can save money or improve their health, looks, or fitness through products that are proven to do nothing at all.[21]

The news media are often accused of bias. That is, people often claim that TV networks, newspapers, Internet sites, or radio programs favor one political perspective over another. In one respect, such bias is incontestable. Not every event, or every facet of an event, can be reported. Journalists and editors must choose which things are "newsworthy" and then select which facts and opinions about the event to include in a story. They must decide how prominent the story should be, whether it should be featured or moved into the background. A number of things influence such decisions. Limitations of space and resources, evaluation of how influential an event will be, expectations of the amount of public interest the story will generate—all factor into decisions about media coverage. Many of these factors are known and acknowledged. But when critics of a media organization allege bias, they are claiming that some of the factors influencing decisions (in particular, favoritism toward a particular party or political point of view) are unacknowledged, that journalists or editors are not themselves aware of how certain factors influence their decisions, or that they refuse to publicly admit the influence of such factors.

People tend to take offense at an allegation of bias, because it implies either that they are not being honest (that is, they refuse to

---

20. See the annual statistics reported by the Small Business Administration at *www. sba.gov*.

21. For a recent example, see reports about the "Power Balance" wristband sold to millions of people with the claim that it would enhance athletic performance and stamina by resonating with the body's "energy flow." David DeSalvo, "Power Balance Scam Shows Again That the Pseudoscience Song Remains the Same," *Psychology Today, http://www.psychologytoday.com/blog/neuronarrative/201101/power-balance-scam-shows-again-the-pseudoscience-song-remains-the-same.*

admit their partiality) or that they literally do not know their own minds (that is, their perceptions and judgments are not under their conscious control). Moreover, people in professional positions tend to take pride in acting according to certain standards, in knowing how to sort through information, distinguishing what is important from what is unimportant, and making decisions based on what is true and good. Financial analysts, for example, are trained to know what is really going on economically, so that they can give sound advice regarding investments. Physicians are trained to examine patients to determine what is causing certain problems and then prescribe a course of treatment. Most professionals, in short, are trained not to be biased—to be able to determine what is true and good.

However, multiple studies of bias reveal its pervasiveness. The fact that one is trained not to let partiality influence one's judgments does not necessarily mean one is less susceptible to bias. In fact, complacency about the influence of partiality because of overconfidence in one's training and ability may increase one's susceptibility toward bias.

It is well known among people who work in fraud detection that successful professionals are more likely, not less, to be victims of fraud. Dennis Marlock, a veteran of the Milwaukee Police Department who has made a career of studying fraud, puts it this way:

> The biggest misconception about fraud is that the victims are stupid. The truth is, con artists prefer intelligent people. First, smart people are more likely to have money. Second, smart people are easier to fool precisely because they think they're too smart to get scammed. We deal with victims who are doctors, lawyers, judges—even cops. The easiest people to deceive are those who think that they are immune to deception.[22]

Con artists typically operate by exploiting people's greed, a form of partiality toward money. Smart, successful people are not more likely than the general population to be greedy; rather they are more likely to think they won't be unduly influenced by their partiality. This, ironically, is precisely what makes them more likely to be influenced

22. Linda Tischler, "Master of Deception," *Fast Magazine*, December 31, 2002, *http://www.fastcompany.com/magazine/66/realitycheck.html?page=0%2C0*.

by their partiality; that is, more likely to be biased and thus more susceptible to fraud.[23]

In a survey designed to measure the perception of bias among physicians, first- and second-year medical residents reported that they did not think promotions from pharmaceutical representatives significantly influenced their own prescribing (61 percent said such promotions have no influence on them, and only 1 percent said promotions influence them a lot). However, when asked whether pharmaceutical promotions influence the prescribing of other doctors, 16 percent said such promotions have no influence on other doctors, and 51 percent said such promotions influence other physicians a lot. In other words a majority of young physicians thought they were immune to the influence of pharmaceutical promotions but believed a majority of other doctors were greatly influenced by them.[24] This example highlights how bias affects the very perception of the world around us and our place in it. Most people tend to think their own actions are rational and deliberate, even though they readily acknowledge that others are commonly influenced by greed, ignorance, desire, fear, and a host of other nonrational factors.

Awareness of bias is important because of the many ways bias influences one's perception of the context in which disagreements about ethical issues takes place. For example, numerous studies of college students indicate that most students believe others drink more alcohol and do so more frequently than is actually the case. Because they believe heavy drinking to be pervasive, they are more likely to engage in that behavior themselves.[25] The widespread

23. See Jack Malvern, "Clever People 'Are Easier to Con,'" *The Times*, March 17, 2008, *http://www.timesonline.co.uk/tol/news/uk/crime/article3564520.ece*.

24. M. A. Steinman, M. G. Shlipak, and S. J. McPhee, "Of Principles and Pens: Attitudes and Practices of Medicine Housestaff toward Pharmaceutical Industry Promotions," *American Journal of Medicine*, vol. 111, no. 7 (2001): 551–557.

25. D. A. Prentice and D. T. Miller, "Pluralistic Ignorance and Alcohol Use on Campus: Some Consequences of Misperceiving the Social Norm," *Journal of Personality and Social Psychology*, vol. 64 (1993): 243–256. See also H. W. Perkins, "College Student Misperceptions of Alcohol and Other Drug Norms among Peers: Exploring Causes, Consequences, and Implication for Prevention Programs," in *Designing Alcohol and Other Drug Prevention Programs in Higher Education* (Newton, MA: Higher Education Center for Alcohol and Other Drug Prevention, Department of Education, 1997), 177–206.

misperception about drinking is itself one of the factors contributing to heavy drinking among college students. Another factor in the misperception of social norms is projection bias, or the tendency to assume that other people act similarly to oneself. For example, people who cheat on their taxes are inclined to think that many others cheat on their taxes too. People who do not cheat on their taxes are inclined to think that relatively few people cheat. People who smoke, recycle, conserve scarce resources, and so on, all tend to think their practices are more common than they actually are.[26]

Thus, figuring out the truth is a difficult task, for it not only requires access to information but also the ability to interpret the information correctly. Personal interests often get in the way of interpreting information in a straightforward, objective fashion.

DISCERNMENT

Finding the truth is not merely a matter of reading the right material or talking to the right people; it also consists of having the proper experience and training to interpret the available information correctly. There is no quick way to learn how to do this. In fact, one could say that the primary function of education in general is simply to help us learn how to make sense of things in the world. This requires that one be able to read (that is, recognize meaning in things), to evaluate sources of information, and to evaluate arguments.

Reading

In his book *Life on the Mississippi*, Mark Twain recounts when he learned as a youth to pilot a steamboat on the river. During his first time at the helm he steers the boat sharply toward shore to avoid what he thinks is a reef. Mr. Bixby, the pilot, orders him to turn the boat back on course and run over the reef. Twain questions the order, but Mr. Bixby is insistent. "I'm taking responsibility," he says. So, the young Twain turns the boat toward the reef.

---

26. See research sponsored by the National Social Norms Institute at the University of Virginia at *www.socialnorm.org*.

I . . . made a straight break for the reef. As it disappeared under our bows I held my breath; but we slid over it like oil.

"Now don't you see the difference? It wasn't anything but a *wind* reef. The wind does that."

"So I see. But it is exactly like a bluff reef. How am I ever going to tell them apart?"

"I can't tell you. It is an instinct. By and by you will just naturally *know* one from the other, but you never will be able to explain why or how you know them apart."

It turned out to be true. The face of the water, in time, became a wonderful book—a book that was a dead language to the uneducated passenger, but which told its mind to me without reserve, delivering its most cherished secrets as clearly as if it uttered them with a voice.[27]

Just as Mark Twain had to learn to read the face of the water, the student of ethics has to learn to read the appearances of things to discern what is happening just under or behind the appearances. This is the first and most important step in ethical reasoning, because everything else depends on it. It is important not only for thinking clearly and consistently about one's own reasons for acting in one way or another but also for communicating with other people. If one person sees a bluff reef just ahead and the other sees a wind reef, it is unlikely they will be able to agree on what to do, regardless of how sophisticated their moral reasoning is.

To know what is really going on, sometimes one has to read people: their words, their facial expressions, their body language, or their actions. Sometimes one has to read policy manuals or legal texts. Sometimes one has to read newspaper or Internet accounts of an event. Being able to pay attention to things and becoming skillful at sorting out the significant from the insignificant takes years to learn. It is a skill that can be improved but never perfected. Because the ability to find relevant information, sort through it, and understand it takes many years to develop, little can be said in this chapter that will improve that ability significantly; nevertheless, it may help to keep in mind a few general ideas.

---

27. Mark Twain, *Life on the Mississippi* (New York: Library of America, 1982), 67.

First, acquiring a habit of regular reading is essential. Reading, like most skills, improves with practice, and the amount of practice is more important than native ability. Reading involves what psychologists term *chunking*, grouping bits of information into coherent patterns. When letters are grouped into a word that one has learned, it becomes fairly easy to remember their order. But it proves comparatively difficult to remember a random string of letters.[28] The same principle applies to the vast amounts of information one encounters throughout the day. The ability to make sense of and recall what one experiences depends on the capacity for grouping the bits of information into coherent patterns, and one acquires this ability through practice.

Robert D. Richardson notes that poet Samuel Taylor Coleridge (1772–1834) distinguished four types of readers: "the hourglass, the sponge, the jelly-bag, and the Golconda.[29] The hourglass gives back everything it takes in, unchanged. The sponge gives back everything it takes in, only a little dirtier. The jelly-bag squeezes out the valuable and keeps the worthless, while the Golconda runs everything through a sieve, keeping only the nuggets."[30]

The goal of reading habitually is to become a Golconda: skillfully sifting through the worthless and retaining the valuable.

Second, reading both contemporary and historical sources can help in overcoming one's culturally acquired biases. We live in a largely ahistorical society. Not only do most of us not know much history; we often think it largely irrelevant, so we do not pay much attention to it.

This results in part from the myth of progress, which dates back in literature to the nineteenth century, with writers such as Herbert Spencer (1820–1903), Charles Darwin (1809–1882), and H. G. Wells (1866–1946). The myth also has roots in the popular effects of the scientific age, in the practical effects of scientific application on society, which inclines us to think that the next new thing inevitably

---

28. Here are two strings of twenty-four letters: "The sun was shining on the sea" and "nudmfihengendkmningeexgp." Which string is easier to remember?

29. Golconda was an ancient city in India, renowned for its diamonds.

30. Robert D. Richardson, *First We Read, Then We Write: Emerson on the Creative Process* (Iowa City: University of Iowa Press, 2009), 8.

improves on the last old thing. For the most part this remains a subconscious attitude, expressed in a multitude of ways: the tendency to value youth and disparage age, attentiveness to trends and fashions, brand consciousness, the desire for the new and improved, preference for the synthetic over the natural, and, most of all, the tendency to read only what has been written in the past few days or months or years.

The danger of relying too much on present sources of information and ideas lies in developing a narrow perspective on our own lives and the challenges facing us. We may forget that we not only live in history, but are, to a great extent, products of history. Having forgotten this, we can begin to think that only our own preferences have value.

We can step out of this preoccupation with the present in a couple of ways. One strategy consists of participation in traditional activities, whether civic celebrations, or the ritual of worship, or the activity of politics, sport, music, or dance. G. K. Chesterton (1874–1936) referred to tradition as "the democracy of the dead."[31] It provides a way of keeping the past alive in our daily activities, of allowing those who have gone before us to have a voice in the way we manage the world.

Another way to avoid this preoccupation with the present is to read old books. It is a wise habit to read one book at least a hundred years old for every contemporary book one reads. For every courtroom drama by John Grisham, one could read a tragedy by Shakespeare; for every Stephenie Meyer thriller a novel by Jane Austen; for every contemporary religious text by Marcus Borg an ancient treatise by Athanasius.

Stepping out of a preoccupation with the present can help one see the contemporary world in a broader context. One may come to see that some ideas that seemed new are actually quite old, that some parts of life that seem accidental are actually fundamental to human nature, that some features of society that seem to demand a quick fix

---

31. "Tradition refuses to submit to the small and arrogant oligarchy of those who merely happen to be walking about. All democrats object to men being disqualified by the accident of birth; tradition objects to their being disqualified by the accident of death." G. K. Chesterton, "The Ethics of Elfland," in *Orthodoxy* (Grand Rapids, MI: Christian Classics Ethereal Library, 1990), 7, *http://www.netlibrary.com/Reader/*.

are actually cyclical and will resolve themselves in time. In short, one will be better able to distinguish the truly significant from the merely urgent and articulate to others a perception of events that comes from a broad and comprehensive understanding of things.

Evaluating Sources of Information

We live in what is sometimes called the information age. Unlike a century ago, when most people had access to only one or two newspapers, or fifty years ago, when people had access to a newspaper, a few radio stations, and perhaps three TV networks, most people today have access to thousands of information sources. Anyone who has Internet access can read, watch, and listen to news from around the world. Millions of books are readily available through digital copy and online booksellers. Magazines, academic journals, blogs, social networking sites, government Web sites—all offer access to more information than a person can possibly comprehend. Nearly anyone or anything can be a reliable source of information, but not everyone and everything is. Some sources prove more consistently reliable than others. Being able to determine what is reliable and what is not is necessary to make ethical decisions on the basis of what is really going on.

To evaluate the credibility of information sources, one must look at a number of factors:

- Are there significant conflicts of interest influencing a source's opinions or conclusions?
- Does the information source have a good track record and a reputation for trustworthiness?
- Can the information the source is reporting be confirmed from other sources?

The first consideration when evaluating the credibility of an information source is whether a conflict of interest exists. A conflict of interest is present when someone has something to gain by convincing people to believe one way or another. Some conflicts are relatively easy to spot, but others take some investigation. TV, radio, and newspaper advertisements are not credible sources of information.

This is not to say they are necessarily false or misleading, just that one should be cautious about relying on them, especially as a sole source of information.

Newspapers tend to be fairly credible sources of information. They hold one another to standards of professional journalism, which stipulate a certain level of objectivity in reporting. This has its limits, however. One rarely finds a negative automobile review in a major newspaper, because newspapers receive a considerable percentage of their advertising revenue from automobile dealerships. Thus when looking for credible information about the reliability of a certain make and model of automobile, it would be wise to consult a source that does not accept automobile advertisements, such as *Consumer Reports*. Another limit is caused by the deadlines under which reporters operate. Reporters often work on several stories at once and have only a limited amount of time to research stories before they go to print. Most newspaper stories are designed to get basic facts about events out to the public quickly. It is important for the reader to know which stories are written quickly and which stories are more deliberate, intended by the reporter to provide an in-depth analysis or overview of events.

Some large city newspapers, such as *The New York Times*, *The Washington Post*, and others, employ investigative journalists who specialize in looking into events in more depth and providing detailed analysis. They may also employ fact-checkers to review stories and look for inaccuracies. However, the chief way inaccuracies are caught in many newspapers is by readers. A newspaper that publishes inaccurate information loses credibility with its readership; thus, an alert readership provides a constant incentive to report the truth insofar as possible.[32]

Occasionally, one hears of journalists who have falsified information in their stories. A notorious example is Jayson Blair, who worked as a reporter at *The New York Times* for four years before the paper discovered he had made up crucial information in his stories, including the location of events, people he had interviewed, what they said to him, and so on. He also claimed to have reported from

32. Exceptions to this rule are newspapers like *The National Enquirer* and *Weekly World News*, whose readership seems not to be interested in accuracy; they are more interested in the fantastic and outlandish.

the site of locations he had never visited.[33] But such cases of outright journalistic fraud are relatively rare. Sooner or later, journalists who rely on making up information to meet deadlines get discovered, and their careers are finished.

TV and radio reports are similar in many ways to newspaper reports. They have credibility within limits, and largely for the same reasons. They are also subject to certain conflicts of interest because of their funding sources, but they have to maintain a level of credibility with their audience to maintain viewership or listenership. Generally speaking, the time window for TV and radio reporting is smaller than for newspapers, so the information tends to be more basic, less detailed, and sometimes less fully researched than in newspapers.[34]

The credibility of commercial magazines varies a great deal. Some carry stories from journalists with excellent reputations and the time and resources to do in-depth analysis; others are designed chiefly as vehicles for advertisers, with the occasional product review and how-to article thrown in. It is important for the reader to look into the reputation of the publication and also of the journalist providing the story.

The most credible sources for information are books and articles that are peer reviewed. "Peer review" refers to a process of a group of professionals with expertise in a relevant field evaluating the quality and accuracy of a submission. If a book or article passes the peer-review process, then it is accepted for publication. Such a process does not guarantee the truth of all the claims made in the publication, but it does assure the reader that independent evaluators familiar with the subject matter find the contribution credible and worthy of consideration. This text, for example, has been peer reviewed by professors who teach in the area of ethics.

The Internet is not a specific source of information. It is simply a means of delivering various types of information, such as conversation, news stories, journal articles, TV programs, radio programs,

---

33. "Correcting the Record; Times Reporter Who Resigned Leaves Long Trail of Deception," *The New York Times*, May 11, 2003, *http://www.nytimes.com/2003/05/11/us/correcting-the-record-times-reporter-who-resigned-leaves-long-trail-of-deception.html.*

34. There are, of course, exceptions. Some TV programs, such as *60 Minutes*, provide reporting of events that is as detailed and well researched as stories in well-established newspapers.

books, and so on. As such, the same considerations apply for judging the credibility of Internet sources as for sources published in other media. However, the Internet has made certain new forms of information available that raise questions about credibility, because it allows for forms of communication not possible with other media. Online forums (such as wikis, blogs, and social networking sites), which allow anyone who has access to the Web site to instantly publish information, have proven to be powerful resources for finding information quickly and easily. Yet they are subject to manipulation by people who are ill informed or determined to misinform others. The likelihood of manipulation increases when people contribute information anonymously. A good rule of thumb with such forums is to use them as sources for getting leads on information but not to accept what one finds on them as authoritative.

Evaluating Arguments

Ultimately, regardless of how credible one's sources of information are, how well rounded one's reading is, or how accurate one's perceptions are, one will also have to develop certain basic skills in evaluating arguments. Arguments are the means by which people attempt to persuade one another of the truth of what they are saying. In fact, any form of communication that attempts to persuade (which means, any form of communication that presents claims it encourages the reader to believe) does so by means of argument. A climatologist presenting evidence that Earth's temperature has been increasing over the past century, a politician urging people to support education reform, a parent trying to get her child to eat more vegetables—all use arguments.

In academic contexts the word *argument* does not refer to a verbal contest between people (that's called a *disagreement*). Rather, an argument is a set of logically connected statements in which some of the statements provide reasons for believing other statements. The statements that provide reasons are called *premises*, and the statements supported by the premises are called *conclusions*. For an argument to be considered sound (that is, a good argument), the premises must be true, and the conclusion must follow logically from the premises.

An example of a sound or good argument is this:

You should respect your neighbor. John is your neighbor. You should respect John.

This is, of course, an elementary sort of argument. It has two premises:

"You should respect your neighbor" and "John is your neighbor." The conclusion is "You should respect John."

Most of the arguments considered in this book are significantly more complex, but the key thing to remember is the same for all arguments: for an argument to be sound, the premises must be true, and the conclusion must logically follow from the premises.

An example of an unsound or bad argument is this:

You should hate your neighbor. John is your neighbor. John is a dirty, rotten nincompoop.

The argument is unsound because, first of all, it is not true that you should hate your neighbor, and, second, it does not follow logically from the first two statements that John is a dirty, rotten nincompoop. (He may, in fact, be a fairly decent sort of nincompoop.)

The first statement in each of the sample arguments is debatable. I (the person putting forth the argument) assert that they are true, and anyone who agrees with me will also agree that the first argument is sound. But someone who doesn't think that you should respect your neighbor will not agree that the first argument is sound. In that case, it would be incumbent on me, as the creator of the argument, to provide reasons for that statement, thus creating a supporting argument for the original argument. For genuine dialogue to take place, there must be agreement between people about the truth of some statement(s) or other.

Common Fallacies

Strictly speaking, any unsound argument is considered a fallacy, but the term *fallacy* normally refers to certain types of unsound arguments that are both commonly used and widely believed to be plausible. Of the dozens of commonly used fallacies, a few frequently appear in discussion of ethical issues.

False Dilemma A false dilemma consists of stating (or assuming) that there are only two sides to an issue when actually more alternatives exist.[35] This kind of reasoning occurs frequently in political debates in which it is assumed that the positions taken by Democratic and Republican candidates exhaust all possibilities for choice. "You should vote for Candidate X because Candidate Y wants to raise taxes on the middle class." Even if you did not support raising taxes on the middle class, you would still want to know Candidate X's position before voting, because of the many possible options when it comes to providing funding for government services. Raising or not raising taxes on the middle class doesn't exhaust the many possible actions a candidate could support. (If you were looking to get a ride to Seattle, and Bob said to you, "Don't go with Fred; he's going to Sacramento," you would not automatically decide to ride with Bob. After all, Bob might be planning to go to Saint Paul.)

The false dilemma fallacy appears frequently in debates about certain issues. For example, a death penalty proponent might say: "Society needs capital punishment to make sure murderers aren't allowed back on the street to kill again." The argument rests on the assumption that the only sentencing alternatives for convicted murderers are execution or a term in prison after which they would be released. The argument ignores the most likely alternative: life imprisonment.

Straw Man The straw man fallacy consists of misrepresenting a position in order to argue against it. (The name comes from the image of setting up a figure made of straw to fight, thus ensuring an easy victory.) Successfully arguing against a false position, however, does not really mean one has won the argument. The fallacy depends upon the audience not noticing the initial deception.

An example of a straw man would be something like the following: "Animal rights activists think animals should have all the same protections that people have. But that's crazy. Do they really think deer, raccoons, pigs, and chickens should be given an education and allowed the right to vote?" The fact is, few (perhaps no) animal rights

---

35. This is also known as the false alternative or either/or fallacy.

activists think such a thing, but by misrepresenting their views in this way, the speaker avoids having to address the real (and difficult) issue of whether and how we should take seriously the suffering to which many animals are subjected.

Ad Hominem An *ad hominem* (Latin for "against the person") argument focuses on the person who makes a claim rather than the claim itself.[36] A famous example of this occurred in a speech given by then-governor of Texas, Ann Richards, at the 1988 Democratic National Convention. She said of George H. W. Bush, the Republican candidate for president of the United States, "Poor George. He can't help it. He was born with a silver foot in his mouth." It was a brilliant line because it drew attention to Bush's inherited wealth and his tendency to misspeak in public; it was also completely irrelevant, because it had nothing to do with his policies or qualifications. But that's the power of the *ad hominem*. When used skillfully it causes the hearer to focus on some negative characteristic of a person rather than on the substance of what the person is saying.

Appeal to Authority Citing an authority in a relevant field is normally a good way to support a claim. For example, saying that it will likely rain tomorrow because, on the evening news, meteorologist Ray Sunny predicted a 90 percent chance of thunderstorms, is perfectly acceptable reasoning. It is considered fallacious to use an authority only when the person referred to is not qualified to give expert opinion on the topic under consideration. To use the opinion of a medical doctor to explain why one should invest in a real estate time-share would be an example of a fallacious appeal to authority.

It is generally easy to know when someone is speaking altogether outside his or her realm of expertise, but when somebody exaggerates his authority or uses her authority irresponsibly, it is often difficult to judge. Just because someone has an advanced degree in, say, political science does not mean he or she is equally and adequately informed on all political issues. The burden is always on the evaluator of an argument to determine whether a presumption of credibility should be granted to someone who claims to be an expert.

---

36. This is more commonly referred to as a "personal attack."

Insufficient Evidence Several fallacies have to do with misuse of scientific studies, statistics, surveys, or other kinds of data, but one of the most common is the fallacy of *insufficient evidence*. This refers to a situation where evidence of some sort is used to support a claim that extends beyond the legitimate range of the evidence. All scientific research is limited in scope, and claims made on the basis of the research findings must be consistent with those limitations. For example, a study on the health effects of eating a diet rich in seafood may compare the cholesterol levels of two groups of fifty people, one of which eats seafood three times per week, and another that eats no seafood. The results of such a study may be significant when considered in light of other similar studies, but no findings resulting from it would warrant the claim that "eating fish reduces heart attacks."

A good rule of thumb when citing studies in support of a general claim is to look for meta-analyses of studies of a particular type and see whether they show trends in the data. (A meta-analysis collects data from several related studies and combines them into a single set of data.) Looking at meta-analyses is especially helpful with topics such as global climate change, where there are so many studies using so many different techniques and approaches that it is difficult to attain familiarity with more than a small fraction of the relevant research.[37] Such an approach tends to compensate for idiosyncrasies and biases in particular studies. When it is not possible to refer to a meta-analysis, it is important to keep in mind the limitations of the evidence and also to make sure the claims made on the basis of the evidence do not exceed the scope of the study.

CONCLUSION

William James, an American philosopher and psychologist, wrote that a baby perceives the world "as one great blooming, buzzing confusion."[38] The more one becomes aware of the challenges of getting an accurate and consistent impression of what is going on in

---

37. An example of a meta-analysis in the area of global climate change is Cynthia Rosenzweig et al., "Attributing Physical and Biological Impacts to Anthropogenic Climate Change," *Nature* 453 (15 May 2008): 353–357.

38. William James, *The Principles of Psychology*, vol. 1 (New York: Holt, 1890), 488.

the world, the more one is inclined to think it is a condition from which human beings never escape. Nevertheless, the effort to know the truth is fundamental to living an ethical life. Although truth may be impossible to achieve consistently and thoroughly, one can become better at knowing the truth by developing certain habits and practices, including careful and selective reading, awareness of one's biases, association with people who challenge one's opinions and interpretations of events, and attention to the common fallacies that frequently mislead people. In this way we may progress toward a shared understanding of things that, in turn, allows subsequent efforts at moral reasoning to proceed with sincerity and goodwill.

SUGGESTIONS FOR FURTHER READING ON TRUTH

Frankfurt, Harry. *On Truth*. New York: Alfred A. Knopf, 2006.

This book is a brief defense of the usefulness of truth. It is written for a popular audience, but contains fairly sophisticated philosophical arguments.

Plato. *Five Dialogues*. Trans. G.M.A. Grube. Indianapolis, IN: Hackett, 1981.

This volume includes five of Plato's dialogues dealing with events leading up to the trial of Socrates, the trial itself, his imprisonment, and execution. Together, they give the reader a good sense of the method of Socratic dialogue that places great significance on consistency of thought and avoiding self-deception.

Weston, Anthony. *A Rulebook for Arguments*. 4th ed. Indianapolis, IN: Hackett, 1988.

Weston's handbook is a concise guide for constructing well-formed arguments and functions also as a guide to clear, consistent thinking. It includes a directory of common logical fallacies.

Consequences

EVERY DAY WE MAKE CHOICES by evaluating the likely consequences of our actions. Sometimes we make careful, deliberate comparisons of the consequences, and other times we make quick, almost sub-conscious judgments based on information we have already gathered and considered. In the morning I go to the bathroom to brush my teeth. Why? Because I want to prevent cavities. I go to the kitchen and make some coffee. Should I drink one cup or two? If I drink too much coffee in the morning, I may run out of energy later in the day. But I have lots of tedious work to do in the morning, so maybe it is more important to be fully awake early, even though I may get sleepy later in the day. What should I eat for breakfast? I really like eggs and toast, but the egg yolks may raise my cholesterol level. Oatmeal is healthier; maybe I will have that. By 6:30 a.m. I have already made half a dozen decisions, based mainly on an evaluation of consequences. And the day has just begun.

Many people would consider the choices just described as per-sonal and not ethical, because the consequences only affect oneself. However, even personal choices may be ethical choices, not only because we have duties to ourselves but also because what we choose for ourselves often has an indirect effect on others. Using consequences as a way of ethical thinking encourages us to look at all the relevant consequences, regardless of whether I experience the effects person-ally. If, in deciding whether to drink coffee, I think not just about the effects of caffeine on my energy levels but also about effects on the farmers who grow and harvest the coffee, then I am thinking ethically. Such an approach may also encourage me to consider whether the coffee I am purchasing is a fair-trade product and whether I should support the company that sells the coffee by consuming its product.

In short we think about the consequences of our actions constantly. What makes such thinking a matter of ethics is whether we have broadened the scope of our deliberation to include more than our narrowly circumscribed immediate and personal interests.

This way of thinking about ethics is called *consequentialism*. Decisions about what is right or wrong, good or bad, are made by considering the widespread effects of possible actions and then weighing the effects of one possible action against those of another. Generally speaking, an action is considered "right" or "good" if it has a more positive effect on those affected than the most likely alternatives.

Deliberating in terms of consequences is a powerful and practical way of ethical thinking. Furthermore, this strategy can be broken down into simple, easily understood questions or steps:

1. What is the situation?
2. What are the (likely) possible actions one can take in response to the situation?
3. Who is affected by the possible actions?
4. What are the positive and negative effects of the possible actions?
5. Which action would have the best overall effects?

The advantage of having simple steps such as these is that they remind those who use them to step back from personal, and often emotional, involvement in a situation and take a broader look. As noted in the beginning of chapter 3, it is common for people to jump to conclusions in cases where some personal interest is at stake. A simple set of questions functions like a checklist to ensure one has not forgotten to account for some factor essential to making a responsible decision.[1] Even asking an obvious question like

---

1. Although a checklist may seem like an insignificant tool, using one in complex situations can have profound effects on how things turn out. For a discussion of the significance and many uses of the checklist, see Atul Gawande, *The Checklist Manifesto* (New York: Metropolitan Books, 2009).

"Who is affected by the possible actions?" can be eye-opening for someone who is so emotionally involved in a situation that she has only considered the effects of possible actions on herself or her family or friends.

Having simple steps to follow also provides people who may have different opinions about what is right or wrong in a particular situation with a place to start their discussion. The steps don't guarantee that everyone will agree in the end, but they supply a common starting point to begin deliberations.

Despite these advantages, however, using consequences in ethical thinking is not quite as simple as it might first appear, for the very idea of a consequence can be problematic. It is necessary to have a way to determine which consequences are significant and which are not.

WHAT MAKES SOME CONSEQUENCES MORE SIGNIFICANT THAN OTHERS?

To compare different possible actions and decide which has the best overall effects, one must have some criteria to use in evaluating the consequences of those actions. The criteria used are what define the different versions of consequentialism. The most widely used type of consequentialism is known as *utilitarianism*, a theory proposed by English philosopher and reformer Jeremy Bentham (1748–1832) in the eighteenth century. Bentham argued that all ethical decisions should be based on what he called the principle of utility.

> By the principle of utility is meant that principle which approves or disapproves of every action whatsoever, according to the tendency which it appears to have to augment or diminish the happiness of the party whose interest is in question. . . . By utility is meant that property in any object, whereby it tends to produce benefit, advantage, pleasure, good, or happiness . . . or . . . to prevent the happening of mischief, pain, evil, or unhappiness to the party whose interest is considered.[2]

2. Jeremy Bentham, *The Principles of Morals and Legislation* (Amherst, NY: Prometheus Books, 1988), 2.

In other words, individuals should consider how their actions affect the happiness of everyone involved, with happiness being measured by how much an action increases the pleasure and decreases the pain someone experiences.

JEREMY BENTHAM (1748–1832)

Jeremy Bentham

Jeremy Bentham was born in London in 1748. The son of a lawyer, he himself studied law at Oxford, though he never practiced it. Instead, he devoted himself to writing treatises on moral, political, and legal philosophy. He was intensely interested in reforming social institutions along utilitarian principles. For example, he spent years devising and trying to implement a revolutionary new prison design which he called the "Panopticon."

Bentham wrote thousands of pages of documents, most unpublished during his lifetime. He was influential in politics and an eager participant in legal debates. But the majority of his time was spent writing, and the many reforms he envisioned came to have their greatest influence after his death. Even today his enduring influence can be detected in the very language of politics and economics, in phrases such as "maximizing return on investment" and "cost-benefit analysis."

His *Introduction to the Principles of Morals and Legislation* was published in 1789 and remains his greatest achievement. In it he set forth a theory for evaluating all actions on the basis of "the greatest happiness principle." Bentham was convinced that morality and politics should be based upon the emerging scientific method. In this way, human beings could be freed from the constraints of superstition, custom, and tradition, all of which he believed led people to behave

Continued

irrationally. If social institutions and policies were based on the systematic calculation of pleasure and pain, he argued, the result would be a world in which much needless suffering is eliminated.

Bentham believed that the basic task of moral education is to get individuals to care about the consequences of actions beyond themselves, because people naturally are motivated more by what affects them directly than by what happens to others. The "greatest happiness principle," which he thought should be regarded as the supreme principle of morality, dictates that one take into account the consequences of one's actions on everyone who may be affected.

When Bentham died he left a considerable sum of money to University College in London to provide an education for Catholic and Jewish students who were often denied admission to other universities. His corpse, in accordance with instructions set forth in his will, was preserved, dressed in one of his suits, and seated on a chair. It can still be seen today, residing in a small room, and occasionally attending meetings, at the university.

The genius of Bentham's formulation is that it allows people who might disagree about which consequences are good and which are bad to focus instead on what actually produces pleasure and pain. This provides a criterion with which to evaluate the consequences, rather than leaving it up to individuals to create their own.

Consequentialist thinking works particularly well in situations where a proposed action affects large numbers of people in different ways. Many political decisions fit into this category. Seat-belt laws, health care reform, tax incentive programs, capital punishment, immigration policies, publicly funded sports stadiums, for example, all affect large numbers of people, but do so in different ways. As human beings, we tend to think first of the ways a proposed action affects ourselves, or perhaps the people we know. Thus, if I am a fan of the Oakland Raiders football team and enjoy going to their games, I would likely support building a new stadium, especially if that would ensure keeping the team in Oakland for the next several decades. But someone who lives in Oakland and doesn't go to football games, who doesn't even like football, may wonder why his tax dollars should be used to support a football stadium rather than another (in his opinion) more worthwhile cause. How can he and I have a discussion about the proposed stadium that goes beyond the obvious facts that I like football and he doesn't?

Consequentialist reasoning provides a way of thinking about this issue that goes beyond mere personal interests by looking at the effects of building a stadium as compared to using the same tax dollars for other purposes or not raising taxes at all. This strategy would take into account how the stadium would affect the regional economy, whether there would be adverse environmental effects, or whether it would increase the quality of life in the region. One would have to ask whether a new stadium would attract more business to the region, whether it would employ more people, or whether it would raise tax revenues for the city. Similar questions could then be asked about projects that could be funded instead, such as, for example, a new art museum, improved public schools, new city parks, and so on.

THE NEW STADIUM

What is the situation? The owner of a professional football team has proposed building a new stadium for the team, but the project depends on funds that would be provided by city tax dollars.

What are the possible actions? The other options being considered by the city are renovating the old stadium, building a new art museum, or renovating public school buildings. The other three options are considerably less expensive than building a new stadium.

Who is affected? There are many people who would be affected by each of the proposed actions. The main groups of people who would be affected are the city taxpayers, professional football players, business owners, students, football fans, and art lovers.

Continued

The New Stadium *Continued*

What are the positive and negative effects? There are many types of effects, some of them very hard to assess, such as the quality of sporting or aesthetic experiences, the lifelong enrichment that comes from a good education, and so forth.

Fill out the chart below using the following symbols:

- + + great positive effect
- + some positive effect
- o negligible effect
- - some negative effect
- - - great negative effect

	BUILD A NEW STADIUM	RENOVATE OLD STADIUM	BUILD A NEW ART MUSEUM	RENOVATE SCHOOL BUILDINGS
Taxpayers				
Football Players				
Business Owners				
Students				
Football Fans				
Art Lovers				

Which action would have the best overall effects?

Note: The above diagram is simply a visual aid to help picture how positive and negative effects are distributed across groups of people; it does not provide enough details to allow one to measure precisely how the effects compare to one another.

In short, consequentialist thinking encourages us to consider the effects on those we might otherwise forget or discount. It reminds us to look at the basic things first—tangible benefits and harms for everyone affected—before reaching a conclusion on an issue. And it provides a criterion to use when evaluating and comparing possible actions.

However, there also are a number of difficulties associated with consequentialism. For one thing, comparing different levels of pleasure and pain is notoriously difficult. If we try to distinguish types of pleasures by the extent to which they contribute to happiness, we find the notion of happiness to be elusive, as well. Another problem is determining whose consequences count. It is easy enough to say that the effects on everyone should be considered, but who does "everyone" include? Does it include infants, embryos, dolphins, sparrows? Where does one draw the line?

Evaluating Pleasure and Pain

Perhaps the most problematic aspect of consequentialism is the difficulty of evaluating different types of pleasure and pain. How does one make reliable evaluations about the comparative worth of different sorts of pleasures? Imagine a school board faced with the difficult decision of cutting programs to balance their budget for the upcoming year. Some board members recommend discontinuing the high school band; others propose cutting the football program. Both cuts would result in approximately the same amount of savings. When they compare the number of people affected, the board discovers that about the same number of students participate in the two activities. Whichever choice they make, the board will disappoint many students and community members by eliminating a valued activity. So should the school board look at which activity, football or band, provides more pleasure for the participants? How could they make that determination?

Perhaps if some studies showed that people who participate in band do significantly better in college than people who play football, the board could make an argument that the band program has benefits beyond the mere fact that some people like music. But such studies are unlikely. The fact is, the decision may just come down to preferences, and it is hard to judge the relative merits of different people's preferences.

Some people have proposed using quantitative ratings of different kinds of pleasures and pains to make objective comparisons, and Bentham himself seemed to think that pleasures and pains could be ranked in such a way. He proposed measuring pleasure and pain in terms of their "intensity," "duration," "certainty or uncertainty," "propinquity or remoteness," "fecundity," "purity," and "extent."[3] Despite different ways of estimating the significance of pleasures and pains, it proves difficult to reliably assign quantitative values to them.

Because there are many kinds of pleasures and pains, which differ not only in quantity but also in quality, they are difficult to compare. We cannot, for example, assign a numerical ranking to them. We can, however, solicit the opinions of people familiar with the different kinds of pleasures and pains, asking which they prefer. John Stuart Mill (1806–1873), a nineteenth-century British philosopher, suggested this way of comparing pains and pleasures, which he expressed in a memorable passage:

> It is better to be a human being dissatisfied than a pig satisfied; better to be Socrates dissatisfied than a fool satisfied. And if the fool, or the pig, are of a different opinion, it is because they only know their own side of the question. The other party to the comparison knows both sides.[4]

Mill's insight was that people will always prefer familiar pleasures over unfamiliar ones, and so the only way to compare the quality of different sorts of experiences validly is to consult those familiar with both. If you ask a person who cannot read whether he would prefer a book or a chocolate chip cookie, he will most likely choose the cookie. But he is not in any position to determine whether, in general, reading is more pleasurable than eating cookies, for he has never experienced the pleasure of reading. Returning to the example of the school board dealing with budget cuts, if the board followed Mill's advice, they might interview students who participate in both music and sports and see which activity they think is most significant. Presumably, these students are best able to make reliable comparisons based on their experience of both activities.

---

3. Ibid., 28–29.

4. John Stuart Mill, *Utilitarianism*, 2nd ed. (Indianapolis, IN: Hackett, 2002), 10.

JOHN STUART MILL (1806–1873)

John Stuart Mill

© Corbis

John Stuart Mill's father, James Mill, was a close friend and collaborator of Jeremy Bentham. Shortly after his son John was born, James started him out on a rigorously designed educational curriculum that would prepare him to continue the radical social reform along utilitarian principles upon which he and Bentham were engaged. The plan succeeded—more or less.

By the age of eight, John Stuart Mill was reading the classical Greek and Roman philosophers in their original languages. By age eleven he had been educated in mathematics and the natural sciences and had studied Sir Isaac Newton's physics. At age fourteen he went to France to study for a year and became familiar with French language, customs, and politics. By age twenty he was fully engaged in the radical political movement that Bentham and his father were leading. He was participating in debates, organizing philosophical societies, and contributing articles to journals.

But then he suffered some kind of breakdown. He referred to it in his *Autobiography* as a "mental crisis" and described his recovery as a gradual awakening that came through reading Romantic literature, especially Wordsworth's poetry. He came to believe that Bentham's insistence on strict rational principles was too limiting and failed to allow for adequate emotional development.

For most of Mill's adult life he worked for the East India Company, a multinational corporation that provided him with a steady income and enough free time to pursue his academic interests. He published influential works in metaphysics, epistemology, logic, ethics, political philosophy, religion, and economics, though it is mainly his ethical and political writings that remain widely read today.

Continued

Jeremy Benthan *Continued*

Mill was intensely interested in pushing the sorts of reforms that would result in greater equality and protection from oppression for all citizens. His book entitled *On Liberty* contains a series of eloquent arguments for freedom of speech. And in *The Subjugation of Women* he argued forcefully for extending full political rights to women. Throughout his political writings he maintained that the only reason either individual people or governments may interfere with the freedom of others is to prevent harm to someone; any other exercise of power is unjustified.

Mill retired from the East India Company in 1857 and shortly after that his wife, Harriett Taylor, died, a loss he felt keenly for the remainder of his life. He spent a peaceful retirement in France until his own death in 1873. He was buried next to his wife.

Can we always find people able to testify about the experience of the different kinds of pains and pleasures we wish to evaluate? Are the judgments of those with both kinds of experiences always the most reliable?

The things that cause pain or pleasure rarely come raw—that is, without some kind of interpretive context. Consider someone who begins feeling nauseated and develops a slight headache. She takes her temperature and discovers it is 100 degrees Fahrenheit. You ask her how she feels. "Terrible," she says. "Could you give me a ride home? I don't think I can drive." Three days later you stop by her house to see how she is doing. She answers the door with a big smile. "How are you today?" you ask. "Much better—at least, so much better than yesterday. The fever was 103, but now it is back down to 100, and the headache isn't nearly so bad." You notice that she has been fixing herself something to eat and that she is in surprisingly good spirits. What has changed for her in those few days? Physically, her symptoms are about the same, but on the first day, she was "getting sick" and on the third day, she is "getting better." On the first day, her 100-degree temperature caused her great distress, but on the third day, the same temperature causes her to be fairly upbeat. The context is different.

How we think about our experiences has a great deal to do with how we rank them in terms of pleasure and pain. Thus, simply having an experience is not always enough to ensure that we can evaluate it reliably. Imagine that you are considering where to go on vacation, and you have narrowed your choices to two possibilities: Disney World or Yellowstone National Park. You have not been to either place, but your friend Cheryl has been to both. She says, "No question. You should go to Disney World. There's nothing to do in Yellowstone. There's just a bunch of trails and stuff, and you might get eaten by a bear. When we were there, I didn't even get out of the car." You are not so sure you should take Cheryl's advice. You don't really like crowds, and you really enjoy spending time alone and hiking outdoors. Even though Cheryl has experienced both places, is she a reliable judge of which vacation site would bring you the most pleasure?

Conceptions of Happiness

Different kinds of pleasure and pain are difficult to compare, because we judge them according to our individual conceptions of happiness. In fact one could say that the process of becoming a moral agent consists in large part of learning how to determine what kinds of actions lead to happiness and what kinds do not. Should a parent encourage her children to play sports or engage in the arts? Should someone take a job that pays more money or one that pays less but is more enjoyable? Should a student take an elective course that may be useful in a future career or one that will provide a better understanding of world cultures and, perhaps, help him become a better citizen?

These are difficult questions to answer because most people are not good at judging which activities ultimately lead to happiness. It is easy to say that individuals all have different ideas about happiness. That's certainly true. But does it follow that different things actually make us happy?

In one respect, yes, people find happiness in different things. One person enjoys golfing, and another enjoys video games. One person likes painting, and another likes music. But we often find that we aren't good judges even of the activities we take special pleasure in. The person who can't wait until retirement so he can fish every day discovers that, although fishing two days a week is great fun, fishing six days a week is as burdensome as work and the loss of his work has deprived him of the companions with whom he used to share fishing stories.

The Greek hero Achilles, whose exploits Homer recounts in *The Iliad*, was given a choice to live a long but unremarkable life or a short but famous life:

> For my mother Thetis the goddess of the silver feet
>   tells me
> I carry two sorts of destiny toward the day of my
>   death. Either,
> if I stay here and fight beside the city of the Trojans,
> my return home is gone, but my glory shall be everlasting;
> but if I return home to the beloved land of my fathers,
> the excellence of my glory is gone, but there will be a
>   long life
> left for me, and my end in death will not come to
>   me quickly.[5]

Achilles chose the short but famous life. If he had not done so, readers more than two thousand years later would not be reading books describing his exploits. His choice is similar to the professional football player who chooses to keep playing after having had several concussions, knowing that the long-term effects of his injuries may lead to an early death.

One thing is certain: what people think will make them happy and what actually does make them happy are two different things. That's why popular sayings such as "The grass is always greener on the other side of the fence" and "Be careful what you wish for, you may receive it" and similar sayings are both timeless and true. Perceptions are biased and unreliable. What seems to promise happiness now may turn out to be a disappointment later on.

---

5. Homer, *The Iliad of Homer*, trans. Richmond Lattimore (Chicago: University of Chicago Press, 1951), 209.

Many of us have had the experience of being mistaken about what we wanted or thought we wanted. As we age we often accumulate regrets: things we wish we had done, or done differently, or not done at all. This may lead to a kind of wisdom over time, an ability to discern the lasting satisfaction from the ephemeral pleasure. For most people, the source of lasting satisfaction turns out to be good relationships with other people, though this is not something people tend to rate as highly as other things.

People's daily behavior also indicates an inability to connect their happiness with their choices. For example, why do people watch television? Presumably, because they enjoy it. In other words, at the time, it is something they want to do. Faced with other forms of available activities, they believe it will give them the most pleasure. But it is not likely to make them happier. In fact, some studies suggest that watching television (and spending time with other forms of electronic media) could lead to increased levels of depression.[6]

Why do people find it so hard to judge accurately what will make them happy or unhappy? There are two chief sources of difficulty: (1) the fact that pleasures and pains are subjective phenomena and (2) the problem of reliably predicting future states.

Subjectivity

The things that cause pleasure and pain are notoriously subjective; they vary from one person to another to such an extent that it would be impossible to create a list of pleasure-producing and pain-producing conditions that all people would agree on. Some people find going to the dentist a painful experience, even if just for a routine exam and cleaning; others don't mind going at all, even to have a tooth drilled and a cavity filled. How can one determine how much pain or pleasure something produces? Only by asking the person undergoing the experience. That is what is meant by *subjectivity*.

Conjoined twins are born with a connected body part, and in many countries they are surgically separated at birth. They are separated because nearly everyone agrees that going through life

---

6. Brian A. Primack et al., "Association between Media Use in Adolescence and Depression in Young Adulthood: A Longitudinal Study," *Archives of General Psychiatry* 66 (2009): 181–188; Marilyn Jackson-Beeck and Jeff Sobal, "The Social World of Heavy Television Viewers," *Journal of Broadcasting* 24 (1980): 5–12.

permanently connected to another person would be intolerable—everyone except conjoined twins, that is. Daniel Gilbert describes the situation of Lori and Reba Schappel, who were born joined at the forehead.[7] When asked whether they would like to have a surgery to separate them, Reba replied, "Our point of view is no, straight out no. Why would you want to do that? For all the money in China, why? You would be ruining two lives in the process." For Reba and Lori, the reasons for not separating are self-evident. They can't seem to understand why someone would even propose such a procedure. Yet, non-conjoined twins would almost universally agree that such a life would be unbearable—not only difficult to endure but perhaps not even worth living.

Because the only way to be really sure of what another finds pleasurable or painful is by asking, decision making is difficult in cases where the decision affects other people, because we can't always ask those affected. Even if we could, how do we know their judgments are reliable? What if conjoined twins mistakenly think they would be happier if they stayed together, because they don't have any experience of living apart, but if they were separated they would soon come to feel that their lives had improved?

Parents often face this type of situation with their children. A parent suggests her daughter take piano lessons. The daughter objects: "I hate playing the piano. Why are you making me do something I don't want to do?" "Because you will learn to like it. It may take a year or two, but pretty soon you will discover that you enjoy playing the piano." Sometimes it turns out that way, and sometimes it doesn't. In the end it depends on what the child actually concludes, perhaps after several years of piano lessons. "You were right. I didn't like the lessons at first, but I'm glad you made me take them. I really love the piano," or "See? I told you so. You made me take lessons for two years, and I hated every minute of it." There is yet another possible response: one day the child says she loves playing the piano, and a few days later she says she hates it, and both times she is sincere.

It is not just that we cannot know for certain how something affects another person—for example, how much pleasure a hike in the woods will produce as compared to reading a poem—we often

---

7. Daniel Gilbert, *Stumbling on Happiness* (New York: Random House, 2006), 31–32.

don't even know how to make such a comparison in our own lives. In the essay "Experience," Ralph Waldo Emerson notes the difficulty of reliably evaluating the quality of even one's own experiences.

> Life is a train of moods like a string of beads, and, as we pass through them, they prove to be many-colored lenses which paint the world their own hue, and each shows only what lies in its focus. From the mountain you see the mountain. We animate what we can, and we see only what we animate. Nature and books belong to the eyes that see them. It depends on the mood of the man, whether he shall see the sunset or the fine poem. There are always sunsets, and there is always genius; but only a few hours so serene that we can relish nature or criticism.[8]

Sometimes we can appreciate certain things more fully than at other times. Our ability to make reliable comparisons among consequences depends not only on whether we have experienced them ourselves but also on the condition of that experience—whether we are in a receptive mood, whether we have the appropriate preparation or background to appreciate it, and, of course, the quality of our own temperament and character.

Sources of pleasure and pain differ not only from one person to the next; they also differ from our past, present, and future selves. Madhu Narayan, an outdoor education manager for the Girl Scouts of America, tells the story of a time she took some urban girls camping for the first time:

> One night, a nine-year-old woke me up. She had to go to the bathroom. We stepped outside the tent and she looked up. She gasped and grabbed my leg. She had never seen the stars before. That night, I saw the power of nature on a child. She was a changed person. From that moment on, she saw everything, the camouflaged lizard that everyone else skipped by. She used her senses. She was *awake*.[9]

---

8. Ralph Waldo Emerson, "Experience," in Emerson, *Essays and Lectures*, (New York: Library of America, 1983), 473–474.

9. Quoted in Richard Louv, *Last Child in the Woods: Saving Our Children from Nature-deficit Disorder* (Chapel Hill, NC: Algonquin Books of Chapel Hill, 2008), 156.

The experience of seeing stars for the first time awakened the young girl's perception to the beauty and wonder of all sorts of things that were already there but that she had simply not noticed before. Before seeing the stars, she had seen grass and trees and birds and lizards, but after seeing the stars, she saw everything else differently, with more focus and intensity. One might say that before and after seeing the stars, she experienced the same things, but she had different experiences of them.

This volatility of experience simply seems to be part of the human condition. It helps explain why it is hard to base ethical decisions only on the appraisals of comparative pleasures and pains. "Gladly we would anchor," says Emerson, "but the anchorage is quicksand."[10]

Prediction

Another difficulty in evaluating pleasure and pain comes from the unpredictability of future states. This stems in part from the complexity of many events, as well as people's general tendency to place greater value on the immediate than on the distant. For example, I may think the greatest thing that could happen to me today is to hit the jackpot in the lottery. But have I considered all the negative consequences that could arise? Would I be any better off in two years than I am now? Studies of lottery winners show that some big winners end up financially worse off than they were before.[11] Benefiting from a windfall like the lottery depends not only on receiving the money but also on knowing how to invest it, how to manage the many demands that come with having sudden wealth, and how to deal with friends and relations who may feel entitled to a share of the winnings.

A famous story coming from the Taoist tradition relates the story of a farmer whose horse runs away:

---

10. Ralph Waldo Emerson, *Essays and Lectures* (New York: The Library of America, 1983), 476.

11. See Bankrate.com, "8 Lottery Winners Who Lost Their Millions," in *MSN Money*, *http://articles.moneycentral.msn.com/SavingandDebt/SaveMoney/8lotteryWinnersWho LostTheirMillions.aspx*. See also Philip Brickman, Dan Coates, and Ronnie Janoff-Bullman, "Lottery Winners and Accident Victims: Is Happiness Relative?" *Journal of Personality and Social Psychology*, vol. 36, no. 8 (1978): 917–927.

His neighbor commiserated, only to be told, "Who knows what's good or bad?" It was true, for the next day the horse returned, bringing with it a drove of wild horses it had befriended. The neighbor reappeared, this time with congratulations for the windfall. He received the same response: "Who knows what is good or bad?" Again this proved true, for the next day the farmer's son tried to mount one of the wild horses and fell, breaking his leg. More commiserations from the neighbor, which elicited the question: "Who knows what is good or bad?" And for a fourth time the farmer's point prevailed, for the following day soldiers came by commandeering for the army, and the son was exempted because of his injury.[12]

Sometimes what looks like a good turn of events has unexpected consequences that lead to misfortune; and sometimes an apparent misfortune leads to something good. This idea—that good and bad are intertwined—is symbolized in the yin-and-yang image. Light pushes into the darkness, and darkness pushes into the light, suggesting that neither is stationary but always moves into the territory of the other. The black and white dots illustrate how light takes up residence in the home of darkness and vice versa.

The yin and yang reminds us that good and bad experiences— we could even say the pleasurable and the painful—are not sharply and permanently separated from each other but are always flowing into and out of one another. This makes future states difficult, if not impossible, to predict with certainty and reliability.

12. Huston Smith, "Taoism," *The World Wisdom Online Library*, *http://www.world wisdom.com/public/viewpdf/default.aspx?article-title=Taoism_by_Huston_Smith.pdf*.

Whose Consequences?

When evaluating various possible actions according to likely consequences, where do we draw the line about which consequences to
consider? Do we have to take into account the consequences for
everyone and everything? What about people in remote areas of the
world whom we have never met and likely will never meet? What
about animals? What about plants, mountains, rivers, and trees?

Other People

Most people consider how their actions affect the people
relatively close to them: parents, children, brothers, sisters, friends,
neighbors, classmates, coworkers, and so on. That is natural and to be
expected, for if I do something to benefit or harm someone close to
me—my brother, for instance—he will let me know. The cause-effect
chain is evident, and communication is direct and immediate. But it
takes effort and attention to consider how our actions affect those
who are remote from us. If my action benefits or harms a stranger
in another state or country, I may not even know about it, and the
stranger will not likely know that I am the cause or be able to tell me
about it.

Many charitable organizations face the challenge of creating a
personal connection between the people they help and the people
who support the organization financially. The personal connection
can be broached in a variety of ways, but it is often hard to sustain,
especially when the contributors live in one country and the recipi-
ents of goods or services live in another.

Most people in the United States are distanced from those who
live in Haiti. Unless they come from Haiti themselves or have family or close friends who live and work there, they do not pay much
attention to what is happening there—except in the rare case of a
political or natural disaster, such as the devastating earthquake that
struck the country in 2010. Even then, the attention to Haiti, and the
serious consideration of how our actions may benefit the people who
live there, are generally short-lived. Thinking about consequences
encourages us to be intentional about how our actions affect others,
even across distances, and to engage in such thinking consistently,
not just when news stories happen to direct our attention.

Beyond just geographical separation, though, people can be distanced or separated by race, gender, class, time, age, political affiliation, or social interests.[13] Distance may be enhanced or lessened by the use of language, power, images, activities, and even social cues.

Sometimes behavior creates artificial distance by directing attention one way rather than another. Several years ago when I taught at a university in a large city, I asked a colleague who had lived in the city for a long time a question about something I had seen in a neighborhood just three blocks away from where we both worked. He had never driven on the streets running through that neighborhood and so had never witnessed the living conditions in that area. He confined his travel to what he considered "safe" streets, even if that meant taking a longer route to get from one place to another. Simply because we drove different routes to the university, different images would come to mind when discussing the neighborhoods and the living conditions in the city. This led to differences of opinion about basic things, such as whether more tax dollars should be used to improve the city streets. In this case the relative distance was not geographical but arose because of different habitual activities.

Factors that create distance between people (or groups of people) tend to make it more difficult to properly consider the ethical consequences of one group's treatment of another. This has been shown both by certain studies, set up to demonstrate this very phenomenon, and by actual present-day and historical examples.

It is a well-documented fact that the Nazis systematically killed more than six million Jews and hundreds of thousands of others (the mentally or physically disabled, homosexuals, gypsies, political opponents, and religious dissidents) in the years between the time they came to power in 1933 and their defeat in 1945.[14] It is less well known that in the years leading up to the genocide, they instituted a variety of educational reforms designed to emphasize the differences between the races and especially to highlight the differences between

---

13. See the Pew Research Center for People and the Press, "Internet Gains on Television as Public's Main News Source," *http://people-press.org/2011/01/04/internet-gains-on-television-as-publics-main-news-source/*.

14. See, for example, the United States Holocaust Memorial Museum Web site, *http://www.ushmm.org/*.

Jews and so-called Aryans.[15] By emphasizing physical, mental, and cultural differences, the Nazis convinced many people that what happens to Jews doesn't count—that the consequences to them are morally insignificant.

In 1830 the U.S. legislature passed the Indian Removal Act, which allowed for the forcible relocation of the Cherokee Nation, along with several other Indian nations—the Chickasaw, Choctaw, Creek, and Seminole—to Indian Territory, in what is today Oklahoma. (The routes taken by the series of relocations became known as the "Trail of Tears.") The Indian Removal Act didn't spring out of nowhere. Rather, it was a product of years of ethnic prejudice, legislation, and court findings that effectively denied the Indians legal means to resist the relocation. In a series of legal decisions, state and federal courts refused to grant protection to Indians on the grounds that indigenous people's interests did not have to be acknowledged, because they were regarded as unlikely to be motivated by civilized considerations, such as laws and contracts. In the words of Chief Justice John Marshall (1755–1835) in 1831, "Their appeal was to the tomahawk."[16] As such, despite legitimate interests in remaining on their own property, those interests had no legal standing. The Indians' objections to relocation, when they were even allowed to be voiced, were not acknowledged as having either moral or legal significance.

How does it happen that people discount the interests of others and see them no longer as human beings with legitimate interests but as obstacles or things to be manipulated? Surprisingly, it doesn't require years of indoctrination or acculturation.

One insight comes from a famous classroom exercise conducted in 1968 by a third-grade teacher in Riceville, Iowa.[17] In response to questions from her students about why Martin Luther King Jr. had been murdered, she decided to give them a practical lesson

---

15. For an excellent account of the educational strategy of the Nazis, see Gregory P. Wegner, *Anti-Semitism and Schooling under the Third Reich* (New York: Routledge, 2002).

16. *Cherokee Nation v. Georgia*, 30 U.S. at 18 (Marshall, C. J., majority opinion), quoted in Walter R. Echo-Hawk, *In the Courts of the Conqueror* (Golden, CO: Fulcrum, 2010), 103.

17. A documentary describing the exercise along with interviews of the children who participated several years later was produced by the PBS program Frontline, *A Class Divided*, produced and directed by William Peters, 1985. It can be viewed at *http://www.pbs.org/wgbh/pages/frontline/shows/divided/*.

in prejudice by dividing the class into two groups: "blue eyes" and "brown eyes." She told the children that blue-eyed people were smarter, better behaved, more honest and trustworthy. Then she had the brown-eyed children wear special collars so they could be easily identified and gave the blue-eyed children special privileges, like being first in line and getting extra time at recess. The teacher, Jane Elliot, commented later: "I watched what had been marvelous, cooperative, wonderful, thoughtful children turn into nasty, vicious, discriminating, little third-graders in a space of fifteen minutes."

Another revealing study, the Stanford Prison Experiment, was performed at Stanford University in 1971 by psychology professor Philip Zambardo, who wanted to look at the psychological effects produced by prison.[18] He built a makeshift "prison" in one of the academic buildings on campus and then recruited volunteers among college students, randomly assigning them the role of prisoner or guard. The study, scheduled to run for two weeks, had to be ended after just six days because the situation had gotten out of control. The "prison guards" were abusing the "prisoners," and the "prisoners" were experiencing severe psychological trauma.

The experiment demonstrated that simply separating people into easily identifiable groups and then distributing power unequally was enough to cause the powerful group to discount the legitimate needs and interests of the other group. All the participants in the experiment were college students, and in normal settings they would never have considered treating one another abusively. The setting of the experiment, however, distanced them from one another—by different types of clothing, by prison bars, by names, by privileges. That distance was sufficient to cause one group of students to disregard the significance of what was happening to the other group over the period of just a few days.

One cause of distance between people is due to the unequal distribution of power. Some terms used for naming the frequent and widespread failures to recognize the legitimate interests of other people are *racism, sexism,* and *ageism.* But, as in the case of the classroom in Iowa or the artificial prison at Stanford, sometimes the prejudice is short-lived or narrowly focused, and in those cases there is no name for what takes place.

---

18. See the Stanford Prison Experiment Web site, *http://www.prisonexp.org/.*

Thinking about ethics in terms of consequences is important precisely because it is easy to overlook the interests of those distanced from us. Such neglect is both natural and habitual and may be reinforced by education, peers, and even prevailing cultural attitudes. Looking first at an action's consequences for everyone and disregarding whose consequences they are, introduces a radical equality into the deliberations. It is an equality based on nothing other than that all people have interests. Thus, for example, if my action affects (or could affect) another person—either positively or negatively—I have a responsibility to take those effects into account. I cannot simply disregard them.

A word of caution is in order here, however. A person's desire to take the interests of others into account doesn't mean he or she actually will or even can do so in a way that is beneficial rather than harmful. Generally speaking, we have greater responsibility for the people who are closer to us—family, friends, neighbors, coworkers— simply because we can more reliably know how our actions really affect them. We also have responsibilities to strangers, of course, but we must take into account the fact that the more distanced a person is, the more difficult it is to accurately evaluate the effects of our actions upon them, especially when differences of language or culture get in the way of mutual understanding.[19]

It would be impractical to completely disregard the distance separating us from other people and to consider all the effects of all our actions on everyone equally. For one thing, it would be impossible to think through how one's actions and potential actions affect everyone. That would require spending all one's time just thinking and not doing anything. Nevertheless, thinking about ethics in terms of consequences requires that we do our best to understand other people insofar as practically possible and consider the effects of relevant actions on everyone affected by them, regardless of potential obstacles to understanding like differences in place, time, race, culture, class, gender, age, and so on.

---

19. There are all sorts of obstacles to understanding other people's interests and expectations, even when language and culture are shared. That is why, when making decisions that have significant effects on other people, it is important to involve them, when feasible, in the decision-making process. Howard Behar, former president of Starbucks Coffee Company, states this as a leadership principle: "The person who sweeps the floor should choose the broom." See Howard Behar and Janet Goldstein, *It's Not about the Coffee: Lessons on Putting People First from a Life at Starbucks* (Penguin, 2009).

Animals

What about nonhuman animals?[20] Are we not morally obligated to take their interests seriously? After all, animals feel pleasure and pain. Anyone who has spent much time with animals knows that they are capable of suffering and also that they have many of the same responses to pleasure and pain that humans do. To disregard animal pain just because it is experienced by a creature different from us seems equivalent to discounting the pain of other people just because they are different from us. Peter Singer, a Princeton philosopher and key figure in the animal rights movement, terms such disregard *speciesism*:

> The fact that some people are not members of our race does not entitle us to exploit them, and similarly the fact that some people are less intelligent than others does not mean that their interests may be disregarded. But the principle also implies that the fact that beings are not members of our species does not entitle us to exploit them, and similarly the fact that other animals are less intelligent than we are does not mean that their interests may be disregarded.[21]

Taking the effects of our actions upon nonhuman animals seriously does not imply that animals should have all the same moral and legal rights that humans do. It would be absurd to argue that animals should receive public education and be allowed to express their political views and vote and so on. Dogs, cats, deer, raccoons, and even chimpanzees do not have (as far as is known) any compelling interests in learning to read and write, and so barring them from school has no negative effect on them. However, such animals do have interests in food, safety, and avoiding suffering. Some animals, in addition, have interests in companionship and the ability to roam freely. So those things should be taken into account.

What does this mean practically? For one thing, it means humans should not discount animal suffering when it comes to scientific experimentation and farming.

---

20. The term *animals* refers to sentient creatures, that is, creatures capable of experiencing pleasure and pain.

21. Peter Singer, *Practical Ethics*, 2nd ed. (New York: Cambridge University Press, 1993), 56.

North Carolina contains approximately thirty-four hundred hog farms, consisting of structures holding four to five hundred hogs each. Many of those hogs spend their entire lives confined indoors in pens of steel and concrete. They are not allowed to move about, because using energy would require more feed, which in turn would make their meat more expensive to produce. They have no straw to lie down on, because the necessity of cleaning out straw-lined pens would require additional labor. Instead, they reside on bare slatted floors through which their waste falls into drainage channels.[22] To increase efficiency and maximize profit for the investors, every decision about how to construct and run the farms is made without regard to the suffering imposed on the hogs. The hogs have interests, which are known (or at least knowable) to anyone who makes the effort to discover them, but their interests are disregarded.

A similar thing happens with animals used in scientific research, although rules regulating such use are stricter than regulations regarding animals used for consumption.

Thinking in terms of consequences requires one to treat similar consequences similarly, regardless of who or what experiences the consequences. Thus, hogs' subjection to unbearably painful conditions is a reason for moral outrage, not because pigs and humans are equals but simply because pigs can feel pain.

Inanimate Things

It is considerably harder to evaluate an action's consequences on nonsentient living things and inanimate objects. Can a tree, mountain, lake, or stream be harmed? In some senses, yes. A tree can be damaged and even killed by poisoning it or cutting it down. But the kind of harm done to the tree is not clear. Cutting down a tree does not cause the tree pain, because trees don't have the neural receptors necessary for feeling pain. So it remains unclear whether we could even say the tree's interests have been disregarded. Can a tree have interests? Even if we could say that depriving any living thing of life is contrary to its basic interest in survival, what do we say of mountains or lakes or streams?

---

22. Matthew Scully, *Dominion: The Power of Man, the Suffering of Animals, and the Call to Mercy* (New York: St. Martin's Press, 2002), 247–249.

In Aldo Leopold's famous essay, "Thinking like a Mountain," he describes the thought that came to him while working for the U.S. Forest Service in Arizona: our efforts to shape the natural world to our liking are often done out of narrow-minded interests and an inability to appreciate the far-reaching consequences of our actions. He recounts the time he shot a wolf and her cubs on the side of a mountain, a common practice in those days in the effort to increase the size of the deer herd:

> I realized then, and have known ever since, that there was something new to me in those eyes—something known only to her and to the mountain. . . . I now suspect that just as a deer herd lives in mortal fear of its wolves, so does a mountain live in mortal fear of its deer. And perhaps with better cause, for while a buck pulled down by wolves can be replaced in two or three years, a range pulled down by too many deer may fail of replacement in as many decades.[23]

Leopold's enduring lesson is this: the basis for living ethically in the world is seeing fully—and accurately—the relationships among things. In *A Sand County Almanac* he sums it up this way: "We abuse land because we regard it as a commodity belonging to us. When we see land as a community to which we belong, we may begin to use it with love and respect."[24] In other words, the consequences to the mountain should be taken into account, because the mountain is part of the community to which we belong. Separating the parts of the natural world into those that count and those that do not count is a result of a faulty moral perception that leads to a miscalculation of consequences.

This is a point made by Vicki Hearne, a philosopher and animal trainer, who wrote an essay about koi, the ornamental carp that are bred for display in Japanese ponds. Hearne notes that "though you can never know how many koi you have at a given moment, if you are properly attentive, you can tell that one of your fish is gone, even out of the corner of your eye, by the changes in the patterns."[25] In other

23. Aldo Leopold, *A Sand County Almanac, and Sketches Here and There* (New York: Oxford University Press, 1949), 130–132.

24. Ibid, viii.

25. Vicki Hearne, *Animal Happiness: A Moving Exploration of Animals and Their Emotions* (New York: Skyhorse, 1994), 17.

words, sometimes what counts is not the number of individuals but rather the relationship of individuals to their community, and in fact it is only in relationship that some individuals make their presence known. For koi the mode of their belonging together is the pond; it is thus the pond that bears moral significance, because it is the pond that suffers the consequences of good or bad behavior.

IS THE CONSIDERATION OF CONSEQUENCES ITSELF UNETHICAL?

Finally, one must ask whether it is morally objectionable to look at the consequences of an action before considering the intrinsic nature of the action itself. A long-standing objection to consequentialist reasoning is that it doesn't consider certain types of actions, such as murder, theft, lying, and abuse, to be wrong regardless of the consequences that result. Isn't there something problematic about even considering whether to steal another person's property, even for the sake of achieving some good result? A story commonly used to illustrate this objection goes as follows:

> Consider the situation of a young man who discovers that his uncle is dying from a mysterious and sudden illness. The uncle is a wealthy industrialist who has willed his considerable wealth to his nephew, his only surviving relation. The uncle happens to be a terrible person—miserly, rude, cynical—unhappy with his own life and determined to do nothing to improve, or even make tolerable, the lives of others. He treats his employees badly, providing low wages, few benefits, and unsafe working conditions in his factory. Many employees have been injured at work over the years. His products have been unsafe too, and though nobody has been able to prove it, the nephew suspects hundreds of consumers may have been sickened by contaminated food products issuing from the plant.
>
> When the nephew learns of his uncle's impending death, he immediately gets in his car and begins driving to his uncle's mansion, which is several hours away. As

he drives he begins to think of his inheritance and all the changes he will make to the factory. The business is healthy and profitable, so he should be able to raise wages and improve benefits for the employees. He will also be able to make considerable improvements in the safety and quality-control procedures at the plant. He thinks of all the lives he will affect by his actions: happier, more productive employees, and consumers who will benefit from safe food products. He also has plans to use much of the money he will inherit to give to charities. As he drives he starts to make a list in his head of the charitable organizations that provide the best return on the dollar for the poor people in his city.

When he arrives at his uncle's bedside, however, he learns that his uncle is beginning to feel better. He is talking for the first time in several days and is asking for something to eat. The nephew's hopes are dashed. All the good things he had hoped to accomplish will have to be postponed. Who knows for how long? Then a thought occurs to him. Nobody else is in the room, and everybody thinks his uncle is about to die. If he would just take a pillow and hold it down over his uncle's head for a bit, his uncle would die easily, and no one would ever know he did it. But could he do that? Could he commit murder? It wouldn't be for himself, he thinks. It would be to improve the lives of countless employees, consumers, and beneficiaries of charity. The more he thinks about it, the more it seems to him that he not only could do it, but that it would be the right thing to do. In fact, it would be unethical for him not to kill his uncle.

Such an example may seem far-fetched, but it poses a significant question for anyone who uses the consequentialist approach to moral reasoning. Are any actions at all simply "out of bounds," that is, so wrong that they should never be considered, regardless of the consequences? Or is any action permissible, as long as it results in more good than harm? This isn't just theoretical. People have to wrestle with such questions frequently, especially when a situation arises where the stakes are unusually high. Should a politician renege on a pledge he made to constituents in order to support a bill he thinks would benefit citizens? Should a military intelligence officer torture a terrorist suspect to prevent a bombing that would endanger hundreds of lives?

On August 6, 1945, the United States dropped an atomic bomb on the Japanese city of Hiroshima. Three days later another was dropped on Nagasaki. The bombs killed approximately one hundred forty thousand people in Hiroshima and seventy thousand in Nagasaki, mostly civilians.[26] Hiroshima and Nagasaki were not typical military targets.[27] The actual reasons for the bombing and the choice of targets generated much controversy. At the time, though, many people agreed that it was the only way to bring a quick end to World War II, because the sole alternative was an American invasion of Japan, which would have resulted in large numbers of casualties on both sides. President Harry Truman, who ultimately made the decision to drop the atomic bombs, believed that American casualties from an invasion would range from two-hundred fifty thousand to a million, with Japanese casualties projected to be three to four times higher.[28] Given the anticipated casualties, the decision to drop the bombs seems justified. It would quickly end the war and thus save many lives. Critics of the decision said (and continue to say) that intentionally targeting civilian populations is unethical, even if it achieves military objectives more quickly and with less cost. Such actions are wrong because they fall outside the scope of legitimate warfare. Targeting civilian populations is not an act of warfare, they argue, but mass murder.[29]

---

26. See the Hiroshima Peace Memorial Museum Web site, *http://www.pcf.city. hiroshima.jp/kids/KPSH_E/frame/hirotop11.html*, and the Radiation Effects Research Foundation, *http://www.rerf.or.jp/general/qa_e/qa1.html*.

27. According to historian Dan Kurzman, Hiroshima was chosen not because of its military significance but because the Target Committee considered it "sufficiently spectacular for the importance of the weapon to be internationally recognized when publicity on it was released." *Day of the Bomb: Countdown to Hiroshima* (New York: McGraw-Hill Book Company, 1986), 394. Quoted in "Hiroshima and Nagasaki," *http://history1900s.about.com/od/worldwarii/a/hiroshima.htm*.

28. For a thorough discussion of the various estimates of casualties made by military experts during preparations for the invasion of Japan, see D. M. Giangreco, "Casualty Projections for the U.S. Invasions of Japan, 1945–1946: Planning and Policy Implications," *Journal of Military History* 61 (1997): 521–582.

29. For an example of this criticism, see G.E.M. Anscombe, "Mr. Truman's Degree," in *The Collected Philosophical Papers of G.E.M. Anscombe*, vol. III, *Ethics, Religion and Politics* (Oxford: Blackwell, 1981), 62–71.

The decision to drop the atomic bombs highlights both the strength and the weakness of consequentialist reasoning: its strength is that it provides a single, readily grasped criterion for making difficult choices; its weakness is that the criterion may be insufficient by itself. Consequentialist reasoning stresses the results of the action without regard to the type of action, and sometimes it is the type of action that is morally objectionable.

CONCLUSION

Thinking about consequences is probably the most intuitive of the four ways of ethical thinking; it is certainly the type of thinking people turn to first and most frequently when debating public issues. It is also easy to define: simply identify possible actions and determine which one has the most favorable results for all. But the simplicity is deceptive for, as we have seen, determining the criteria for evaluating consequences is far from simple, nor does the question of who "counts" have an obvious answer. Despite its power and simplicity, thinking in terms of consequences is a blunt instrument when it comes to certain kinds of choices. It doesn't help resolve interpersonal conflict very well, nor does it help guide decisions about developing character.

None of the four ways of thinking is sufficient in itself to guide ethical decision making; the others must be taken into account, as well. Truthfulness, fairness, and character are limitations on the consideration of consequences: truth is important, because one must know the truth to make an accurate estimation of what the effects of various actions might be; fairness is important, because how one obtains results is often as important as the results themselves; and character is important, because in ethical reasoning one evaluates not only actions in themselves but also the people who perform the actions and the quality of life in which actions take place. None of this diminishes, of course, the importance of consequences as something one must consider to develop a robust conception of how to act; it merely puts the significance of consequences in context.

SUGGESTIONS FOR FURTHER READING
ON CONSEQUENCES

Bentham, Jeremy. *The Principles of Morals and Legislation*. Amherst, NY: Prometheus Books, 1988.

This is the first attempt to present and defend the utilitarian approach to ethics systematically. The prose can be challenging, and it helps to read it with a dictionary close by, but it is an indispensible work in the history of ethics.

Mill, John Stuart. *Utilitarianism*. 2nd ed. Indianapolis, IN: Hackett, 2002.

Mill provides a nuanced articulation and defense of utilitarianism in this work. Many of the misunderstandings and criticisms of the theory that are still voiced today could be answered by an attentive reading of Mill.

Singer, Peter. *Practical Ethics*. 2nd ed. New York: Cambridge University Press, 1993.

Singer's classic work on ethics is easy to read, engaging, and also highly controversial. He takes a consistent and uncompromising utilitarian approach to addressing problems like the treatment of animals, abortion, euthanasia, and distribution of wealth.

5

CHAPTER

Fairness

EVERY CULTURE HAS SOME CONCEPT OF FAIRNESS, usually expressed succinctly in a version of the Golden Rule. The versions of the rule differ slightly, and they derive from different contexts, so they cannot be interpreted as meaning precisely the same thing. But the very fact that similar expressions of fairness have appeared across so many of the world's cultures suggests it is a fundamental insight of human nature.

Here are a few examples of the Golden Rule, though many more could be cited:

"Let no man do to another that which would be repugnant to himself." (Hindu)[1]

"None of you [truly] believes until he wishes for his brother what he wishes for himself." (Muslim)[2]

"Hurt not others in ways that you yourself would find hurtful." (Buddhist)[3]

"That nature only is good which shall not do unto another whatever is not good for its own self." (Zoroastrian)[4]

---

1. *Mahabharata* 5.49.57, quoted in Jeffrey Wattles, *The Golden Rule* (New York: Oxford University Press, 1996), 4.

2. *An-Nawawi's Forty Hadith* 13, quoted in ibid., 4.

3. *Udana-Varga*, 5.18, quoted in ibid., 192.

4. *Dadistan-i-Dinik*, 94.5, quoted in ibid., 192.

"Each one should do unto others as he would have others do unto him." (Inca)[5]

"O man, what you do not like, do not to your fellows." (Bacongo)[6]

"Avoid doing what you would blame others for doing." (Greek)[7]

"That which is hateful to you, do not do to your fellow. That is the whole Torah; the rest is the explanation." (Hebrew)[8]

"Do to others as you would have them do to you." (Christian)[9]

"Do not impose upon others what you yourself do not desire." (Confucian)[10]

The essence of the Golden Rule is the idea that all people are equal. I must value your needs and desires just as I value my own. I cannot give preference to my own needs and ignore yours, just because I am me and you are you. To do so would be to think of myself as more important—morally more significant—than you. It would be a failure to acknowledge our moral equality.

Other historical codes and principles also express some idea of fairness, though not in quite the same manner as the Golden Rule. These codes comprise the earliest attempts to set forth a model of justice. For example, the Code of Hammurabi, which dates from 1760 BCE, states: "If a man put out the eye of another man, his eye shall be put out. If he break another man's bone, his bone shall be broken."[11] The book of Leviticus (24:17–21) states:

---

5. Garcilaso de la Vega, *The Incas*, trans. Maria Jolas (New York: Orion, 1961), 9, quoted in ibid., 192.

6. C. C. Claridge, *Wild Bush Tribes of Tropical Africa* (no publication data given), 259, quoted in ibid., 193.

7. Attributed to Thales by Diogenes Laërtius, *The Lives and Opinions of Eminent Philosophers*, I, 36.

8. Babylonian Talmud, *Shabbat* 31a. This is sometimes referred to as the "Silver Rule."

9. Luke 6:31.

10. Confucius, *Analects* 15.24, trans. Edward Slingerland (Indianapolis, IN: Hackett, 2003), 183.

11. "The Code of Hammurabi," trans. L. W. King (1910), at *Exploring Ancient World Cultures, http://eawc.evansville.edu/anthology/hammurabi.htm.*

Anyone who kills a human being shall be put to death.
Anyone who kills an animal shall make restitution for it, life
for life. Anyone who maims another shall suffer the same
injury in return: fracture for fracture, eye for eye, tooth for
tooth; the injury inflicted is the injury to be suffered. One
who kills an animal shall make restitution for it; but one
who kills a human being shall be put to death.

These are expressions of *lex talionis*, or the "law of retaliation."
They were intended to limit the extent of vengeance a person could
seek in response to an injury. They imply that justice consists in
maintaining or restoring balance among people, and thus, like the
Golden Rule, express a form of equality as a basic moral principle.

This way of thinking about ethics focuses on the nature of the
action itself rather than on the consequences that follow from the
action. Philosophers refer to this way of thinking as *deontology*, that
is, the study of duty, for by appealing to the idea of fairness, one can
specify what types of actions are intrinsically right or wrong. One can
provide criteria for describing the types of actions that are permit-
ted or prohibited and in this way, generate a set of duties, rights, or
obligations. Fairness isn't the only basis for rights, duties, and obligations; however, it is central to the theories of most deontologists. In
particular, it is central to the thinking of the German philosopher
Immanuel Kant (1724–1804), who is widely considered to have provided the most substantial and influential deontological theory.

Before taking a closer look at Kant's theory, it is important to
look at other historical ideas about fairness, for theories do not arise
out of nowhere. They arise out of and in response to questions that
people struggle to answer. The question people have tried to answer
regarding fairness is this: Where does the universal commitment to
fairness (as expressed in the Golden Rule) come from? Does it derive
from a perception of the way the world actually is or from the way
people think the world should be?

The earliest written reflection on this question comes from the
Greek historian Thucydides (c. 460 BCE–c. 400 BCE). In retelling
the story of the Athenian invasion of Melos, he poses a challenge to
the notion of justice—and the commitment to fairness that underlies
the notion of justice—that continues to resonate today.

THUCYDIDES'S CHALLENGE

In a well-known passage from his *History of the Peloponnesian War*, Thucydides describes a debate that took place in 416 BCE between Athenian representatives and the leaders of the small island of Melos. The Athenians were trying to persuade Melos to join the alliance in their war against Sparta, an alliance which, in effect, would have put the island of Melos under the rule of Athens. Melos historically had been allied with Sparta, but it had so far remained neutral in the war, and it had enjoyed self-rule for seven hundred years.

The Melians argued that it would be contrary to justice to force them to accept Athenian rule; the Athenians replied that justice was irrelevant, that "decisions about justice are made in human discussions only when both sides are under equal compulsion; but when one side is stronger, it gets as much as it can, and the weak must accept that."[12] After debating the issue for some time and failing to persuade the Melians to surrender, the Athenians laid siege to the island, killed all the adult males, and took the women and children as slaves.

What could the Melians have said to convince the Athenians that they were acting unjustly and that therefore they *must* not use force to compel the Melians to join their alliance? The painful truth is that they said nearly everything they could have said.

First the Melians responded to the Athenians' claim that justice is irrelevant in this situation and that the only relevant principle is self-interest by arguing in the following way: justice is in everyone's interest, and because it is a natural law that everyone acts in his or her own interest, the Athenians must act according to justice. The Melians argued that there is a "rule which is good for all: that a plea of justice and fairness should do some good for a man who has fallen into danger. . . . And this rule concerns you no less than us: if you ever stumble, you might receive a terrible punishment and be an example to others."[13] The Athenians replied that they were more concerned that their other subjects would perceive them as weak if they allowed Melos to keep its independence, so it was in their self-interest to force the Melians into the alliance.[14] The Athenian reply

---

12. Thucydides, *On Justice, Power and Human Nature: Selections from the History of the Peloponnesian War*, trans. Paul Woodruff (Indianapolis, IN: Hackett, 1993), 103.
13. Ibid., 103.
14. Ibid., 104.

points out a problem with all such attempts to derive justice from rational self-interest: justice is regarded merely as a means to some other end. If justice is what you seek in order to get something else you want, there is always the possibility that you can get what you want without justice. Because the Athenians are interested primarily in security, and they believe they will be more secure by conquering Melos, they choose that course of action. It seems to them to be more practical than just.

Then the Melians tried another tactic: "The gods are on our side, because we stand innocent against men who are unjust."[15] (In short, a sort of magic power—the gods, or fortune, or luck—protects those who are in the right.) The Athenians remained unconvinced:

> The favor of the gods should be as much on our side as yours. . . . Nature always compels gods (we believe) and men (we are certain) to rule over anyone they can control. We did not make this law, and we were not the first to follow it; but we will take it as we found it and leave it to posterity forever, because we know that you would do the same if you had our power, and so would anyone else.[16]

The Athenians claimed to have discovered a psychological law, and they correctly noted that "they will leave it to posterity forever." The dialogue between the Athenians and Melians has influenced political thinking about power struggles for centuries. When former U.S. president Richard Nixon was asked in 1993 about attempts to broker a peaceful resolution to the conflict in the former Yugoslavia, he remarked: "You cannot work out a settlement unless there is a correlation of forces."[17] In other words, concerns of justice come up only when it is in the interest of both sides to reach an agreement. According to this way of thinking, justice is not a matter of determining what the two parties ought to do. Rather, the practical business of "working out a settlement" can be accomplished only when it is in the mutual interest of the parties in conflict (or potential conflict). So justice exists only when there is a balance of power, and it consists in a negotiated settlement or contract between both sides.

---

15. Ibid., 106.
16. Ibid.
17. William Safire, "The Last New Nixon," *The New York Times*, March 8, 1993, A17.

If the Athenians are correct, then basic moral equality does not underlie a concept of fairness. Human beings may achieve equality with others by acquiring power of some sort, but there is no equality independent of power. The practical implications of this view are considerable. Without basic moral equality, claims of racism, sexism, ageism—any claim of discrimination based on natural or cultural differences—have no moral basis. Nor would charges of injustice against nations at war have any moral force. Such claims might point out differences of power between groups, but they wouldn't point out injustice, unless some law or policy had been violated.

RESPONSES TO THUCYDIDES

Over the centuries, there have been three basic kinds of responses to the view expressed in the dialogue by Thucydides. Some philosophers have defended and even expanded on the argument that fairness is a function of power. Some have argued instead that fairness is inescapable, that contrary to appearances, the world really is fair. Others, like Kant, have argued that fairness is a genuine moral obligation, something we have a duty to bring about in the world through our individual actions and social institutions. To understand how the idea of fairness functions as a distinct way of ethical thinking, it is necessary to see how Kant's deontological theory provides an alternative to the other two responses to Thucydides.

Fairness as a Function of Power

In Plato's *Republic* the character Thrasymachus states a view nearly identical to that expressed by the Athenians in the Melian dialogue. He says that ". . . justice is nothing other than the advantage of the stronger."[18] In other words, the laws and procedures that constitute justice in a society do not derive from an inborn sense of fairness; rather they are invented to protect the interests of the people who make and enforce the laws.

---

18. Plato, *Republic*, trans. G.M.A. Grube, rev. C.D.C. Reeve (Indianapolis, IN: Hackett, 1992), 338c, 14.

Similar ideas have been expressed throughout history. The Italian philosopher Niccolò Machiavelli (1469–1527), for instance, observed, "Since there cannot be good laws without good arms, I will not consider laws but speak of arms,"[19] echoing the Athenian ambassadors' assertion that justice issues not from a sense of fairness but from the possession of power.

The English philosopher Thomas Hobbes (1588–1679) argued that justice consists of a social contract that people agree to because they fear the consequences of anarchy. People surrender their liberty to the power of the state because that is preferable to a "war of all against all." In such a contest, everyone would lose, because no human being has a significant advantage of power over the others:

> Nature has made men so equal in the faculties of the body and mind as that, though there be found one man sometimes manifestly stronger in body or of quicker mind than another, yet, when all is reckoned together, the difference between man and man is not so considerable as that one man can thereupon claim to himself any benefit to which another may not pretend as well as he. For as to the strength of body, the weakest has strength enough to kill the strongest, either by secret machination or by confederacy with others that are in the same danger with himself.[20]

Human beings thus have natural equality, according to Hobbes, but this is not the same as moral equality. This is a radical view, because it is generally assumed that people are not naturally equal (that is, they differ in strength, talents, and intelligence) but they are morally equal (that is, they deserve equal treatment). Hobbes, however, insists that prior to the social contract, no concept of fairness governs interactions among human beings. Hobbes explains that the very idea of right and wrong derives only from the laws, not the other way around:

> To this war of every man against every man, this also is consequent: that nothing can be unjust. The notions of right and wrong, justice and injustice, have there no place. Where

19. Niccolò Machiavelli, *The Chief Works and Others*, trans. Allan Gilbert (Durham, NC: Duke University Press, 1965), 47.

20. Thomas Hobbes, *Leviathan* (Indianapolis, IN: Bobbs-Merrill, 1958), 104–105.

there is no common power, there is no law; where no law, no injustice. . . . Justice and injustice are none of the faculties neither of the body nor mind. If they were, they might be in a man that were alone in the world, as well as his senses and passions. They are qualities that relate to men in society, not in solitude.[21]

According to Plato's character Thrasymachus, Machiavelli, and Hobbes, claims of fairness are significant only when backed up by force. People agree to abide by laws of the state (or rules and policies of the workplace, school, or community) because it is in their interest to do so, either to get something they want or to avoid something they fear. The idea of fairness alone has no power to motivate people.

Fairness as a Feature of the World

The Greek and Roman Stoics had a different concept of fairness.[22] According to them, whatever happens is a matter of fate. Events always turn out the way they must turn out. Epictetus, one of the best-known Stoics, said that "just as a target is not set up to be missed, in the same way nothing bad by nature happens in the world."[23] The only thing human beings can do is adjust their attitude toward events. Thus complaints of injustice, either in the way natural events turn out or in the way other human beings act, are unfounded. According to Epictetus, you should not "seek to have events happen as you want them to, but instead want them to happen as they do happen."[24]

> Remember that you are an actor in a play, which is as the playwright wants it to be: short if he wants it short, long if he wants it long. If he wants you to play a beggar, play even this part skillfully, or a cripple, or a public official, or a private citizen. What is yours is to play the assigned part well. But to choose it belongs to someone else.[25]

---

21. Ibid., 108.

22. Stoicism thrived in the Mediterranean region during the first and second centuries, though the earliest writings date from a couple of centuries before that and its influence survived well into the Middle Ages.

23. Epictetus, *The Handbook*, trans. Nicholas P. White (Indianapolis, IN: Hackett, 1983), 19.

24. Ibid., 13.

25. Ibid., 16.

There is something admirable in the advice to take charge of one's own feelings and attitudes and make the best of whatever situation one finds oneself in. In this respect, much of what Epictetus and other Stoics say can be quite helpful. In fact, Epictetus's *Encheiridion* (or "Handbook") often reads like the world's first self-help book.

However, the Stoic outlook may result in complacency toward inequalities and injustices that take place in the world. For example, according to the Stoics, if I get passed over for a promotion at work because of my gender or race, I should not file a discrimination complaint. Instead, I should examine my own attitude and accept the result as something that was meant to be. If somebody points out that the clothes being sold in a local store were produced by a factory that forces young children to work long hours, depriving them of the education and social development that all children need and deserve, the Stoic outlook gives one no basis for objecting that such a thing violates human rights and that a boycott or a protest should be organized. If children are being forced to work in deplorable conditions, well, that's just the way the world is. Perhaps they can learn to make the best of their situation.

EPICTETUS (C. 55–135 CE)

Epictetus

© Bridgeman-Giraudon/Art Resource

Epictetus was born into slavery and spent most of his youth serving a wealthy household in Rome. He was given an early education in Stoic philosophy and was freed at age eighteen. A few years later the Emperor Domitian banned all philosophers from Rome, so Epictetus moved to Nicopolis in Greece where he established his own school. He quickly earned a reputation for the quality of his teaching, and people traveled from all over the Mediterranean to learn from him.

Continued

Epictetus *Continued*

There are many stories about Epictetus that circulated after his death, but it is impossible to know whether they are historically accurate. Most of the stories provide examples of him living out his basic principles. What we know for sure is that he lived very simply, in a modest hut with few possessions—perhaps a pad for sleeping, a table and a lamp. He never married, though late in life he may have adopted a child in order to save the child from neglect.

Epictetus's writings consist of two books, the *Discourses* and the *Encheiridion* (or "Handbook"), the latter an abridged version of the former. The books were composed after his death by his student Arrian, and most scholars agree that they are probably transcriptions of Epictetus's own words.

The central theme of Epictetus's teachings is living well, something that can only be accomplished through learning how to control one's thoughts, emotions, likes, and dislikes. That is easier said than done however, so Epictetus provides practical advice about how to think and act. In the *Encheiridion* he tells the reader how to think about things so one doesn't lose self-control in cases of disappointment. He says, for example, if you are fond of a particular ceramic cup, tell yourself that it is ceramic cups in general that you are fond of. Then you won't be upset when it breaks. The idea is that if you can practice control over your emotions during common, everyday situations, you will be better able to practice self-control when a crisis arises.

One early source reports that after his death someone paid three thousand drachmae for his lamp (a large sum of money). If true, it would have been an ironic tribute to the departed philosopher, for the consistent message of his teachings was that possessions are worth nothing; only his words, which were free, would be worth going out of one's way to possess.

In short, the problem with Stoicism is its failure to acknowledge the existence of real wrongs in the world, real injustices that need to be addressed.

Another attempt to articulate an idea of fairness as a natural feature of the world was made by Ralph Waldo Emerson in his essay "Compensation." There he relies upon popular expressions or sayings to demonstrate the widespread belief that fairness or moral balance is part of the order of things. Or, as people sometimes say today: "What goes around, comes around." Emerson does not go as far as the Stoics in suggesting that injustice never occurs, but he does say that the tendency to cry foul, that is, to complain of unfair treatment, or that somebody else has an unfair advantage, is frequently shortsighted. A broadened perspective on events would reveal a moral balance in the world. Every supposed benefit carries some cost; every apparent setback brings with it some gain that will become clear sooner or later.

Such a belief is sometimes referred to as karma.[26] It is the notion that the laws of cause and effect operate according to a moral principle. If I help you, someone will eventually help me. Perhaps if I help someone change a flat tire, someone will eventually help me change my flat tire when the time comes. Sometimes that does, in fact, happen. Of course, actions are rarely returned in direct proportion, but the idea of karma, or as Emerson calls it, "compensation," is that balance is inevitable, even though it may not take place in ways that are immediately clear or that match one's expectations:

> All things are moral. That soul which within us is a sentiment, outside of us is a law. . . . Justice is not postponed. A perfect equity adjusts its balance in all parts of life. . . . The dice of God are always loaded. The world looks like a multiplication table, or a mathematical equation, which, turn it how you will, balances itself. Take what figure you will, its exact value, not more nor less, returns to you. Every secret is told, every crime punished, every virtue rewarded, every wrong redressed, in silence and certainty.[27]

According to such a view, justice is built into the structure of the universe. People should be good because otherwise they are trying to

---

26. A related concept in Hindu and Buddhist teaching is *dharma*, which refers to the norms or principles one should follow to act in accordance with nature.

27. Ralph Waldo Emerson, "Compensation" in *Emerson: Essays and Lectures* (New York: The Library of America, 1983), 289–290.

cheat the universe, and there is no possibility of getting away with that. Eventually, they will be "caught." All kinds of folk proverbs express this idea: "Cheaters never prosper"; "Honesty is the best policy"; "You reap what you sow"; "What goes up, must come down"; "The bigger they are, the harder they fall"; "When you point your finger at someone, three fingers are pointing back at you"; "A good deed is never lost."

But the fact that people frequently use such expressions does not indicate that they are fully convinced the world does in fact balance itself. People may instead use such expressions to insist that the world should be balanced and thus to urge people to act in ways that help make it so. It is to such a view of fairness that we turn next.

Fairness as a Moral Prescription

Is the world really as immoral and power-driven as Thucydides insisted, or as just and ordered as the Stoics believed? No; the truth seems to lie somewhere in-between. Sometimes wrongdoers do benefit from their misdeeds, and sometimes they are punished. Sometimes good people benefit from their actions, and sometimes they do not. However, most people agree that good behavior should be rewarded and that bad behavior should be punished. We seem to have an inborn sense of fairness that tells us how things ought to be, whether or not that's what we actually observe happening in the world.

That is the central insight of Immanuel Kant's moral philosophy, which he described in a brief book entitled *Grundlegen zur Metaphysik der Sitten* (Groundwork of the Metaphysics of Morals), published in 1785. Kant argued that we can take our moral guidance neither from how people actually act nor from observations of what happens to people when they do act in one way or another. Instead, moral guidance should come from the dictates of reason, which tell us that we should treat everyone equally. Why does reason tell us this? Because insofar as human beings are rational creatures, we are all equal. We are not equal when it comes to our physical bodies, possessions, social standing, education, cleverness, or personality. When it comes to those things, we all differ. Some people have natural or social advantages or disadvantages compared to others. But those things are all incidental to who we are. They come and go and change over time, but our essential nature remains the same. Essentially, we are rational creatures, with the ability to think abstractly, to reason from premise to conclusion, to be self-aware and choose to act one way or another, and in that respect we are equal. The rules of logic that apply to you are exactly the same as the ones that apply to me.

IMMANUEL KANT (1724–1804)

Immanuel Kant

© Nicku/Shutterstock

Immanuel Kant was born in Königsberg, the capitol of Prussia. His father was a harness maker who always struggled to make a living. By all accounts his parents were deeply religious. They were Lutheran Pietists, a movement that emphasized personal conversion and inward examination of the soul. Kant rebelled against the emphasis on soul-searching, but for the rest of his life he was influenced by his parents' example of self-sacrifice, discipline, and inner peace.

At age sixteen he entered the university at Königsberg and fell in love with natural philosophy. After graduating he served as a tutor for several years before returning to the university as a teacher. He spent the next forty-two years there, never venturing more than a few miles from the city. Yet he was said to be fascinated by travel and would encourage guests at his dinner parties to tell stories of foreign lands and customs. During the course of his career he taught a wide range of topics, including philosophy, science, and mathematics.

Although Kant was early recognized as a promising scholar and engaging lecturer, his reputation did not extend very far until late in life when he published a series of books that revolutionized the philosophical world: the *Critique of Pure Reason* (which dealt with epistemology); the *Critique of Practical Reason* (which dealt with ethics); and the *Critique of Judgment*

Continued

Immanuel Kant *Continued*

(which dealt with aesthetics). These three works, all published in a period of nine years, established his international reputation as one of the world's greatest philosophers.

Kant attributed his prodigious output to a decision he made around age forty to impose a strict physical and intellectual discipline upon his life. He began following a strict routine of waking, eating, lecturing, and writing at precisely fixed times. He was so diligent in this effort that he became a standing joke among the residents of Königsberg, where people claimed to set their clocks by Kant's daily walk along the city streets. He also began to employ the same sort of discipline to his work, systematizing his studies until he achieved a universal theory in which every aspect of experience could be explained.

He lived a quiet life in retirement, though his old age was not peaceful. He suffered nightmares and continual worries about his failing health. He died just before turning eighty. His last words were spoken to a friend who had handed him a glass of wine. "It is good," he said.

Kant calls the dictate of reason that we should treat everyone equally the "Categorical Imperative." (Actually, that is an early English translation of Kant's original phrase. A more up-to-date translation would be something like "Universal Command.") The Categorical Imperative is the single moral principle that guides behavior in every instance. However, it can be expressed in different ways.[28] The most commonly used version is that *you should always act in the way that you would want anyone else in the same situation to have to act.*[29] But such a principle may not be as easy to apply as it seems.

---

28. In the *Grundlegen* Kant provides several slightly different versions of the Categorical Imperative. They are simply different ways of expressing the same basic moral principle.

29. Immanuel Kant, *Grounding for the Metaphysics of Morals*, trans. James W. Ellington, 3rd ed., (Indianapolis, IN: Hackett, 1993), 30. Kant actually expresses it this way: "Act as if the maxim of your action were to become through your will a universal law of nature." However, the purpose of this book is not to present a thorough analysis of Kant's ethics but merely to refer to Kant as one important source of thinking about fairness, so I have presented a simplified version of Kant's formulation.

Imagine you are planning to sell a car. It is a ten-year-old Ford Taurus with high mileage and a number of minor mechanical problems; however, it runs well, and there is no reason to think it won't continue to run well for the foreseeable future. One thing bothers you, though. Occasionally the car fails to start. It doesn't happen often, about once a month or so. If you just leave it and try to start it the next day, it is fine. You have taken the car to some mechanics, and they could not find anything wrong with it, so you don't know if it is a serious problem or not. Then someone sees your ad for the car and asks to take it for a test drive. You wonder: Should I tell the person it occasionally fails to start? Or should I just let him test drive it and hope it starts fine, which it probably will. If you tell him that sometimes it doesn't start, he may not buy the car, or he might ask you to take less money for it. If you don't tell him, he won't know the car has that problem. If it fails to start for him after he buys it, he will probably assume the problem only recently developed.

According to Kant, in such a situation you should ask yourself: "If I were the buyer, what would I want the seller to do?" What another seller probably would do remains irrelevant; the only thing that matters is what you would want the seller to do if you were the buyer. The fact is, you most likely would want the seller to tell you everything relevant to your ability to make a good, informed decision about buying the car. That the car sometimes fails to start certainly affects that decision. Somebody might object to this and say: "You don't have to tell the buyer what's wrong with the car; it's his responsibility to have it checked out." Even if that is a common practice, however, it doesn't matter. What matters is how you would want to be treated in such a situation. If you would want to be told everything wrong with the car, then you must treat the actual buyer the same way. To do otherwise is to act as if you are more important than the other person—as if your concerns matter and his do not.

But the Categorical Imperative requires one to take ethical considerations beyond simple reversibility (i.e., "putting oneself in another person's shoes"). It asks us to think universally—that is, to imagine what would happen if everyone acted in a certain way. In the case under consideration, that would mean asking, "What would happen if everyone who had something to sell withheld relevant information; would I want to live in such a world?" The answer is "no." I would not want to live in such a world because sometimes I am a buyer, and whenever I am a buyer, I want access to all available information that will help me make a good decision. Moreover, a world in which sellers always withheld relevant information would be a world in which sellers' claims were never believed. That would not be good for sellers either.

This provides a way of thinking about a problem that is difficult to resolve when thinking in terms of consequences, namely, the "free rider" problem. Imagine that you get onto a city bus and the driver forgets to collect your fare. Are you obligated to pay anyway? If you look at it from the point of view of consequences, it doesn't seem to make much difference whether you pay or not. The bus company will mostly likely not even notice the missing revenue. But isn't it wrong to ride the bus without contributing your fair share? The Categorical Imperative requires you to ask, "What if nobody paid their bus fare? Could I wish that to be the case?" Obviously, I could not, because then the buses wouldn't run at all.

The Categorical Imperative is an ethical principle, that is, it provides a criterion for determining what is right and wrong. But it does not provide specific rules for behavior. It does not state specifically that murder, lying, cheating, or stealing is wrong. Rather, it provides a way of understanding why such actions are wrong—namely, they always treat others in ways the actor would not want to be treated. Another thing that distinguishes principles from rules is that the same principle may be expressed in quite different ways. Kant actually provides several versions of the Categorical Imperative, all of which should lead to the same conclusion about whether particular actions are right or wrong. One of the alternative versions goes like this: *Always treat people as ends in themselves and never only as a means.*[30] This means always treating people as inherently valuable, as if they themselves are more important to you than whatever it is that you can get from them. To treat someone only as a means to an end is to use them to get something you want without regard to their own needs or desires.

When you go to the bakery to buy a loaf of bread, you use the baker as a means to an end. Your end (or purpose) is a loaf of bread, and you need the baker in order to get it. The baker also uses you as a means to an end. Her end is to make money, so she needs customers

---

30. Ibid., 36.

to buy her bread. But neither of you use each other *only* as a means. You each freely choose to engage in a trade: if you think the price is too high or the bread seems stale, you don't have to buy it; if you won't pay enough, or if you are causing a disturbance in the bakery, the baker doesn't have to sell the bread to you. Because you each freely engage in a trade, and you both understand the terms of the agreement, you are treating each other also as ends, that is, as free and equal moral beings. The situation is different if a store is selling clothes produced in a sweatshop (where people are forced, often against their will, to work long hours in deplorable conditions for very low wages). In that case the purchaser can choose whether to buy the clothes, but the people who make the clothes don't have the same choice. They serve only as a means, and thus the transaction is unfair. Notice that buying the clothes would also be unfair according to the first version of the Categorical Imperative. The sweatshop workers are not being treated the way you would want to be treated. Because it is a version of the same principle, one should always reach the same conclusion, no matter which version is used to evaluate a situation.

Fairness operates as a function of moral equality. Because all people are morally equal to one another (insofar as they are rational beings), everyone's legitimate concerns and interests have equal importance. That doesn't mean people must always do what others want; it just means that they must always give others the same amount of respect and consideration they would want themselves.

THE SCOPE OF FAIRNESS

Kant's notion of personhood has been tremendously influential, both by grounding the notion of moral equality in the metaphysical status of human beings as moral agents (that is, as beings who are self-aware and capable of recognizing and acting on a concept of duty) and also by drawing a sharp line between the moral status of human beings and the nonmoral status of all other creatures. For Kant moral status does not depend on actual cognitive ability; it depends rather upon the potential for rationality of the species. Thus each human being, whether conscious or in a coma, whether an infant or a mature adult, is a person. Nor does moral status depend on sentience (the ability to feel pleasure and pain) as it does for utilitarians. It is not the ability to feel that confers moral status but rather the ability to recognize obligations, what we sometimes call the possession of a conscience. This justification is often invoked when extending the notion of moral rights to human embryos and those who have suffered brain injury and are in a permanent vegetative state. To say an embryo is a person is to assert that an embryo has a certain moral status, and that is different from asserting that an embryo is a member of the species Homo sapiens. Membership in a species may be determined genetically, but personhood is an ethical concept. There is no genetic test to determine personhood.

One way to examine how far ethical obligation can be extended is to ask whether any nonhuman creatures qualify as persons. One can imagine that we may someday discover—or be discovered by—intelligent creatures from other planets who communicate, act, and form communities, much as we do. We would presumably consider them to be persons. But what about nonhuman creatures here on Earth? What about dolphins, whales, apes, and elephants? Should the Golden Rule apply to them as well? After all, they are intelligent beings, even though they cannot communicate in the variety of ways human beings do. What about dogs and cats, or even fish, snakes, and clams? Is there moral equality among all sentient creatures?

Kant thought that, because duty derives from our nature as rational beings, and because nonhuman animals do not possess rationality, we have no moral duties, as such, toward animals. Therefore, claims of fairness do not apply to them.

> Beings whose existence depends not on our will but on nature have, nevertheless, if they are not rational beings, only a relative value as means and are therefore called things. On the other hand, rational beings are called persons inasmuch as their nature already marks them out as ends in themselves, i.e., as something which is not to be used merely as means and hence there is imposed thereby a limit on all arbitrary use of such beings, which are thus objects of respect.[31]

This is perhaps the most significant weakness of Kant's theory, for it provides no basis for claiming that anything done to an animal

---

31. Ibid., 35–36.

might be wrong, except insofar as the animal has some relationship to human beings. That is, it would be wrong for Tom to kick Harry's cat because Tom would not want Harry to kick his (Tom's) cat. But Kant's theory provides no basis for saying that Harry's cat itself has been wronged by being kicked. Since in Kant's view a cat is a thing, and things do not have moral status, a cat cannot be morally wronged. In short, cats do not have rights.

But this runs contrary to most people's moral sensibility, not to mention many animal protection laws based on those sensibilities that aim to protect animals from undue suffering, not just from theft or damage (the way in which one might seek to protect one's possessions). Harry doesn't object to Tom kicking his cat because he is worried that the cat may be "damaged"; he objects because he cares about his cat and doesn't want to see it hurt. He might even say to Tom, "How would you like it if I kicked *you*?" The fact that it is possible to thus apply the Golden Rule to other species, to put oneself in the place of a dog or a cat and imagine what it would feel like to be treated in a certain way, reveals that there is no reason the idea of fairness cannot be extended to members of other species. However, Kant himself did not extend his moral theory in that way.

Extending the Categorical Imperative to other species has its own difficulties, of course. While one may be able to intelligibly ask, "If I were a cat, would I mind being kicked?" it is not so clear whether the question, "If I were a clam, would I mind being eaten?" makes any sense. Can one even imagine what it is like to be a clam?[32] However, the important thing to recognize is that the deontological approach to ethical questions does allow for the consideration of the moral status of nonhuman species, even if Kant himself did not think so. Furthermore, without extending the notion of fairness to intelligent beings of other species it is difficult to explain the moral status of human beings who have marginal rationality or self-awareness, such as embryos, the comatose, or those with severe cognitive impairments. The idea of fairness comes into play not only with regard to those who are precisely like me but most significantly

---

32. For a compelling essay on the implications of such questions, see Thomas Nagel, "What Is It Like to Be a Bat?" in *Mortal Questions* (New York: Cambridge University Press, 1979), 165–180.

with regard to those whose lives I can with some effort imagine and yet not, perhaps, be readily sympathetic toward.

The notion of fairness doesn't easily resolve all questions about moral status, but it gives us an approach to take, that is, a way of thinking about the extent of moral obligations to those who are unlike ourselves.

THE PRINCIPLE OF AUTONOMY

Another contemporary development of Kant's theory has to do with thinking about rights and duties in terms of autonomy. *Autonomy* means, literally, "self-rule," the ability of a person to choose for himself or herself. The principle of autonomy has been widely used in professional ethics to provide justification for certain kinds of laws or policies that protect people's rights. For example, the "right to free speech" in a political context is sometimes defended as necessary for allowing individuals to decide for themselves what to believe, for whom to vote, and so on. The "right to privacy" provides a person with the ability to decide what personal information others may have access to. The principle of autonomy, just like Kant's Categorical Imperative, provides a way of applying the notion of fairness to particular actions. Moreover, it directs attention to the ways in which fairness is most often violated, namely by denying individuals the ability to choose for themselves. The three most common ways of denying a person's autonomy are coercion, deception, and manipulation.

Coercion

To coerce somebody means to force them to do something without their consent or even against their will. Any exercise of power over another person to which he or she does not consent is a form of coercion. Bullying, hazing, rape, and torture are all forms of coercion. Such actions use force in ways that violate a person's autonomy.

Not every use of force is coercion. Legitimate punishment is not considered coercive if it results from a fair application of laws to which a citizen consents. If Joe is caught shoplifting, given a fair trial, and sentenced to pay a fine and serve some time in jail, the punishment is legitimate, because Joe lives in a society governed by laws to which he consents by his own actions. If he benefits from the laws by having his own property protected from would-be thieves, then he cannot protest when the same laws punish him for stealing another person's property. In this way the punishment (if lawful) is fair because he agrees to it (in general) even though he might object when it is applied specifically to him. The important consideration is whether the punishment is fair, that is, whether it proceeds from an appropriate application of the laws to which citizens, either by their direct action or inaction, consent.

Does this apply also to children? Yes and no. Children reach the age of consent in stages. They can understand and agree to some things at a fairly young age but cannot consent to other things until they are older. Once people reach the level of maturity at which they fully understand situations affecting them and take responsibility for their decisions, it is no longer fair to force them to do things for their own good unless they agree to it. For example, most states in the United States recognize eighteen as the age at which people can marry without their parents' consent. The age at which children may refuse to eat their vegetables usually comes much earlier (though there is no generally agreed-upon age at which that milestone is reached). It is considered fair for parents to force their children to do certain things, even against the child's will and using the threat of punishment, to ensure that their children are raised safely and in good health. Parents, for example, may force their children to do their homework, brush their teeth, and eat healthy food. But at a certain age, it is no longer permissible for parents to use coercion; they must instead use persuasion (as they must with any other mature person) if they wish to change their children's behavior.

Persuasion is generally considered legitimate, because it attempts to influence another person's beliefs or actions through the presentation of reasons, which allows a person to consent freely. Persuasion, though not always welcome, is fair, because it respects the other person's autonomy. Exceptions to the legitimacy of persuasion arise only when the person being persuaded cannot independently evaluate the soundness of reasons being presented, either because of youth or cognitive impairment, such as dementia. To see why this is so, one need only consider Kant's Categorical Imperative. There are forms of persuasion you might consider perfectly acceptable if applied to you as a mature, clear-thinking adult and yet unacceptable if you imagined yourself as a young child. Certain advertisements, for example of alcohol or tobacco products, are considered inappropriate for TV programs or magazines that are aimed at children, and yet they are considered fine for adult viewers and readers.

Deception

Kant believed that lies of any kind are morally prohibited. Because lying creates a false impression of something, it denies other people the opportunity to perceive a situation in the same way the speaker does and, thereby, creates a condition of inequality. Lying denies the other person's autonomy and contributes to a world in which all speech is distrusted. It is also self-defeating. A lie works only if people believe speech is trustworthy. But telling a lie makes speech untrustworthy, which undermines the possibility of it being effective. "For a lie always harms another; if not some other human being, then it nevertheless does harm to humanity in general, inasmuch as it vitiates the very source of right. . . . To be truthful (honest) in all declarations is, therefore, a sacred and unconditionally commanding law of reason that admits of no expediency whatsoever."[33]

One of Kant's early critics raised an objection using the following scenario: Suppose a friend comes to you and says she is being chased by someone who intends to kill her. She asks you to hide her, and you agree to do so. A short time later there is a knock upon your door. You open it and there stands the person who has been chasing your friend. He asks if your friend is in the house. What should you do?

Most people would probably agree that in such a situation it would not only be permissible but morally required to lie. You should say anything you could to throw the pursuer off the track to ensure your friend's safety.[34] But even in the face of an example such as this, Kant remained insistent. One should never tell lies. You may refuse

---

33. Immanuel Kant, "On a Supposed Right to Lie," in *Grounding for the Metaphysics of Morals*, trans. James W. Ellington, 3rd ed., (Indianapolis, IN: Hackett, 1993), 64–65.

34. Notice that if we think about this situation only in terms of consequences, you should do whatever is most likely to ensure your friend's safety, and if you can do that most effectively by telling a lie, you should tell a lie.

to answer; you may refuse to let the person come into your house; you may do any number of things to try to protect your friend, but you may not tell a lie. Just because one refuses to lie does not mean one has to accept meekly the negative consequences that might seem to follow from telling the truth.

Examples of accepting restrictions on certain types of behavior while still trying to act in ways that provide good results may be found in any community that takes the duty of truth-telling seriously.[35] Most early Christians, for example, would have agreed with Kant that it is always wrong to tell a lie. Even in life-and-death situations, they considered it necessary to tell the truth. That doesn't mean they didn't care about what happened as a result of their truth-telling. A story passed down about Athanasius (c. 296–373), the fourth-century Bishop of Alexandria, illustrates this point. One day Athanasius was in a boat on the Nile River, being chased by the emperor's soldiers. The rowers of his boat were exhausted and in danger of being overtaken, so after they had rounded a bend in the river, Athanasius instructed the captain to turn the boat around. As they headed back downriver and the pursuing boat approached them, one of the soldiers cried out, "Have you seen Athanasius, the bishop?" Athanasius knew he had to answer them truthfully, so he shouted back, "Yes, he's not far." His pursuers thanked him and rowed with renewed energy up the river and out of sight.[36] The story illustrates an important point about adhering to moral rules. Even though the duty to comply with a rule may be strict, the way in which one complies may still allow for inventiveness. Committing oneself to telling the truth does not require checking one's imagination at the door. It does not require one simply to give up and accept whatever consequences follow. It just means that one option, namely lying, is removed from consideration.

Manipulation

Manipulation falls roughly between deception and coercion. It consists of arranging circumstances in such a way that people do

---

35. See, for example, Richard Brandt, *Hopi Ethics: A Theoretical Analysis* (Chicago: University of Chicago Press, 1974).

36. For a brief biography of Athanasius, see F. A. Forbes, *Saint Athanasius* (Rockford, IL: Tan Books, 1998).

what one wants them to do, often contrary to their own interests and without regard to their well-being. It can be contrasted with persuasion, which attempts to get people to agree to something by presenting them with good reasons. Persuasion is legitimate, because it enhances people's autonomy by giving them greater clarity or additional relevant information about something. Manipulation is illegitimate because it seeks to take advantage of people's ignorance, confusion, fear, desire, or anxiety in order to sway their will. Swindles, con games, and blackmail are common forms of manipulation.

Sales techniques also frequently employ some degree of manipulation. For example, pushing a prospective customer to close a deal because "this price is good today only" is sometimes used to pressure a customer into making a hasty decision. Another technique consists of asking a series of probing questions before the sales pitch begins, to determine a prospective customer's emotional vulnerabilities. One person may respond well to pleas of sympathy and feel sorry for the salesperson who is friendly and badly needs to make a sale. Another person may be intimidated easily and respond better to a more forceful approach. Another technique involves diverting objections to the sale by changing the subject or putting off the answer in hopes that the customer forgets to raise the question again. All such techniques attempt to convince the customer to buy something that he probably neither needs nor wants. Legitimate persuasion, on the other hand, would provide the customer with information to make a wiser, more informed decision.

In the Pulitzer Prize–winning play *Glengarry Glenn Ross*, by David Mamet, four real estate agents compete with each other to become top earners for their company. One scene takes place in a bar where the top seller, Ricky Roma, meets a man named James Lingk. Roma quickly sizes up Lingk as an insecure person whose life is stuck in a rut. He never even mentions the potential investment value of the land he wants to sell him; instead he talks philosophically about taking chances and finding "opportunity":

> How can I be secure? Through amassing wealth beyond all measure? No. And what's beyond all measure? That's a sickness. That's a trap. There is no measure. Only greed. . . . I do those things which seem correct to me today. I trust myself. And if security concerns me, I do that which today I

think will make me secure. And every day I do that. When that day arrives that I need a reserve, (a) odds are that I have it, and (b) the true reserve that I have is the strength that I have of acting each day without fear. . . . Stocks, bonds, objects of art, real estate. Now: what are they? An opportunity. To what? To make money? Perhaps. To lose money? Perhaps. To "indulge" and to "learn" about ourselves? Perhaps. So . . . what? What isn't? They're an opportunity. That's all. They're an event. A guy comes up to you, you make a call, you send in a brochure, it doesn't matter. "There're these properties I'd like for you to see." What does it mean? What you want it to mean.[37]

Notice that Roma doesn't try to deceive Lingk, and he doesn't do anything that could be construed as forcing him to purchase some land. In fact, he doesn't even bring up the topic of a sale until well into the conversation. But everything he says is designed to get Lingk to be receptive to his pitch: Don't think about the consequences; we worry too much about things anyway. Money, security, comfort—these things don't have any real meaning. They're just words that mean different things to different people. Trust yourself. Act without fear. Have a drink.

It isn't always clear where the line between manipulation and persuasion should be drawn. But that isn't as important as understanding the principle of autonomy that underlies the distinction. Does an action help a person make a better, more informed decision, or does it push a person in a certain direction, without regard to the person's own best interests or wishes?

Informed Consent

Kant's Categorical Imperative may be applied to any action one considers. However, there is not always time to think through all the implications of an action in detail. Furthermore, not everyone has studied Kant's theory (or other deontological theories), and so it may be difficult to get everyone in an organization or a community to

---

37. David Mamet, *Glengarry Glenn Ross*, 1984, scene 3.

agree on how to think about what actions are fair and what actions are unfair. That is why it is useful to put in place certain kinds of rules or policies, ensuring that people will be treated fairly. Thus, in some areas of society where people are especially vulnerable to coercion, deception, or manipulation, special protections are put in place to ensure that autonomy is respected; in other words, to make certain that people are given the opportunity to understand and either agree to or refuse certain kinds of actions that would affect them. This is known as informed consent.

For example, the bar associations of the various states have ethics rules for lawyers. These rules protect clients from various forms of deception or manipulation by requiring disclosure of fees, accurate billing, avoidance of conflict of interest, and so on. When lending money or issuing credit cards, banks must follow certain consumer protections, such as providing information about interest rates and penalty fees. Not only must they provide the information but, in many instances, consumers must also sign documents stating that they have read, understood, and agree to the terms of the loan or service being offered. (That's the "consent" part.) In health care facilities and universities where research on human subjects frequently takes place, the U.S. Department of Health and Human Services requires that all biomedical and behavioral research be approved by an institutional review board (IRB).

Policies regarding informed consent did not arise simply out of thin air. They developed over time because people were harmed in persistent ways, sometimes intentionally and sometimes unintentionally. As certain patterns of harm were repeated, lawmakers intervened to pass laws protecting people from abuse, and in some cases members of a profession got together to make policies governing professional conduct among their members. Like many policies that develop out of ethical principles, the policy of requiring informed consent is generally a good thing, but it does not solve all ethical problems. It serves to constrain certain kinds of irresponsible behavior, but it does not, on its own, guarantee that the right thing is done.

Two areas where concerns about informed consent are particularly important serve to illustrate how the practice is grounded in a commitment to fairness: the practice of health care and research on human subjects.

Informed Consent in Health Care

In the case of a child who needs medical treatment, for example, who needs to be informed of the diagnosis, the prognosis, possible forms of treatment, and the risks and benefits associated with the possible treatments, including the amount of pain involved and possible long-term effects? Who, in the end, should decide what to do? Can parents decide for their children, even despite or contrary to their children's wishes? What if the parents choose a course of treatment that medical professionals think will harm the child? These questions prove difficult to answer because children reach cognitive and emotional maturity gradually and at different rates. An infant has no role to play in decisions about his or her health care. A fifteen-year-old has a significant role to play. What about a thirteen-year-old who has been brought up to distrust doctors?

What if you were being raised by irrational, gullible, ill-informed, or self-centered parents? What if they made decisions that could lead directly to your death, but—because they are your parents and because you have no other reliable form of reference by which to judge their decisions—you tended to believe what they said? In such a case, would you want the state to intervene on your behalf to save your life, even if that meant forcing you to do something you believed at the time was wrong?

In 2009 thirteen-year-old Daniel Hauser was diagnosed with Hodgkin's lymphoma, a form of cancer that typically responds well to treatment. In fact, patients Daniel's age have a 95 percent success rate if they receive appropriate treatment. However, Daniel and his parents refused chemotherapy and radiation, the forms of treatment recommended by specialists at the University of Minnesota and the Mayo Clinic. Instead, the Hausers turned to alternative medicine, including herbs, vitamins, and ionized water. Daniel explained his reasons for refusing the treatment: "I am opposed to chemotherapy because it is self-destructive and poisonous. I want to live a virtuous life, in the eyes of my creator, not just a long life."[38] The county attorney charged Daniel's parents with child neglect and endangerment.

---

38. Maura Lerner, "Sleepy Eye Parents, Teen Fight to Refuse Chemo," *Minneapolis Star Tribune*, May 7, 2009, *http://www.startribune.com/lifestyle/health/44568447.html?page=1&c=y.*

In an interview the attorney explained why he filed the charges: "If he were eighteen years old and made the decision that his parents are making for him, we would not be in court. Since the boy just turned thirteen in March, I felt the judge needs to take a look at this and make a decision."[39] In other words, the county attorney did not make a judgment about which action would have the best consequences for Daniel; instead he was concerned about fairness. Thus he applied a deontological principle to the case that would respect Daniel's autonomy by having a judge assess whether Daniel was capable of making an informed decision.

Cases such as this are difficult because, on the one hand, Daniel seems to have a good understanding of his situation, but, on the other hand, thirteen-year-old children may not be capable of understanding all the implications of their decisions and may be too easily swayed by the wishes of their parents. Daniel Hauser's case is just one of many that exist on the borderlines where it is difficult to determine just how best to ensure a person's autonomy and welfare. Applying Kant's Categorical Imperative is a helpful way to proceed in such cases, because it helps one think thoroughly and consistently about how individuals should be treated. If I were a thirteen-year-old with Hodgkin's lymphoma, would I want a judge determining whether to enforce cancer treatment even against my will and the will of my parents? Could I will that all thirteen-year-olds in similar situations should have a judge make the final decision?

Informed Consent in Human Research

There have been thousands of cases involving questionable treatment of human beings, many involving various degrees of deception, coercion, or manipulation. Some involve only one person or family; other cases involve many people over an extended period of time. Two well-known and controversial cases led to the creation of ethics committees and IRBs at hospitals and universities, because they demonstrated serious disregard of the principle of fairness. This has led to a greater emphasis on respecting the autonomy of research subjects by enforcing informed consent policies.

---

39. Ibid.

The Tuskegee Syphilis Study

In 1928, the U.S. Public Health Service (PHS) collaborated with the Tuskegee Institute, located in Tuskegee, Alabama, to offer free health examinations to African American men in Macon County, Alabama, in conjunction with research into the effects of syphilis. Men diagnosed with syphilis were not told that they had the disease so researchers could study the progression of untreated syphilis and compare it to various treatments. Study subjects were tracked even after they left Macon County, and the PHS worked to ensure that they were not given treatment by other health care providers. The study continued until 1972. John Heller, director of the Venereal Diseases unit of the PHS during a portion of the study, remarked during an interview: "The men's status did not warrant ethical debate. They were subjects, not patients; clinical material, not sick people."[40]

When an official from the PHS leaked information to a reporter about the forty-year study, it made front-page news across the country. The study was halted, a class action lawsuit was filed in U.S. District Court on behalf of the study subjects and their families, and a process was begun to rewrite policies and regulations governing the research of human subjects. One significant result was the Belmont Report, drafted by the U.S. Department of Health, Education, and Welfare (which later became the Department of Health and Human Services) in 1979. The Belmont Report, subtitled "Ethical Principles and Guidelines for the Protection of Human Subjects of Research," set forth three basic ethical principles that continue to serve as guidelines for research in the United States: respect for persons, beneficence, and justice.[41] The principle of "respect for persons" arises directly out of the principle of fairness and concerns about autonomy. Universities and health care institutions are now required to inform all potential human research subjects of any risks or inconveniences posed by the research so they may decide for themselves whether they wish to participate.

---

40. James Jones, *Bad Blood: The Tuskegee Syphilis Experiment, a Tragedy of Race and Medicine* (New York: The Free Press, 1981), 179.

41. See "The Belmont Report," Office of Human Subjects Research, *http://ohsr.od.nih.gov/guidelines/belmont.html*.

The Milgram Experiments

In 1961 Yale University psychologist Stanley Milgram began a series of experiments designed to determine whether ordinary people would obey an authority figure even if they were told to do something they believed was wrong. This was a significant question because the Eichmann trial was taking place in Jerusalem that year. Adolf Eichmann was a Nazi officer in charge of coordinating the transportation of Jews in Germany to killing centers throughout Europe during World War II. He defended his actions by saying he was just following orders. His defense raised profound questions. Did Eichmann participate in the Nazi war crimes because he believed in the cause, or was he sincere in saying he was just following orders? If an ordinary citizen was placed in Eichmann's situation, would he or she do the same thing? That's what Stanley Milgram wanted to determine.[42]

Milgram solicited volunteers and told them the experiment was designed to test the effects of electrical shocks on memory. He said the volunteers would be randomly selected into two groups—the "teachers" and the "learners." The learners would be asked to memorize word pairs, then the teacher would say one of the words and the learner would be asked to recall the matching word. If the learner did not recall the right word, he or she would be given an electrical shock, and the shock would be increased by fifteen volts for each wrong answer. The volunteers did not realize the selection of teachers and learners was rigged. All of the volunteers were teachers. The learners were actors hired to play the role. They did not receive actual electrical shocks; they just acted as if they were receiving shocks. The experiment was not intended to test memory at all; it was intended to determine how far ordinary people would go in delivering electrical shocks to strangers just because they were told to do so.

When groups of people were asked independently how many people they thought would deliver shocks all the way up to the maximum level of four hundred fifty volts, most thought only a very small percentage would do so, perhaps 1 or 2 percent. However, in Milgram's first set of experiments, 65 percent of the volunteers continued

---

42. Stanley Milgram, *Obedience to Authority: An Experimental View* (New York: Harper Collins, 1974).

to deliver shocks up to the maximum level, even after the learners pleaded with them to stop, said they had a heart condition, and finally became completely unresponsive to the teacher's questions.

The Milgram experiments are significant for two reasons: (1) the results greatly increased understanding of how people respond to authority, and (2) they could only be obtained by violating the subjects' autonomy. We all like to imagine that if put in the position of the teacher in such an experiment, we would not give shocks—certainly not up to the point where they inflict severe pain and possibly death. But the results are incontrovertible. Most people will give shocks to the maximum level, and almost everyone gives shocks to a higher level than they would predict. This forces us to acknowledge the uncomfortable truth that we really don't know how we would act in certain situations until they actually arise.

The results of the experiments reveal a considerable gap between one's moral beliefs and one's actions (at least in certain circumstances). This raises questions about what it means to say, for example, "I believe in the Golden Rule" or "I believe in Kant's Categorical Imperative." Does it mean we think people *should* act in the way they would want others to act toward them? Does it mean that we actually do act in that way? Does it mean we try to act in that way? Eichmann himself testified that he had read Kant's moral writings and believed them, but then he added that after he was given lawful orders to carry out the Final Solution, he resigned himself to no longer being "master of his own deeds."[43]

Another significant result of the Milgram experiments was the emotional distress it caused the participants after they discovered they were the real subjects of the experiment and that they had acted contrary to their own moral convictions. They were deceived by the researcher and manipulated by being placed in a situation that impressed on them the importance of following through with the tests. Milgram was conducting an experiment to see whether people would do something to others that they would not want done to themselves, and to test that, he did something to the participants that he (most likely) would not want done to himself—he deceived them

---

43. Hannah Arendt, *Eichmann in Jerusalem: A Report on the Banality of Evil* (New York: Penguin, 1963), 136.

and manipulated them. Like the Tuskegee syphilis experiments, this led to a reaction among the public and fellow scientists to create stronger ethical guidelines on research involving human subjects, and informed consent became the cornerstone of those guidelines.

JUSTICE AS FAIRNESS

Since Immanuel Kant proposed his theory of ethics, a number of other philosophers have set forth interesting variations on the same general theme. The best known of these is John Rawls. He has tried to show that fairness ought to be the fundamental principle of justice in society and that it should be used as a basis for deciding what kinds of legal rights, duties, and obligations should be established to ensure that society is just. Rawls proposed that many of the political disputes that arise in a democracy can be settled by engaging in a thought experiment called the "veil of ignorance."[44] To do this, one tries to deliberate about general principles governing conduct without regard to one's particular circumstances, such as race, gender, social standing, wealth, education, and so on. Adopting the veil of ignorance is a way of trying to take one's biases and prejudices out of play when making moral decisions.

For example, imagine a group of people arguing about raising local property taxes to pay for a new school building. Some people in the group have children and are concerned about the deteriorating building. They stress the necessity of building a new one. Others do not have children and own large houses. Their taxes would go up the most, and they don't see why they should have to pay for other people's education. Some in the group rent apartments, and their rent would not be significantly affected by the increased tax. Still others live on fixed incomes, and an increase in taxes could make it difficult for them to pay their other bills. In such a situation, Rawls proposes that each person set aside for a moment their actual circumstances— how much money they have, whether they own a house, whether they have children, and so on—and deliberate without regard to such

---

44. John Rawls, *A Theory of Justice* (Cambridge, MA: Harvard University Press, 1971), 136–142.

factors. They should try to decide general principles, such as who should have the authority to set tax rates, what criteria they should use, what process there should be for settling disputes, and so on. They should make such deliberations knowing that after they have made a decision, they will find themselves affected in different ways, but not knowing beforehand whether the effect will be positive or negative. Such an approach encourages people to deliberate honestly and thoroughly and to focus more on coming up with a fair process for making a decision rather than just focusing on how the results affect them.

Rawls's approach is significant because it provides a way of thinking about how fairness may be applied to difficult social problems that affect many different people in different ways. Such problems tend to invite a consequentialist approach, which provides a relatively clear step-by-step method for considering possible effects on different groups of people. Kant's theory, by contrast, may be applied in a straightforward fashion to interpersonal conflict but not so easily to large-scale societal issues. It is fairly easy to imagine how I would feel if you did something to me, but to think about how to vote on an issue such as health care, taxes, or military actions proves a much more challenging task. Rawls's approach provides a way to use the idea of fairness to think through such difficult and complex situations.

CONCLUSION

The notion of fairness as a basic way of ethical thinking is common to all cultures and all historical periods. Yet precise expressions of fairness differ, and even within cultures there may be significant disagreements. Fairness seems to be most important when considering how individuals are treated, perhaps because the most intuitive way of thinking about fairness is in terms of the Golden Rule, in which one imaginatively takes the place of another to evaluate whether one is regarding the other as an equal. Such an approach has limitations in circumstances where large numbers of people are affected in disparate ways. It is also difficult to apply the principal of fairness to those who are different from ourselves, such as the unborn, the cognitively impaired, or other species, because they often cannot speak adequately for themselves and tell us how they perceive a situation, how they are feeling. In the absence of such communication, it may be difficult imaginatively to exchange positions with them. That is one reason why a virtues, or "character," approach provides an important complement to fairness. Being fair requires a basic perception of moral equality. Such perception is the result of having developed a certain type of character, as will be discussed in the following chapter.

SUGGESTIONS FOR FURTHER READING ON FAIRNESS

Epictetus. *The Handbook*. Trans. Nicholas P. White. Indianapolis, IN: Hackett, 1983.

A collection of fragments from the teachings of Epictetus, this book is easy to read, provocative, and loaded with useful advice on how to practice self-control. It begins with a distinction between the inner and outer self that persists through the centuries and turns up later as a basis for Protestant ethics and Kant's formulation of the Categorical Imperative.

Kant, Immanuel. *Grounding for the Metaphysics of Morals*. Trans. James W. Ellington. 3rd ed. Indianapolis, IN: Hackett, 1993.

This book is challenging to read, but worth the effort because it is essential for understanding contemporary accounts of deontology. Every serious student of ethics should read this book, especially the first section.

Rawls, John. *A Theory of Justice*. Cambridge, MA: Harvard University Press, 1971.

It would be hard to overestimate the profound effect this book has had on contemporary political and legal philosophy. One should pay particular attention to chapter 1, "Justice as Fairness"; chapter 3, "The Original Position"; and chapter 8, "The Sense of Justice."

Sandel, Michael J. *Justice: What's the Right Thing to Do?* New York: Farrar, Straus, and Giroux, 2009.

This book includes excellent chapters on the ethics of Immanuel Kant and John Rawls (among others) along with engaging and relevant applications to many contemporary issues.

6

CHAPTER

Character

CHARACTER AND THE VIRTUES

WHEN THE ALLIES LIBERATED MAUTHAUSEN, a concentration camp in Austria, on May 6, 1945, Martin Weiss found himself, along with about a half dozen other Jewish survivors of the camp, walking out the gates and down the road, sick, malnourished, without possessions, and with no idea where to go or what to do. They came across an overturned truck and searched it, finding a small tub of lard and an assortment of cow hides. They took the lard to cook with, and they took the hides, thinking they might be able to have some shoes made from the leather. None of them had shoes.

A little farther down the road they saw a farmhouse. They knew that Germans lived inside. They regarded all Germans as Nazis, and they hated the Nazis for what they had done to them and their families. They were ready to kill any German they saw.

They walked up to the farmhouse and knocked on the door. When a woman answered, they asked her for eggs and flour, which she gave them. Then they went to the barn, found a kettle, started a fire, and cooked some dumplings with the lard, eggs, and flour. After they had finished eating, one of the men suggested they should take some of their hides and give them to the woman as payment for the food. Years later, Weiss reflected on that moment: "To this day I have a hard time understanding why we behaved so ethically. I could tell you it was because we were nice guys . . . baloney! We were mad. Yet, without any discussion, we all agreed to do the same thing."[1]

This story illustrates the significance of character. The men didn't believe they owed the German woman anything. In fact, they believed that all Germans owed them a debt greater than could be repaid, and yet, faced with a particular situation in which they had asked for something and received it, they responded the way they had been brought up to respond, by paying the woman for what she had given them.

Character does not conform itself to one's beliefs. It goes deeper than that. Character is formed through repeated actions, often beginning at a very young age, until the behaviors become habits, and the habits shape the way we perceive ourselves and others. Aristotle called character our "second nature." It is not who we are born to be, or even who we wish to be, but who we become over time.

There is a long-standing debate among researchers (including biologists, psychologists, and sociologists) over whether character is shaped more by "nature" (i.e., genetic inheritance) or "nurture" (i.e., environment and upbringing). A great deal of evidence has accumulated over the years to show that both nature and nurture are critical components. Everybody is born with certain dispositions, tendencies to act and respond to situations in certain ways. So there is a sense in which character is grounded in our biological makeup. Yet, perhaps the most significant characteristic shared by all young children is the ability to learn new ways of perceiving, acting, and even feeling. This means that character is always in the process of development, as long, that is, as a person is still learning, finding new ways of acting and interacting with others.

Character is not necessarily good. It consists of virtues, which are positive traits, and vices, which are negative traits. Virtues are regarded as positive because they tend to lead to happiness, at least in the long run. Vices lead to unhappiness in the long run, though they often bring short-term gains. Generosity serves as a good example: giving to others always costs one something immediately, but it brings long-term rewards in the form of gratitude and friendship and a sense of belonging within a community. Greed, on the other

1. Lecture at Viterbo University, March 23, 2010.

hand, may save one from incurring some immediate expenses, but a lifetime of greed leads to unhappiness, due to impoverished relationships with others. One rarely finds an old greedy person who looks back on his life with satisfaction.

Virtue ethics is an approach to thinking about ethical issues from the perspective of character. Instead of simply looking at what a person does (i.e., a person's actions), one considers how he or she does something (i.e., a person's character in acting). This involves looking at how a person perceives a situation, how he or she responds emotionally, and, finally, what the person does. Virtue ethics requires looking at a person's behavior from the "inside" as well as the "outside."

This makes the study of virtue ethics problematic, for one may think one knows what a virtue is, based on descriptions of the virtuous person's actions and yet not really have an understanding of what it is like to see things the way the virtuous person does. Descriptions of virtuous actions get us in the neighborhood, so to speak, of the virtues, but they do not get us in the door. That is why character traits tend to be acquired from people who are close friends, family members, teachers, people one spends time with, talks with, whose inner understanding of events and situations can be at least partially grasped. Sports figures, movie stars, politicians, and other celebrity figures who are often hailed as role models have, in comparison, little effect on the spectator's character, because their inner world is inaccessible.[2]

Partly because of this emphasis on the inside perspective, people often speak of values rather than virtues when talking about character traits. Values are those traits that one believes to be important. The term *value* was imported into ethics fairly recently from the field of economics, and it is a much more limited term than *virtue*. Whereas *value* implies a mental assessment of relative worth, *virtue* refers to a

---

2. Novels also prove to be a significant influence on character development because they often allow the reader to "get inside the head" of the characters and both perceive and emotionally respond to situations in the same way the characters do. For compelling discussions on the significance of literature for moral development, see Wayne C. Booth, *The Company We Keep: An Ethics of Fiction* (Berkeley: University of California Press, 1988), and Martha C. Nussbaum, *Love's Knowledge: Essays on Philosophy and Literature* (New York: Oxford University Press, 1990).

character trait. Many people value courage, yet not everyone is able to face dangerous situations bravely. That is why courage is not a value, but a virtue; it is a way of actually responding to dangerous or fearful situations.

Values language has become popular because most people find it fairly easy to say what they value, that is, what they believe to be important. Unfortunately, people often don't act according to their values. People act according to their virtues and vices—according to the character traits that have become part of who they are through their habits and upbringing. Martin Weiss didn't value the Germans after he was liberated. Still, he acted with justice, despite the injustice done to him, because that is the kind of person he had become.

Virtues and Happiness

If virtues lead to happiness, then figuring out which traits are virtues and which are vices would seem to be fairly easy. However, it is not quite as easy as that. Aristotle said that one should not demand more precision than the subject matter allows.[3] And happiness is one of those subjects that does not allow much precision. We even have trouble defining the word. In Aristotle's time the Greek word for happiness was *eudaimonia*, which meant, literally, having a "good spirit." It is often translated as "blessedness" or "fulfillment" because those words imply a long-lasting or deep-seated condition. The biggest problem with using happiness as a criterion, however, is that most of us don't really know much about what makes us happy, and therefore we aren't very good at answering questions about how happy we are or what would make us happier or less unhappy. In fact, Aristotle said that no one may be considered happy until he is dead.[4] In other words, the relative happiness of a person can be evaluated only by considering the totality of life, not by looking only at moments here and there.

At some level, most people know that happiness is not a superficial condition. It consists of establishing and maintaining deep,

---

3. Aristotle, *Nicomachean Ethics*, 3, trans. Terence Irwin (Indianapolis, IN: Hackett, 1985), [1094b14].

4. Ibid., 1 [1100a5–19].

meaningful relationships with people. People nonetheless also have a tendency to make daily choices that frustrate these attempts to achieve happiness as a lasting, more or less stable condition.

According to Tom Rath, a researcher at the Gallup organization, people who have a "best friend" at work are seven times more likely to express high levels of job satisfaction.[5] Yet, "friendship" rarely even rates among the things that workers seek when choosing employment. When seeking a new job, people tend to look for the sorts of things they want, such as type of work, pay level, benefits, vacation time, location, opportunities for advancement, and so forth. But those things are not nearly as highly correlated with happiness as the quality of one's social relationships.

Not only do people not think about friendship as a key factor in their own satisfaction at work, they tend to discount its value in their personal lives. Daniel Gilbert, a Harvard psychology professor who wrote *Stumbling on Happiness*, says that "social relationships are the single most important ingredient of happiness," and yet when he asked people what they would do if they had to choose between losing their best friend and losing their eyesight, they overwhelmingly said they would prefer to lose their best friend. This is despite the fact that people who are blind tend to be just as happy as people with sight, but people who do not have friends are miserable in comparison to people who have significant friendships.[6]

Virtues lead to happiness because they allow one to have deeper, more meaningful relationships with other people. The generous person, for example, finds joy in sharing with others. The courageous person will not abandon a friend in times of trouble. However, virtues also make one more vulnerable to unhappiness for the very same reason. Only the person who has a deep friendship can experience the sorrow of the loss of a friend. Only a person who cares deeply about something can feel the despair of loss.

The classic Frank Capra film *It's a Wonderful Life* covers the life of George Bailey, depicting him as a virtuous person: he is brave (he saves his brother from drowning in a pond); he is prudent (he saves

---

5. Tom Rath, *Vital Friends: The People You Can't Afford to Live Without* (New York: Gallup Press, 2006), 53.

6. Daniel Gilbert, *Stumbling on Happiness* (New York: Knopf, 2006).

a woman who is issued a wrong prescription by acting on his own and against the advice of adults); he is moderate in his habits (he turns down opportunities for wealth, lives in an old house, and is generous to others). But near the end of the film, George considers taking his life because he despairs: he faces imprisonment because of an apparent misuse of funds at his building and loan company; he thinks his life amounts to nothing. He is saved by the intercession of an angel who gives him a vision of what the community of Bedford Falls would have been like had he never lived. He is also saved by his family and friends, who, in the final scene, come to his aid, assuring him that he is loved and that they will help him out of his financial troubles.

The other principal character in the film is Mr. Potter, a thoroughly bad person. He is greedy, insensitive, and ill-tempered. When things do not go according to his plans, he gets angry and plots revenge. But he never despairs. Only the good person despairs, because he cares deeply; Mr. Potter cannot despair, because he cannot lose anything he really cares about.

Mr. Potter would consider himself happier than George, but when people acquire character traits, their conception of happiness changes. Mr. Potter has become incapable of recognizing true happiness. It always seems like something else to him—foolishness, naiveté, lack of ambition, or, in his own words, "sentimental hogwash."

This peculiar feature of virtues and vices makes virtue ethics problematic: those who possess the virtues know they are virtues. People who have the vices disagree; they tend to think their vices are virtues. Establishing who is right and who is wrong in the debate requires one to focus on the whole of a person's life in relationship to others. Only then can one begin to see how the various character traits both contribute to and shape conceptions of happiness and unhappiness.

Virtues in Context

Perhaps the most challenging thing about studying the virtues is that they cannot be easily and succinctly defined apart from their particular contexts. This makes it hard to precisely enumerate the virtues. Consider the following list: accountability, assertiveness, caring, cleanliness, commitment, compassion, confidence, consideration, contentment, cooperation, courtesy, creativity, dependability, determination, devotion, diligence, discernment, discretion, eloquence, enthusiasm, flexibility, forgiveness, frugality, generosity, gentleness, gratitude, helpfulness, honesty, honor, hospitality, humility, humor, idealism, impartiality, integrity, joy, kindness, loyalty, moderation, open-mindedness, patience, peacefulness, perseverance, reliability, resourcefulness, respect, responsibility, sensitivity, service, simplicity, tact, thankfulness, tolerance, toughness, trustworthiness, truthfulness, understanding, wit, wonder, zeal. Are all of these distinct virtues? It is hard to say. What is the difference, for example, among caring, compassion, helpfulness, and kindness? Does each word denote a separate character trait, or does each simply point to a different aspect of love? Or perhaps they refer to different ways love may be expressed.

Character traits considered essential to living a good life vary in different places and shift over time. For example, in his twenties Benjamin Franklin selected thirteen virtues that he regarded as important for his self-development. He carried a notebook in which he recorded instances when he either lived up to or failed to act according to the thirteen virtues. Among his selected virtues were cleanliness and order, two characteristics that few people would consider today to be among the most important.[7]

In the corporate world today, one of the most highly prized character traits is integrity. Leaders are praised when they exhibit integrity and criticized for lacking it, and yet it is not a virtue that Franklin would have recognized. Although integrity has become recently popular in discussions of ethics and leadership, it usually doesn't refer to anything distinct from more traditional words such as *honesty* or *courage*.[8]

Talking about the virtues becomes even more complicated when referring to different cultures. A character trait such as generosity will

---

7. See Benjamin Franklin, *Autobiography and Other Writings* (New York: Oxford University Press, 2009).

8. *Integrity* often is used simply as a synonym for *honesty* or *courage*, but other times it is used to refer to something like consistency or wholeness of character, in which case it seems to stand in for the notion of virtue as a whole. Thus, when somebody is said to be a "person of integrity," it usually suggests that he or she is somebody one can trust, somebody whose words and actions go together. For a good discussion of this character trait using a wealth of examples, see Stephen L. Carter, *Integrity* (New York: HarperCollins, 1996).

have one meaning in a wealthy society like the United States, where it often refers to people's willingness to share a portion of their abundance. Thus, in America, a person who regularly supports a variety of charitable organizations with a percentage of her disposable income and who spends some time after work or on weekends volunteering at a soup kitchen or at the local library may rightly be considered generous. She is generous because she gives away some of her extra money and time for the benefit of others. Yet in a country where resources are scarce and few people have what would be considered extra money or time, generosity consists of sharing one's necessities. In Senegal, in West Africa, for example, the practice of *teranga* (or "hospitality") requires a willingness to share with others at every opportunity. It requires that one always place people before possessions. Because *teranga* is central to all of the social interactions in the culture, it is not clear that the Western notion of generosity has any equivalent. In a place like Senegal, the willingness to share a portion of one's extra resources but not one's necessities would be considered selfish.[9]

Although there are many virtues, only a few require in-depth consideration, for the virtues are closely related to one another. In the process of examining some virtues, one needs to consider other character traits, as well. We can think of the virtues in terms of families, with the chief virtues as heads of families and other virtues as closer or more distant relations.

THE SEVEN CLASSICAL VIRTUES

The chief virtues in the Western tradition are known as the "classical virtues": the four cardinal virtues of wisdom, courage, temperance, and justice; and the three theological virtues of faith, hope, and love.

The Cardinal Virtues

The cardinal virtues (named after the Latin word *cardes*, or "hinge") have been considered the pivotal characteristics of human flourishing since classical Greece. Plato's *Republic* provides the first thorough

---

9. See Katie Krueger, *Give with Gratitude: Lessons Learned Listening to West Africa* (Madison, WI: Gratice Press, 2009).

The Cardinal Virtues

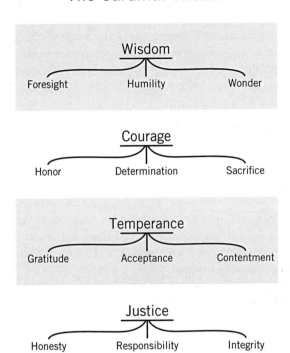

Wisdom
Foresight　Humility　Wonder

Courage
Honor　Determination　Sacrifice

Temperance
Gratitude　Acceptance　Contentment

Justice
Honesty　Responsibility　Integrity

argument for the significance of the four virtues, claiming that justice, both for individuals and societies, proceeds from a harmony of mind, body, and spirit, and that harmony is achieved when each of the three parts of the person achieves excellence in its respective functioning. The excellence (*arête*, or "virtue") of the mind is wisdom, the excellence of the spirit is courage, and the excellence of the body is temperance.

Wisdom

Wisdom consists of the ability to distinguish the true from the false and to make decisions based on what is true.[10] It is often

---

10. The Latin term for wisdom is *prudentia*, which is why this virtue is often translated as "prudence."

considered to be enhanced with age. As one gets older, one accumulates life experiences that allow one to put situations into a richer context. (In fact, the English word *old* derives from a verb meaning "to grow" or "nourish.") Because many decisions are moral decisions, one can see why the ancients considered wisdom the most significant of the four cardinal virtues. Without wisdom, one's actions are "blind"; they have no guidance. All of the other virtues require wisdom to guide action appropriately.

Robert K. Greenleaf, an AT&T executive and founder of the "servant leadership" movement, wrote about "seeing things whole," by which he meant stepping back from the immediacy of a situation and looking at it in its entirety.[11] Some people refer to this as "big picture" thinking, which is another way of referring to the traditional concept of wisdom. Wisdom has as much to do with attitude as with information retention and quickness of wit. Paying attention, questioning oneself and others, seeking advice, thinking thoroughly, persisting when confronted with intellectual difficulties—all of these are part and parcel of wisdom.

Greenleaf tells the story of his father, who was known in his family's community as an expert in the repair of steam engines (this was in the early 1900s). If an engine broke down in one of the factories in the area, Greenleaf's father would be called. One Sunday afternoon he was asked to come out to a large dairy that had recently installed a new pump powered by a steam engine. The operators could not get it to run.

> This pump had a small engine that had come from the factory in a crate and had been connected to the live steam by a local plumber. When the steam was turned on, the engine made no response at all—a curious reaction for a steam engine that would be expected to make some movement, even if it did not work well. I remember Father just standing there and looking at that engine for several minutes . . . , not listening to the chatter of the operators of the dairy. Finally he said, "Unless somebody has invented an

---

11. Robert K. Greenleaf, "Seeing Things Whole," in *Seeker and Servant: Reflections on Religious Leadership*, ed. Anne T. Fraker and Larry C. Spears (San Francisco: Jossey-Bass, 1996), 131.

engine the likes of which I have never seen, this is the first steam engine I ever saw that had a bigger intake than it had exhaust." All that was wrong was that they were putting the live steam into the wrong end of the engine.[12]

As Greenleaf tells the story, his father always approached problems the same way, by first stepping back and observing, taking in all the raw data that his senses could provide before attempting to come up with a solution. This became a habitual practice for him, and he used it not only when repairing machines but also when confronted with political conflict and natural disasters. It was a pattern of thinking that developed over time and became part of his character.

Henry David Thoreau gave expression to the nature of wisdom when he said, "You only need sit still long enough in some attractive spot in the woods that all its inhabitants may exhibit themselves to you by turns."[13] Quieting the mind and paying attention—the practice of contemplation—is not itself wisdom but rather one of the conditions of wisdom. In contemplation, one silences the distractions and tries to seek a harmony of the outward senses (sight, hearing, taste, touch, smell) and the inward senses (cognition, intuition, imagination, common sense, memory) so that what appears (outwardly) is consistent with what one thinks (inwardly).[14] It is a way of removing distraction so that one is able to pay attention.

The ancient Greeks considered wisdom to be the most significant of the four cardinal virtues because it serves as a guide to every other aspect of character. Without wisdom, any trait, such as cleverness, courage, creativity, or determination, may be used for destructive purposes. Wisdom is collaborative; it comes from the ability to listen to other people, to really pay attention, to discern the truth, and then put the truth into action. One test of wisdom is whether one's actions further the common good.

---

12. Robert K. Greenleaf, *My Life with Father* (Indianapolis, IN: Greenleaf Center for Servant Leadership, 1988), 8.

13. Henry David Thoreau, *Walden; or, Life in the Woods* (New York: Library of America, 1985), 505.

14. The idea of inner senses originated in Aristotle (*De Anima*) but can be traced through Augustine and many of the medieval theologians, including Avicenna, Albert the Great, and Thomas Aquinas.

American society tends to value other forms of intelligence more than wisdom. Standardized tests in schools, IQ tests, the ACT, and the SAT, all measure the ability to recall and manipulate information. We tend to lump the different forms of intelligence together (primarily memory and cleverness) and call it "being smart." The odd thing about our society's fascination with "being smart" is that it has relatively little to do with happiness. Good decision making is more important, and that requires long-term thinking, foresight, and the ability to sort through the mass of detail and pay attention to what is really significant. In short, good decision making requires wisdom.

Carol Dweck, a Stanford University psychologist and author of *Mindset: The New Psychology of Success*, has spent a career researching why some people succeed and others fail in a variety of endeavors. She concludes that people are greatly affected by their attitudes about intelligence. People who have what she terms a "fixed mindset" (that is, they think of themselves as consistently smart, or consistently dumb, or somewhere in between) tend to have trouble when they encounter challenging situations, because they don't explore ways of overcoming difficulties. But people who have a "growth mindset," regardless of how smart they think they are, look for ways of acquiring new skills and information that will allow them to succeed.[15]

Wisdom may be thought of as consisting, at least in part, of having a "growth mindset," an attitude that allows one to discover the truth when it seems difficult to obtain. The wise person cares for truth above all else: above power, above recognition, above pleasure. Love of truth is not easy to achieve, however, because the insecurities of the ego constantly interfere. Acknowledging the truth requires one to face criticism, to see oneself as others do and not the way one wants to be seen. For this reason wisdom, although practically oriented, is rooted in the practice of contemplation. It requires being at peace so one can listen to and learn from others.

The vices corresponding to wisdom are ignorance and arrogance. Ignorance proceeds either from a lack of confidence in one's ability to learn or from simple laziness, not bothering to think things through thoroughly or to pay attention to things. Laziness may

---

15. Carol S. Dweck, *Mindset: The New Psychology of Success* (New York: Random House, 2006).

consist of simple inactivity or of staying very busy doing inconsequential things.[16] The person who plays solitaire on her computer all day long may be very busy setting new personal records, and yet the activity doesn't accomplish anything worthwhile. The "busyness" just serves as a way of passing time, of putting off meaningful activity.

Multitasking is a way of engaging in many activities at once that may appear to be productive but is actually a form of laziness leading to ignorance. Multitasking keeps the outward senses aroused but keeps the inward senses functioning at a superficial level, neither requiring nor allowing for sustained attention. Moreover, the more one engages in multitasking, the more distraction itself becomes a habit. Recent research by a group of Stanford psychologists explains why multitasking, ironically, makes one less able to handle multiple tasks effectively:

> Individuals who frequently use multiple media approach fundamental information-processing activities differently than do those who consume multiple media streams much less frequently. . . . HMMs [heavy media multitaskers] have greater difficulty filtering out irrelevant stimuli from their environment . . . , they are less likely to ignore irrelevant representations in memory . . . , and they are less effective in suppressing the activation of irrelevant task sets (task-switching).[17]

The other vice opposed to wisdom is arrogance, which is a refusal to acknowledge one's limitations. The arrogant person refuses to learn new things, either because he doesn't think he needs to or

---

16. See Rebecca Konyndyk DeYoung's *Glittering Vices* (Grand Rapids, MI: Brazos, 2009) for an interesting discussion of sloth and how both laziness and busyness may be symptoms of the same vice.

17. Eyal Ophir, Clifford Nass, and Anthony D. Wagner, "Cognitive Control in Media Multitaskers," *Proceedings of the National Academy of Sciences*, vol. 106, no. 37 (2009): 15585. Other researchers have found that media use enhances some areas of cognitive function while diminishing others. See, for example, Patricia M. Greenfield, "Technology and Informal Education: What Is Taught, What Is Learned," *Science*, vol. 323, no. 5910 (2009): 69–71, in which she argues that visual spatial skills tend to be improved by use of video games, but higher-order cognitive processes, such as mindfulness, reflection, inductive problem solving, critical thinking, and imagination, tend to be diminished.

because he doesn't want others to see him as lacking in some capacity. In a recent HBO documentary, former NFL coach and sports analyst John Madden recalls attending a workshop given by the legendary Green Bay Packers' coach Vince Lombardi. Madden says he attended the workshop but didn't believe he had anything to learn; he already knew everything Lombardi was going to discuss. Then Lombardi proceeded to spend eight hours covering every aspect of one running play, the Packers' "sweep." Madden says he realized then that he didn't really know anything compared to the great coaches like Lombardi.[18]

The well-known Hans Christian Anderson story, "The Emperor's New Clothes," serves as a parable about the mental insecurity that constitutes arrogance and the foolishness that results. An emperor is approached by two con artists, who offer to make him a new suit of clothes. They tell him they will make the clothes from a special cloth that will be invisible to anyone who is either stupid or unfit for their position. The con artists simply pretend to be making the clothes, but because the emperor worries that he might be perceived as stupid or unfit to be emperor, he doesn't admit that he can't see them. Instead he pronounces the clothes the most beautiful he has ever seen. Word passes throughout the kingdom of the new clothes, and when he appears in a parade wearing nothing at all, everyone assures him that his clothes look wonderful, until a child shouts out, "The emperor is naked!" The emperor, when he hears this, realizes it is true, but he can't admit it before the crowd, so he holds his head even higher than before and continues to walk proudly down the street.

The child in the story is not the smartest person in the crowd; he is just a child, not remarkable for cleverness, experience, or social standing. But he has the advantage of trusting his own eyes, because he is not insecure. He has nothing to lose by perceiving (and thinking) for himself and then acting on the basis of what he sees. Though he may not yet have developed the virtue of wisdom, he has the advantage of not yet having developed the vices of ignorance or arrogance either.

---

18. *Lombardi.* First broadcast December 11, 2010 by HBO Sports and NFL Films.

Courage

Of the four cardinal virtues, courage is most readily recognized in contemporary Western societies. That we still employ the concept regularly indicates that it refers to a type of conduct that is widely valued and praised. The term *courage* comes from the Latin word *cor*, or "heart," because the heart was regarded as the seat of the emotions. In times of crisis, the person of courage gathers herself, evaluates the situation, and does what needs to be done. The courageous person is never "faint of heart."

Plato regarded courage as the virtue of the spirited part of the person. He meant "spirited" in the same sense that one speaks of a horse being "spirited" or "lively," of a crowd at a pep rally showing "team spirit," or of a person who feels he can "take on the world" as being in "high spirits."

Aristotle regarded courage as falling somewhere between two vices: cowardice (a deficiency of spirit) and rashness (an excess of spirit). Modern society tends to think of courage mainly in opposition to cowardice, defined as the inability or unwillingness to face danger in times of crisis. But we retain certain expressions of folk wisdom, such as the saying "Fools rush in where angels fear to tread," which

VIRTUES AND THEIR CORRESPONDING VICES

Think of five virtues and list them in the middle column.
For each one try to think of a vice of deficiency and a vice of excess.

VICE OF DEFICIENCY	VIRTUE	VICE OF EXCESS

Does every virtue have two corresponding vices?

acknowledge, at least, Aristotle's view that a rash character who disregards danger altogether is no more praiseworthy than a cowardly one.

Courage is characterized by attention to the task at hand. This explains why people interviewed after performing a heroic action are often reluctant to talk in terms of heroism, instead dwelling on what steps were taken and why they needed to be done. The perception of acting courageously will seem out of place to the person who performed the action.

On January 15, 2009, U.S. Airways Flight 1549 lost both engines when it flew into a flock of birds shortly after takeoff from LaGuardia Airport in New York City. The pilot, Captain Chesley "Sully" Sullenberger, managed to successfully land the 155-passenger jet on the Hudson River, saving the lives of all the passengers and crew. The landing became known as the "Miracle on the Hudson," and Sully was hailed as a hero. When asked afterward about what he was thinking during the crisis, he talked about going through the steps to try to restart the engines, calculating the speed and altitude required to turn back to LaGuardia, then deciding to glide the plane to a landing on the river. He was aware of the urgency, and he said that "the physiological reaction I had to this was strong, and I had to force myself to use my training and force calm on the situation." Yet because he had many years of flight experience and had trained for emergency situations, he was able to focus on the task at hand and not be distracted by fears of what could go wrong.[19]

Training and preparation do not seem to be necessary to act courageously, however. There is story after story of ordinary people acting quickly and decisively in dangerous situations, and nearly all of them reveal the same sort of response. For example, in Florida Chris Locke rescued a sixty-year-old woman who had crashed her car into a neighborhood pool. When he was interviewed about it later, he said simply, "Everything just went right. We just did what we had to do."[20] In a similar incident in Saint Louis, Todd Gilliam

---

19. "Flight 1549: A Routine Takeoff Turns Ugly," *60 Minutes*, July 4, 2009, *http://www.cbsnews.com/stories/2009/02/08/60minutes/main4783580_page3.shtml?tag=contentMain;contentBody*.

20. J. D. Gallop, "Car Smashes Fence, Lands in Satellite Beach Pool," *Florida Today*, December 30, 2010, *http://www.floridatoday.com/article/20101230/NEWS01/12300311/Car-takes-out-fence-plunges-into-pool*.

was driving down the highway when he witnessed a car swerve off the road and into a river. He recalled that his first thought was "I better get in there."[21] Such firsthand accounts of courage are remarkable for their simplicity and directness.

Although we tend to look for courage in stories about people in heroic circumstances—burning buildings, crashing airplanes, battlefields—in fact, courage can be found wherever people face something dangerous and do what should or must be done despite their fears. Because there are many kinds of danger, there are many occasions for courage in one's life. Physical injury is one kind of danger, but loss of work, money, affection, or reputation are also dangers that may require courage to face. A child standing up to a bully at school, an employee reporting an ethics violation at work, a politician taking an unpopular stand on an issue, a friend asking forgiveness for a betrayal: all require varying degrees of courage.

Like all the virtues, courage does not simply consist of a way of acting in response to circumstances; it is a *way of seeing* the circumstances that make extraordinary behavior seem possible and even natural. The courageous person doesn't place herself in danger because she fails to recognize risk. Nor does she face danger because she is overly confident in her own ability to overcome it. The courageous person weighs the danger to self against the greater good to be achieved (or greater harm to be avoided) and acts accordingly. Courage requires knowing what things are worthy of personal sacrifice. In this way, it depends on wisdom.

Temperance

While courage is the most readily recognized of the cardinal virtues in contemporary society, temperance is the least recognized. In fact, few even use the word today, and when they do so, often use it so misleadingly that some philosophers think it better to substitute the term *moderation*. Yet *moderation* is not a satisfactory term either, because it implies something like "half measures" or "holding back." The virtue that the Romans called *temperantia* and the Greeks

---

21. Patrick M. O'Connell, "River Rescue Leaves Lasting Impact," *STLToday*, December 3, 2010, *http://www.stltoday.com/news/local/metro/article_815032b8-cc93-5bbc-9e30-dd04a5b46e0b.html.*

called *sophrosyne* (literally, "sound-mindedness") was a much richer and more positive concept, something along the lines of "harmony of desire." Because no English word succinctly expresses this idea, it is perhaps better to stick with *temperance*.

Although the term may sound strange to contemporary ears, temperance is the virtue concerned with physical desires. Anyone who has ever dieted knows what it is like to want to eat something that one has decided not to eat. You walk past a bowl of potato chips and start to reach out for some. Then you remind yourself, "I can't eat this; I'm on a diet." You draw your hand away and keep going. This is known as willpower. Sometimes you might take a few chips and pop them in your mouth without thinking. They taste so delicious that you say to yourself, "Just a few more won't hurt," and proceed to take a few more handfuls. This is known as weakness of will. Willpower, although closely related to temperance, is not the same thing. Temperance is not the virtue of overcoming one's desires, but the virtue of having well-ordered desires so one doesn't need to overcome them. That is why it is useful to think of temperance as "harmony of desire." The goal consists of having one's desires directed by one's idea of the good—in other words, not to have one's thoughts about what is good struggling against one's thoughts about what is pleasurable.[22]

Three aspects of temperance are especially worth noting. First, temperance is concerned with proper enjoyment of physical pleasure, especially the pleasures involved in satisfying desires for things necessary to survival: food, drink, and sexual intercourse.[23] Second, one can satisfy these desires in many ways that are not necessary for survival—they may, in fact, even be satisfied in ways that become self-destructive. Finally, temperance is closely tied to the notions of freedom and self-control.

---

22. The struggle of the self against the self is a recurrent theme in Christian literature, beginning with the Apostle Paul: "For I do not do the good I want, but the evil I do not want is what I do" (Romans 7:19). Augustine's *Confessions* also contains a famous passage in which he expresses contradictory desires in a prayer: "Grant me chastity and continence, but not yet." Augustine, *Confessions*, Book 5, VII, trans. F. J. Sheed (Indianapolis, IN: Hackett, 1993), 139.

23. All three are necessary for survival of the species; food and drink are necessary for survival of the individual.

Aristotle regarded temperance as the virtue consisting of the proper enjoyment of pleasure—neither overindulging nor being entirely insensible toward things like food, drink, or sex. The temperate person, he said, would enjoy physical activities in the right ways, in the right amounts, and at the right times. Temperance, he insisted, falls somewhere between an excess of desire, which, depending on the type of pleasure, may be called gluttony, lust, or insatiability, and a deficiency of desire, which could be called insensibility or austerity.[24]

Learning to take the proper kind of enjoyment in things requires knowledge of what is good for one in the long run along with the ability to train one's body to enjoy those things that are good. To a certain extent, physical sensations of pain and pleasure provide information about what one needs to stay healthy, but they are not entirely reliable guides. It is possible to enjoy things that are harmful and be pained by things that are good for us. Generally speaking, however, we get thirsty when our bodies need hydration, we get hungry when our bodies need nutrition, we get sleepy when our bodies need rest, and so on. Temperance serves an important function, because our bodies do not say precisely how various desires should be satisfied. If I'm thirsty, what should I drink, and how much, and in what situations? A person needs to know something about what is healthy to answer those questions. Beer might taste great, but if I'm dehydrated, it could make my condition worse. A big piece of cake looks like it will satisfy my hunger, but if I've been lifting weights, my body needs protein, not simple carbohydrates. Our bodies give us a general push in the direction we ought to go, but it also takes good judgment and discipline to develop temperance.

It is also possible for desires to become seriously out of alignment with what is good for us individually and good for others, as well. What we take pleasure or pain in changes as we habituate ourselves to certain kinds of activities, so we may become unable to take pleasure in things in a healthy manner or amount. One who regularly overeats, for example, may become so accustomed to eating large amounts that only overeating is satisfying. This was the case with Philoxenenus of Leucas, a famous glutton of ancient Greece, who is

24. Aristotle discusses temperance in Book VII of *Nicomachean Ethics*, trans. Terence Irwin (Indianapolis, IN: Hackett, 1985).

reported to have wished he had a neck as long as a crane's so that the pleasure of swallowing his food could be prolonged.[25]

The body may also learn to take pleasure in different kinds of sensations that are neither naturally pleasant nor healthy. Few people, for example, like coffee the first time they taste it (unless it is loaded with additives like sugar, cream, or cocoa), and yet millions of people drink coffee daily. I look forward to the first cup of coffee each morning, but there is nothing natural about it. Like millions of other people, I have simply become habituated to the activity of drinking coffee in the morning.[26]

Some activities prove especially harmful because they are addictive. The causes of addiction are multiple and complex, but certain substances stimulate the pleasure centers in the brain so effectively that people quickly habituate to them and find it difficult to experience satisfaction without repeating their exposure. In such cases, whether one is addicted to nicotine, methamphetamine, or alcohol, the person's ability to experience pleasure in healthy sorts of activities is also seriously impaired.

By nurturing the development of temperance, one is more likely to be able to avoid or recover from addictions. That's because once one begins to take genuine pleasure in the sorts of activities that are healthy, the need for other sources of pleasure diminishes. For example, the person who learns to enjoy eating fruits and vegetables as part of a balanced diet is not only less likely to eat junk food, she is less likely to *want* to eat junk food. The same goes for cigarettes, or drugs, or alcohol, or even video games. The catch is that healthy activities are often not as immediately pleasurable as unhealthy activities. Reading a book is not as immediately engaging—it is not as intense or as thrilling—as a good video game. But once one learns to read well, and learns to appreciate the sorts of pleasures that good books offer, one learns that it is often more enjoyable than activities involving fast-paced electronic media. Books engage the imagination more fully, and they often leave one more, rather than less, energized.

---

25. Athenaeus of Naucratis, *The Deipnosophists, or, Banquet of the Learned of Athenæus*, Book 1, ch. 10, trans. C. D. Yonge (London: Bohn, 1854), 9. Available at the University of Wisconsin Digital Collections, *http://digital.library.wisc.edu/1711.dl/Literature.AthV3*.

26. Admittedly, habituation to coffee drinking is complicated, involving the ritual of making coffee, the aroma, the taste, the effect of caffeine, and so forth.

A common misconception is that the temperate person has less freedom than others: he is overly concerned with what he shouldn't do, for example, that he shouldn't do drugs, or shouldn't have sex, or shouldn't drink alcohol, or shouldn't eat junk food. But in fact the opposite is true. The intemperate person is the one who is driven by desires that often threaten to get out of control. But the temperate person can freely choose what pleasures to enjoy; she is not compelled by her own desires to engage in activities her judgment tells her are destructive.

Temperance requires the ability to distinguish between needs and desires, so one doesn't confuse the two. In a capitalistic society, this proves challenging, because the consumption of goods drives the economic engine. It doesn't matter much whether the goods are necessary. What's important is that people keep producing and consuming them. Consider these facts quoted from the Worldwatch Institute:

- The United States, with less than 5 percent of the global population, uses about a quarter of the world's fossil fuel resources—burning up nearly 25 percent of the coal, 26 percent of the oil, and 27 percent of the world's natural gas.

- As of 2003 the United States had more private cars than licensed drivers, and gas-guzzling sport utility vehicles were among the best-selling vehicles.

- New houses in the United States were 38 percent bigger in 2002 than in 1975, despite having fewer people per household on average.

- Calculations show that the planet has available 1.9 hectares of biologically productive land per person to supply resources and absorb wastes—yet the average person on Earth already uses 2.3 hectares' worth. These "ecological footprints" range from the 9.7 hectares claimed by the average American to the 0.47 hectares used by the average Mozambican.

- An estimated 65 percent of U.S. adults are overweight or obese, leading to an annual loss of 300,000 lives and at least $117 billion in health care costs in 1999.[27]

---

27. Worldwatch Institute, "The State of Consumption Today," *http://www.world watch.org/node/810.*

Such statistics about American consumption are often cited as a way of demonstrating the inequality of the distribution of resources in the world, but they prove even more revealing as evidence of pervasive intemperance. As people become more accustomed to warm houses in the winter, cool houses in the summer, traveling on a whim, living in large spaces, eating fresh fruit in the winter, and so on, they become increasingly unable to feel satisfied without such luxuries.

In his well-known sonnet "The World Is Too Much with Us," the English poet William Wordsworth reflected on the intemperance of his age:

> The world is too much with us; late and soon,
> Getting and spending, we lay waste our powers;
> Little we see in Nature that is ours;
> We have given our hearts away, a sordid boon!
> This Sea that bares her bosom to the moon,
> The winds that will be howling at all hours,
> And are up-gathered now like sleeping flowers,
> For this, for everything, we are out of tune;
> It moves us not.—Great God! I'd rather be
> A Pagan suckled in a creed outworn;
> So might I, standing on this pleasant lea,
> Have glimpses that would make me less forlorn;
> Have sight of Proteus rising from the sea;
> Or hear old Triton blow his wreathed horn.[28]

If Wordsworth thought his fellow residents of nineteenth-century England were "out of tune," wasting their powers by "getting and spending," what would he say of Americans today, who typically regard the conspicuous consumption of goods and services as a sign of success? Yet overconsumption, far from leading to happiness, tends to do just the opposite. As one becomes more focused on the effort to satisfy the demands of physical sensation continually, one neglects to attend to those creative and relationship-building activities that alone provide lasting happiness.

---

28. William Wordsworth, *Complete Poetical Works*, *Bartleby.com*, *http://www.bartleby. com/145/ww317.html*.

ARISTOTLE (384–322 BCE)

© Panos Karapanagiotis/Shutterstock

Aristotle

Aristotle's books are so tedious to read that many scholars believe them to be the lecture notes taken by his students. They certainly do not seem like the finished works of a great philosopher. And yet the ideas contained in them, despite their lack of polish, have engaged readers for centuries.

Aristotle was born in Stagira, a city in Macedonia. When he was seventeen years old he traveled to Athens and entered Plato's Academy, where he remained for twenty years, first as a student and then as a teacher.

When Plato died his nephew Speusippus was selected to run the Academy, and Aristotle, most likely disappointed not to have been chosen to lead the school, left Athens to take up his own studies. He began the systematic observation of the natural world, inventing a way of classifying plants and animals according to genus and species. Some of his writings from that period include descriptions of marine animals so detailed that his findings were not be confirmed until centuries later, after the invention of the microscope.

In 343 BCE Phillip II, the ruler of Macedonia, invited Aristotle to serve as tutor to his son Alexander, which he did for three years, forming a close bond with the king and members of the Macedonian court.

Years later he returned to Athens and established his own school, called the Lyceum. His students were much like the research assistants of modern graduate schools, carrying out experiments, documenting results, and holding debates. They were known as the "Peripatetics" for their custom of holding classes while walking about the courtyard of the school.

In 323 BCE Alexander the Great died of a fever while campaigning in Asia, and a series of uprisings took place in cities throughout the Macedonian empire. Aristotle, fearing

Continued

Aristotle *Continued*

that he might be put to death by the Athenians because of his association with Alexander, fled the city. Alluding to the execution of Socrates, Aristotle is reported to have said, "I will not allow the Athenians to wrong philosophy twice." He died a year later of natural causes.

Aristotle's literary production was tremendous, yet he was not nearly as influential as Plato among ancient Greek and Roman philosophers. It wasn't until his writings were rediscovered and translated in the Middle Ages that Aristotle's philosophical influence began to spread. His influence during that time became so great that scholars such as Saint Thomas Aquinas referred to him simply as "the Philosopher."

Justice

The cardinal virtues culminate in justice, which consists of right relations with others. *Right relations* is a broad notion, and that makes justice a difficult virtue to define. But examining how the other three cardinal virtues contribute to justice provides some insight.

In Book II of the *Republic*, Socrates proposes that the best way to discover justice is to look for it in a city, and so he describes a city in which the citizens live a simple life, growing food, making clothes, building houses, raising children, and celebrating moderately. "And so they'll live in peace and good health, and when they die at a ripe old age, they'll bequeath a similar life to their children." But Socrates' conversation partner, Glaucon, objects. Such a city is fit for pigs, he says: "If they aren't to suffer hardship, they should recline on proper couches, dine at a table, and have the delicacies and desserts that people have nowadays." Socrates responds:

> It isn't merely the origin of a city that we're considering, it seems, but the origin of a *luxurious* city. . . . Yet the true city, in my opinion, is the one we've described, the healthy one, as it were. But let's study a city with a fever, if that's what you want. . . . The things I mentioned earlier and the way of life I described won't satisfy some people, it

seems, but couches, tables, and other furniture will have to be added, and of course, all sorts of delicacies, perfumed oils, incense, prostitutes, and pastries. We mustn't provide them only with the necessities we mentioned at first, such as houses, clothes, and shoes, but painting and embroidery must be begun, and gold, ivory, and the like acquired. Isn't that so?[29]

Because all these things have to be added to the city, the city needs more people to provide goods and services and, most importantly, it will need to acquire more land to support itself. "Then we'll have to seize some of our neighbor's land if we're to have enough pasture and ploughland. And won't our neighbors want to seize part of ours as well, if they too have surrendered themselves to the endless acquisition of money and have overstepped the limit of their necessities?"[30]

This conversation illustrates how intemperance leads to the sorts of conflicts that bring the virtue of justice into play. An important aspect of justice is figuring out what belongs to whom, and that is problematic whenever there is not enough—enough land, enough water, enough food, enough gold. If we act intemperately, that is, if we are the sort of people always driven to have more, who cannot impose limits on our desires, then there will never be enough, and conflict is inevitable. The negotiation of conflict (or potential conflict), whether through war, contracts, or bargaining, is the stuff of justice.

Intemperance is not the only vice that leads to injustice. Plato argued that injustice also results when people lack wisdom or courage.

Imagine, for example, an agency dedicated to feeding hungry populations in a foreign country. The agency persuades farmers in that country to plant a new crop with better yields than the crop they currently grow. It turns out, however, that the new crop lacks an essential nutrient that the population in that country depends on and for which they have no other affordable source. The new crop feeds more people, but it leads to widespread illness, something the agency directors did not foresee. The agency did not intend to harm anyone—in fact, it intended to help—but because it acted out

---

29. Plato, *Republic*, trans. G.M.A. Grube, rev. C.D.C. Reeve (Indianapolis, IN: Hackett, 1992), 47–48 [372a–373b].

30. Ibid., 48 [373d].

of ignorance and did not take prudent steps to ensure that the new crop would actually benefit that specific group of people, it ended up harming them.

Another example might be the case of a person working at a waste treatment facility who makes a mistake that releases untreated sewage into a city's drinking water. He knows he should report it, and although too late to fix the mistake, the agency has time to alert the public to boil tap water before drinking or to use bottled water until the water supply is safe again. But he fears losing his job if he tells his supervisor what happened. He thinks of his mortgage, of his kids, of what his wife will say to him. He doesn't think he will be able to find another job that pays as well. So he says nothing at all. Several residents of the city get sick before the contaminated water is discovered. He never intended for anyone to get sick; he just didn't have enough courage to admit his mistake.

In both cases, people take something from others—their health—that they have no right to take. They act unjustly, not because they are bad people, but simply because they happen to lack important virtues essential to being just.

The French philosopher Simone Weil defined justice in this way: "seeing that no harm is done to men."[31] Her definition suggests two things: first, that one should *see*, as in "take care" or "ensure," that no harm is done, a suggestion implying the role of responsibility in justice; second, that one should *see*, as in "perceive" or "take notice of" harms that are done, a suggestion implying an active awareness of the effects of actions upon others.

The just person is one who takes responsibility for her actions
Taking responsibility, while sometimes thought of as the mere willingness to admit to one's faults or misdeeds, is actually much more substantial than that. It implies both knowledge and ability. Knowing the effects of an action and having the ability to change them puts one in a position to take responsibility for those effects. There are limits, of course, to how much responsibility one person can take—limits of time, resources, and energy. But the just person does

---

31. *Simone Weil: An Anthology*, ed. Sian Miles (London: Virago, 1986), 91; quoted in Peter Winch, *Simone Weil: "The Just Balance"* (New York: Cambridge University Press, 1989), 183.

not shirk responsibility. If my neighbor's house is being broken into, and I can prevent it—either by confronting the intruder or calling 9-1-1—then I should do it. It may not be my house, but it is (the just person would say) my responsibility.

The just person is one who sees clearly her relationship to others
What is my relationship to others? How do I know the terms of that relationship? What do I owe my father and mother, my spouse, my children, my pets, my neighbors, my colleagues, my fellow citizens, strangers, birds in the trees, fish in the stream? Answering these questions gets at the heart of justice. Yet, who can answer these questions adequately?

The difficulty of answering such questions is addressed in the parable of the Good Samaritan (Luke 10:25–29):[32]

> Just then a lawyer stood up to test Jesus. "Teacher," he said, "what must I do to inherit eternal life?" He said to him, "What is written in the law? What do you read there?" He answered, "You shall love the Lord your God with all your heart, and with all your soul, and with all your strength, and with all your mind; and your neighbor as yourself." And he said to him, "You have given the right answer; do this, and you will live."
>
> But wanting to justify himself, he asked Jesus, "And who is my neighbor?"

The lawyer asks for a definition. He wants the rule clarified by means of an objective definition of *neighbor*, something that can be understood regardless of one's attitude toward neighbors. Jesus tells a story instead of providing a definition. He does so presumably because a definition of a sort that the lawyer wanted could not be given. To give a definition would make the neighbor into an abstraction, and it would place the listener outside of the relationship to the Samaritan. It would draw our attention away from that which can provide a real understanding of what it means to be a neighbor to someone. Giving a definition would take attention away from the *face* of the neighbor; it would, so to speak, efface the neighbor and

---

32. I am indebted to an article by Peter Winch for the interpretation of this parable. See "Who Is My Neighbour?" in *Trying to Make Sense* (Oxford: Blackwell, 1987).

make a stranger of him.[33] Jesus proceeds to tell the story of the Good Samaritan and then asks: "Which of these three, *do you think* [italics added], was a neighbor to the man who fell into the hands of the robbers?" (Luke 10:36). In this context the question "Who is my neighbor?" becomes "What is it to *see* someone as my neighbor?"

The idea of perceiving the other as neighbor also provides a way of understanding how the virtue of justice is central to understanding certain approaches to environmental ethics. Aldo Leopold, perhaps the most important figure in the modern environmental movement, maintained that human beings will continue to mistreat Earth and its nonhuman inhabitants until people begin to change their perceptions. After a career spent trying to get landowners to improve their soil conservation practices and to get state officials to change their environmental and wildlife regulatory policies, Leopold began to take a different approach. He started writing a series of personal reflections describing his relationship to wild things. The resulting book, *A Sand County Almanac*, was published a year after his death in 1948. In the final essay of the volume, titled "The Land Ethic," he writes: "All ethics so far evolved rest upon a single premise: that the individual is a member of a community of interdependent parts. . . . The land ethic simply enlarges the boundaries of the community to include soils, waters, plants, and animals, or collectively: the land."[34]

The idea that ethics originates in the recognition of membership in a community is significant. One must be willing to enter into the relationship of neighbor to comprehend what it is one owes others. Justice doesn't end with the acknowledgment of others as neighbor, but it certainly begins there. One cannot provide an adequate definition of *right relationship* that fully describes one's obligations to others. However, by entering into meaningful relationships with others, one begins to perceive their significance from the "inside" and thus experiences the change in emotional response and behavior that eventuates in the virtue of justice.

---

33. The notion of the face has rich ethical implications in the writings of the French philosopher Emmanuel Levinas. For a relatively clear and succinct introduction to Levinas's writings on the ethical significance of the face, see Merold Westphal, "Levinas and the Immediacy of the Face," *Faith and Philosophy* 10 (1993): 486–502.

34. Aldo Leopold, *A Sand County Almanac, and Sketches Here and There* (New York: Oxford University Press, 1949), 203–204.

When people refer to injustice, they invariably refer to the vice of deficiency. There are, after all, so many ways in which a person can demonstrate a lack of right relationship to others, whether by violent crime, theft, denial of rights, or disregard. But it is difficult to even imagine an excess of justice. How can one's relationship to others be "too right"?

However, if one thinks of right relationship on the model of neighborliness, one can imagine a situation in which a neighbor is overly considerate, too insistent on being involved in others' affairs. Such a person would fail to appreciate the limits established by other people's autonomy, perhaps out of an overbearing desire to be helpful. Different kinds of relationship, after all, require different degrees of closeness or distance. Justice does not demand the same thing in every relationship. What a person owes a close friend is greater than what one owes an acquaintance or a stranger, but what one owes acquaintances and strangers may still be much greater than one is accustomed to acknowledge.

Because the most frequent cause of unhappiness in life is due to the failure to develop and maintain quality relationships with others, it should be obvious how living a just life leads to happiness. Getting one's relationships with others right means living in harmony with others, understanding one's proper role as parent, child, citizen, neighbor, coworker, teacher, student, or friend. It requires the other cardinal virtues also, because one must be able to maintain good relationships despite the threat of betrayal that can come from danger, of folly that can come from ignorance, or of selfishness that can come from desire. So if justice is thought to be the virtue most essential to happiness, it is partly because the other virtues are already comprehended within it.

THE THEOLOGICAL VIRTUES

The theological virtues first appear together in Saint Paul's First Letter to the Corinthians: "And now faith, hope, and love abide, these three; and the greatest of these is love" (13:13). The theological virtues are characteristics essential to the Christian idea of human flourishing, although they are not exclusively Christian. One finds correlates in all the major religious worldviews, inasmuch as the theological virtues arise out of views about the human relationship to the divine. For example, the notion of faith (*saddhā*) is significant in Buddhism, but functions somewhat differently than faith in the Christian tradition. It refers to an initial willingness to trust in the Buddha's teachings as one sets out on the path toward enlightenment, but it is regarded as instrumental for achieving right understanding, not a component of such understanding itself. Because the different religions originate in different cultural contexts, they each have slightly different definitions of similar virtues, and different stories and examples illustrating what they are and how they may be developed.[35]

The Theological Virtues

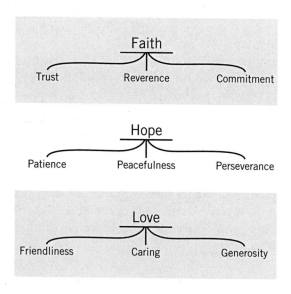

Faith

Trust Reverence Commitment

Hope

Patience Peacefulness Perseverance

Love

Friendliness Caring Generosity

---

35. In the following sections on the theological virtues, most of the illustrations will refer to the Christian tradition, not because it is the only source of the virtues, but because a comprehensive study of the theological virtues in all of the major religious worldviews would require a book length treatment in itself. For the student interested in learning more about the major religious traditions and how they compare to one another, a good place to start is Huston Smith's *The World's Religions* (New York: HarperCollins, 2009).

Faith

Faith is a controversial virtue: first, because it seems irrelevant (and perhaps even irrational) in a modern world characterized by scientific attitudes; second, because the content of faith is closely tied to beliefs of a particular religious viewpoint. So, in a pluralistic, scientific culture, should faith be considered a virtue—or a vice?

The idea that faith primarily consists of holding certain religious beliefs is actually a misleadingly narrow conception of faith. Faith is not simply a matter of belief. Like all the virtues, the test of it lies in a person's actions. Faith implies a trusting relationship, not epistemological certainty. Thus, one does not demonstrate this virtue by the strength of one's beliefs but by the quality of one's actions in relation to another. To have faith in someone entails giving control of one's life (or certain crucial aspects of one's life, say, one's prospects for happiness) over to another. To have faith in someone is to trust the person with something important—an important secret, your life's savings, your prospects for happiness.

Economists speak of the importance of consumer confidence as one of the major indicators of a healthy economy. *Confidence* means, literally, "shared faith." The value of stocks traded on Wall Street is determined more by investor confidence than by analysis of a company's financial prospects. Investing in stock means placing something you value in the hands of others. It is an act of faith.

In the Hebrew and Christian traditions, the paradigmatic story of faith is that of Abraham and Isaac. The story is familiar. Abraham and Sarah cannot conceive. God promises them a child, but the promise is delayed for years. Finally, when they are both in their nineties, they have a son and name him Isaac.

> After these things God tested Abraham. He said to him, "Abraham!" And he said, "Here I am." He said, "Take your son, your only son Isaac, whom you love, and go to the land of Moriah, and offer him there as a burnt offering on one of the mountains that I shall show you." So Abraham rose early in the morning, saddled his donkey, and took two of his young men with him, and his son Isaac; he cut the wood for the burnt offering, and set out and went to the place in the distance that God had shown him. On the third day

Abraham looked up and saw the place far away. Then Abraham said to his young men, "Stay here with the donkey; the boy and I will go over there; we will worship, and then we will come back to you." Abraham took the wood of the burnt offering and laid it on his son Isaac, and he himself carried the fire and the knife. So the two of them walked on together. Isaac said to his father Abraham, "Father!" And he said, "Here I am, my son." He said, "The fire and the wood are here, but where is the lamb for a burnt offering?" Abraham said, "God himself will provide the lamb for a burnt offering, my son." So the two of them walked on together.

When they came to the place that God had shown him, Abraham built an altar there and laid the wood in order. He bound his son Isaac, and laid him on the altar, on top of the wood. Then Abraham reached out his hand and took the knife to kill his son. But the angel of the Lord called to him from heaven, and said, "Abraham, Abraham!" And he said, "Here I am." He said, "Do not lay your hand on the boy or do anything to him; for now I know that you fear God, since you have not withheld your son, your only son, from me." And Abraham looked up and saw a ram, caught in a thicket by its horns. Abraham went and took the ram and offered it up as a burnt offering instead of his son. (Genesis 22:1–13)

This story is emblematic of faith because all meaningful relationships require the willingness to make sacrifices, often of that which we hold most dear. For Abraham and Sarah, Isaac is everything to them, the culmination of everything they have accomplished in their lives and their only connection to the world that will continue after their deaths. Thus, the story illustrates the notion that to have faith in God is to place one's relationship with God before everything else.

Two vices correspond to faith. The vice of excess is gullibility—or being too ready to place control in the hands of another who is not necessarily trustworthy. The vice of deficiency consists of unwillingness to trust, which often takes the form of skepticism. The skeptic refuses to enter into a relationship without having proof that the relationship will turn out well, but that standard of certainty is rarely possible. It is like refusing to invest in the stock market until one knows for sure what the return on the investment will be.

When two people marry, their faithfulness to each other is a matter of trusting each other with their happiness. Betrayal in a marriage relationship is not just the breaking of a promise; it is the refusal of a shared commitment to life together. Such betrayals may take place in a variety of ways, but they all involve some kind of turning away from the spouse, either turning toward another person instead, or turning inward toward oneself.

The *Tragedy of Othello*, by William Shakespeare, gives an example of faithlessness brought about by jealousy.[36] Othello does not betray his wife, Desdemona, by having an affair; he betrays her by suspecting her of loving someone else, his lieutenant Cassio. Instead of trusting Desdemona and turning toward her, his vice consists of skepticism— his unwillingness to surrender his fate to her and his insistence on having proof of her fidelity before he will trust her. By insisting on having proof as a condition of his love, he opens the door to doubt, suspicion, and finally jealousy, which becomes fixed in his mind.

Christians consider faith a virtue, because happiness rests, ultimately, on one's ability to trust God rather than one's own ability, power, wealth, or reputation. One's happiness also rests on one's ability to distinguish the true prophets from the false. This applies not just to religious contexts. Many occasions require faith; they demand that a person know how and when to enter into a trusting relationship with another and give over control of something important. In fact, the virtue of faith functions the same way in both cases, for the ability to distinguish the true prophet from the false prophet is in many respects the same as the ability to distinguish the true friend from the false friend or the loyal business partner from the con artist.

Augustine's *Confessions* may be regarded as the story of learning the virtue of faith. It chronicles, first of all, a series of relationships: genuine friendships, misguided friendships, erotic loves, passions, losses, disappointments, and, eventually, the promise of enduring love. In the middle of the story, Augustine tells of his infatuation

---

36. For an interpretation of *Othello* as a tragedy of skepticism, see Stanley Cavell, "Othello and the Stake of the Other," in *Disowning Knowledge in Six Plays of Shakespeare* (New York: Cambridge University Press, 1987), 125–142.

with the teachings of Manes (the founder of Manichaeism). He studies the writings of Manes for nine years, and he looks forward to meeting Faustus, the famous Bishop of the Manichees, for he has been assured that all of the questions that trouble him will be answered. But when he finally meets Faustus, he is disappointed. He discovers that he likes Faustus for his humility, education, and thoughtfulness, but he cannot maintain the faith he had placed in the Manichees. Augustine says:

> The keenness with which I had studied the writings of Manes was thus somewhat blunted; and I was the more hopeless about their other doctors, now that, upon many matters which troubled me, the famous Faustus had shown so ill. . . . [A]ll my effort and determination to make progress in the sect simply fell away through my coming to know this man.[37]

How do we know when and how to place our faith in someone? There is no rule for that, no foolproof set of guidelines or instructions, just as there are no sure guidelines for how to act courageously, temperately, wisely, or justly. To learn the virtue of faith, the best one can do is to find a faithful person, one neither gullible nor skeptical, who seems to have figured out how to have meaningful, trusting relationships with others, and then try to live in the same way. This usually involves small steps, relying upon others and allowing others to rely upon us in minor matters, until we begin to see a trusting relationship take root.

Hope

Hope is faith directed toward the future. It is confidence that things will turn out well. In the Christian tradition, one's confidence that things will turn out well rests on God's promises and the knowledge that God creates and sustains the universe. In other words, things will turn out well because God is good and all-powerful. However, Christian hope also acknowledges that things may not work out the way individuals would like them to, because desires

---

37. Augustine, *Confessions*, Book 5, VII, trans. F. J. Sheed (Indianapolis, IN: Hackett, 1993), 75.

fluctuate, understanding is partial, and imagination is constricted. But things will work out for good somehow, someway, because God promises they will.[38]

Hope thus depends on humility. One must be aware of one's own shortsightedness and limitations to have hope. Otherwise, one may be optimistic—that is, one may believe things will work out according to plan (that is according to one's wishes and expectations)—but not necessarily hopeful. Hope requires acknowledgment that one's wishes may be frustrated, that one's expectations may turn out to be wrong, and yet that things may work out for the good nonetheless.

The notion that things may turn out well despite the frustration of one's plans is reasonable, especially considering the limited foresight one has of future events. There are few people whose life turns out even remotely similar to their expectations. People sometimes look back after many years to realize that some of their disappointments turned out to be blessings in disguise, but that generally happens only after their expectations have changed.

How this happens can be illustrated by imagining the life of a young woman who has just graduated from a university with a degree in accounting. Sarah has applied for several job openings and has two interviews coming up in the next week. One of the interviews is with a large firm in a city she has visited a couple of times and really likes. She has a friend who lives in that city and thinks it would be great to move to a place where she already knows someone. In addition, the salary is impressive, considerably more than most firms pay for similar entry-level positions. She really wants this job. The other interview is with a much smaller firm in the suburb of a midsized city. She doesn't know anyone who lives in the area, and the pay is reasonable but nothing out of the ordinary. She would take the job if it is the only offer she gets, but she isn't excited about it. As the days go by and the dates for her interviews approach, all she can think about is what her life will be like in the large firm. She pictures herself in the tall, glass-walled building, sitting at her desk, having meetings with her new coworkers. She imagines the apartment she will live in and going out on the weekends with her friend in the city.

---

38. For example, the Apostle Paul writes in Romans 8:28: "We know that all things work together for good for those who love God, who are called according to his purpose." Paul refers to hope frequently in his letters.

She thinks about the car she will be able to buy with the large salary. She pictures herself taking a vacation in the Bahamas. The more she thinks about it, the more real it seems. In fact, she *knows* she is going to get the job; it just feels so right.

A week after the interviews she gets a phone call. The large firm, although impressed by her, had several highly qualified candidates. They are sorry, but they decided to hire someone else. They wish her the best of luck in pursuing her career. Sarah is devastated. Then the other firm calls to offer her a position. Sarah accepts it, but she is not thrilled. It is better than nothing.

Twenty years later Sarah looks back on those days. Now married for fifteen years and with three children, she thinks about how fortunate she was to get rejected by the large accounting firm. The small firm turned out to be better than she expected. She really enjoyed the people she worked with and made some lifelong friends, including her husband. The work she did there, though often boring, helped her gain needed experience to advance in her career. Eventually she and her husband decided to move to a different part of the country, and she found a job in health care administration. She couldn't imagine what her life would be like if she had taken a position with the large accounting firm. It's not that things turned out better than she thought they would; rather, she herself has changed over the years. She now has a different sense of what she wants out of life. She has learned to appreciate things that she neither sought nor anticipated in her earlier life.

The hopeful person takes the long view, recognizing that goodness awaits in the future if one has the persistence to keep moving forward and the patience to wait for its unveiling. That is why hope takes a long time to learn. It is sometimes difficult for young people to be hopeful, because they haven't yet experienced the way life responds to expectations. As Ralph Waldo Emerson (1803–1882) says, "The years teach much which the days never know. The persons who compose our company converse, and come and go, and design and execute many things, and somewhat comes of it all, but an unlooked-for result."[39] The years teach that happiness does not result from the fulfillment of expectations; it comes from the relationships

---

39. Ralph Waldo Emerson, "Experience," in Emerson, *Essays and Lectures* (New York: Library of America, 1983), 483–484.

formed along the way. The virtue of hope is seen most vividly in the lives of those who focus their attention on the quality of their relationships with others and not only on the achievement of their goals.

Yet it is possible to be excessively positive in one's attitude toward the future. Just because one is confident that things will ultimately turn out well does not mean that proper concern about future outcomes is never warranted. The overly positive person is susceptible to the vice of complacency. It is the attitude that no effort is required for things to turn out well. All one has to do is wait. Relax. Take it easy. Don't worry. The Dude, in the Coen brothers film *The Big Lebowski*, is complacency personified. Things happen to him, but he doesn't initiate anything. The Dude never gives up, but he also doesn't really take charge of things. He just goes along as the story of his life unfolds.

Despair is the other vice correlated with hope. It is the attitude that things cannot possibly turn out well. Despair proceeds from a lack of faith, an unwillingness to persist in looking for the good. It comes from a refusal to allow one's well-being to rest upon the goodness of others, instead turning away or turning inward. The voice of despair is cynicism—words that do not invite a response but that shut off the possibility of further conversation.

Love

Love is generally considered the greatest of the theological virtues; here the virtues of faith and hope find their culmination. Even though Aristotle did not consider love a virtue, he did consider *philia* (often translated as "friendship") to be one of the fruits of virtue and an essential component of happiness.

Loves comes in many different forms: sexual love, friendship, love of a child, love of country, love of animals, and love of strangers. What they all have in common is attraction. To love something is to be drawn toward it. Loving a person means wanting to be with him or her. Yet there are many ways of "being with," some that lead to happiness and others that do not.

Contemporary society tends to use the word *love* in two misleading ways. The first is thinking about love as an emotional event. It becomes something that happens, like "falling in love," rather than something one does. Emotional attraction does occur, and for reasons that are only dimly understood. It is through the process of pursuing relationships sparked by emotional attraction that one discovers the potentiality of deep and lasting friendship with other people. But emotional attraction is just the doorway one passes through; it is not the goal. If a person tries to make the feeling of "falling in love" into a permanent condition, he is bound to be disappointed.

The other common error our language can lead to is thinking of love merely as the satisfaction of physical desire—as in "I love chocolate," "I love hanging out at the beach," or "I love this new phone." Such language turns love into a desire for commodities, something that can be purchased and possessed. There is nothing wrong with desiring, for example, a new phone, but thinking of it (or anything that can be possessed) as something one "loves" is problematic. First of all, anything that can be possessed can provide—at most—a temporary spike in the level of pleasure that one experiences, but it doesn't provide true and lasting happiness. Second, and more importantly, the vice of excess in regard to love is to want to turn everything, including other people, into one's possessions. This possessive form of love is also known as narcissism, or self-love. It rejects the mutuality of a healthy loving relationship in favor of a love that excludes the genuine personhood of the other.

The vice of deficiency in regard to love is sometimes thought to be hatred, because if love is attraction, then hatred must be its opposite, namely, rejection. But this is to misunderstand how hatred functions. Genuine hatred always depends on a strong emotional connection. It is actually a form of narcissism, a desire to make the other into something of one's own making, even if that means destroying the other.[40] The vice of deficiency is thus not hatred, but rather neglect or indifference. In the parable of the Good Samaritan, the first two travelers do not fail to love their neighbor because they hate the injured man by the roadside; they simply can't be bothered to help him. He is not worthy of their attention.

Thus, the virtue of love falls somewhere between possessiveness and neglect. It is regarded as the greatest of the theological virtues because it is more directly and intimately tied to happiness than the others.

---

40. See Sigmund Freud on the "narcissism of minor differences," in *Group Psychology and the Analysis of the Ego*, ed. James Strachey (New York: Norton, 1959).

Genuine happiness comes from developing the capacity to have direct concern for the well-being of others. This is love. It is an expansion of the self, so that who I am is not limited by the reach of my arms or the extent of my possessions; it is defined by my attachment to others and my desire for their good. When I love another, I double myself.

Thomas Aquinas noted that the more we enhance our capacity for love, the more we make ourselves susceptible to sorrow. We suffer whenever harm comes to someone we love. When we lose someone we love, we lose a part of ourselves—not the self that we were when we were born, but the greater self that we became when we began to love.

SAINT THOMAS AQUINAS (1225–1274)

Thomas Aquinas

© Scala/ArtResource

Thomas Aquinas was born into the Italian nobility, received his education at a Catholic monastery, and decided at age eighteen to join the Dominican order. His family had different plans and kept him captive for over a year in an effort to change his mind, but he held out until he escaped in 1245 and joined the Dominicans in Paris.

While studying there Thomas was introduced to the recently rediscovered writings of Aristotle by his teacher and mentor Albertus Magnus. He was enamored of the new ideas found in those writings, especially the emphasis on reason and the powers of observation. He spent most of his life studying, translating, and commenting upon Aristotle's work, eventually integrating that work into a complete theological worldview.

The relationship between faith and reason was a controversial topic at the time, and Thomas's contribution to the

Continued

Saint Thomas Aquinas *Continued*

debates was to insist on the ultimate compatibility of faith and reason without subordinating either of them to the other. Faith provides starting points for rational inquiry, which, in turn, reinforces and confirms faith. Such a position placed Thomas at odds both with the Averroists, who argued for the supremacy of reason, and the Augustinians, who argued for the supremacy of faith.

Thomas's writings cover a wide range of theological and philosophical topics, and include a series of detailed commentaries on Aristotle. The *Summa Theologica* is generally considered his greatest and most influential work; a third of it is devoted to ethics.

Thomas stayed in Paris teaching at the university until 1256 when he was called to lecture to the papal curia at several locations in Italy: Anagni, Orvieto, Rome, and finally Viterbo. He returned to Paris in 1268 and then went back to Italy again in 1272 for the final time.

In 1273, while attending mass, he had a mystical vision, after which he put away his pen and refused to write anymore, saying that since the vision everything he had accomplished in his life seemed like "straw." The third part of the *Summa* was never finished.

In 1274 he fell ill while travelling to the Council of Lyon and died at the Cistercian abbey at Fossanova. Just three years after his death, the masters of Paris condemned several of Thomas's theses, but the condemnation was short lived; in 1323 he was canonized a saint. This vacillation between acceptance and rejection of his ideas, both inside and outside the Catholic Church, has been Thomas's legacy ever since.

That is why the Stoics of ancient Rome warned against love. The best way to keep sorrow out of one's life is to avoid emotional attachment, and the Stoics thought it better to avoid suffering than to experience love. But by choosing not to love, one opts for a small and impoverished life. This is perhaps no worse than valuing possessions over relationships or superficial feelings over deep commitment, but certainly it is no better.

Depictions of love in the popular media suggest that love is natural and that we are born with the ability to love others deeply and fully, that it is just a matter of finding the right people to love. But like all of the virtues, love is not completely natural. It is rather "second nature." Although born with the disposition to love, one must learn how to do it well. One must develop, through practice, the ability to love deeply and consistently. This means that one can become better (or worse) at loving. It also means that some people may be unable to love because they have developed character traits that incline their hearts and minds in other directions. Just as some people prove incapable of generosity, courage, or hope because they have become accustomed to greed, cowardice, or despair, so some people are not capable of love, because they have become so habituated to possessiveness or indifference that they no longer recognize the occasions for genuine love.

Hospitality as the Form of the Virtues

Within early Christian communities, the practice of hospitality illustrated the distinctiveness of Christian love; it gave shape to a particular way of life and understanding of the world.[41] Early Christians valued hospitality both because it expressed the love of others as beings created in the image of God and because it was necessary for the development of all the other virtues. Hospitality, in short, was regarded as the *form* of the virtues: each of the virtues comes to fruition in the practice of hospitality, and the practice of hospitality in turn transforms the way in which the virtues are comprehended.[42]

Hospitality consists of a family of practices that opens the door to understanding how the theological virtues of faith, hope, and love, and the cardinal virtues of courage, justice, temperance, and wisdom lead to a life of happiness or fulfillment. It does this by bringing people into relationships with one another in a way that subverts the usual conception of social roles. Hospitality as a practice allows one

---

41. See Amy G. Oden, *And You Welcomed Me: A Sourcebook on Hospitality in Early Christianity* (Nashville: Abingdon, 2001).

42. I would like to thank David Solomon of Notre Dame's Center for Ethics and Culture for suggesting that hospitality could be considered as the form of the virtues.

to experience and thus develop an understanding of the virtues, and, in that way, acquire a conception of happiness rooted in relationship with others.[43]

Taking the virtues seriously gives one a new perspective on the favored values of contemporary society. For example, civility and tolerance are important, and even necessary, traits for a healthy pluralistic society, but they do no more than set minimal standards for social relationships. Hospitality is a more demanding practice because it welcomes a relationship with the whole person, not just an aspect of the person. In doing so, it leads to a transformation of the self. We do not know in advance who is lovable and who is not. Only by seeking relationships with others do we discover the depths of human connectedness. Civility and tolerance express respect for people whose relationships to our own lives are distant and will likely remain so, but hospitality invites strangers into deeper relationship. Said another way: civility and tolerance consist of using words and behaviors to allow people to go their own way; hospitality consists of using words and behaviors to bring oneself and others into relationship *and thus change self and other*. While civility and tolerance respect other peoples' beliefs, hospitality welcomes other people, not just their beliefs. If we tolerate one another, you can go your way and I can go mine; we simply agree not to harm one another. If we show hospitality to one another, we enter into a genuine relationship, and genuine relationships with strangers are risky.[44]

---

43. It is interesting to note that the practice of hospitality is highly valued in many poor countries, but as a society becomes wealthier, people tend to value it less. In the United States, the term *hospitality* is used most often in the hospitality industry, for businesses such as hotels and restaurants. But whereas hospitality is traditionally understood as inviting the guest into one's home, hotels and restaurants allow the needs of visitors to be taken care of without entering into anyone's home. Thus, ironically, the hospitality industry that flourishes in wealthy societies eliminates the need for the practice of hospitality in the way that both requires and helps one to develop the virtues.

44. Portions of this section on hospitality appeared in "Hospitality in the Franciscan Tradition: A Distinctive Ethical Vision and Practice," *The AFCU Journal: A Franciscan Perspective on Higher Education*, vol. 1, no. 1 (2004).

APPLYING THE VIRTUES TO CASES

Thinking about ethics in terms of character complements the other three ways of thinking. It is a different way of looking at things, not really a different method (or theory) of figuring out right and wrong. It provides a way of looking at things that is perhaps more suited to understanding people and situations than solving ethical problems. Thinking in terms of consequences or fairness works well for resolving disputes about what to do in particular cases, because it provides people who may not agree with a common principle to figure out what to do, but character thinking doesn't provide a common principle.

The virtues and the vices are character traits, not principles, and thus they describe ways of seeing things, not ways of solving problems. One can of course propose questions like, "What would the courageous person do in this situation?" or "What would a wise person say about that?" But character thinking really excels in the *prevention* of ethical problems rather than the resolution of them. Character focuses on the development of relationships, and because so many ethical disputes are caused, or at least exacerbated, by poor relationships, good character can prevent situations from arising that could lead to problems. A family, a business, or a community that is concerned about ethics would be well advised to focus first on building a culture of good relationships by focusing on character.

One may of course use character thinking to propose solutions to cases, but its application is not as straightforward as using the other three ways of thinking (truth, consequences, and fairness). For one thing, as already noted, cultural differences affect the determination of which traits are considered virtues and vices. But considerable differences also exist even among individuals within particular cultures. Even when two people agree that honesty, for example, is a virtue, they may have widely divergent views about what constitutes an honest action. That derives in part from the fact that virtues have to be acquired to be acknowledged. In other words, a habitual liar will not recognize honesty as a virtue—or at least not in quite the same way as an honest person will. This has to do with how one learns character traits.

A child brought up in a good household will be taught to tell the truth. She will most likely believe that it is good to tell the truth, but she will not have an understanding of why.[45] If asked to explain why she should tell the truth, she might say something like "because it is wrong to tell lies" or "because my mom told me I should always tell the truth." After a time, if the child becomes accustomed to telling the truth, even in cases where a lie would be more convenient, she will begin to reflect on her experiences. She will notice that people trust her because they know she won't deceive them or betray confidences. She may notice that she does not want to enter into friendships with people who do not tell the truth, because she cannot trust them, and then she may begin to notice that the quality of friendships differs, that those who are honest tend to have deeper, more meaningful relationships with others and that those who are dishonest have more superficial relationships that often end in quarrels and disappointment. She won't notice this all at once, of course, but over the years she will begin to figure such things out so that, by the time she is older, if she is asked why she should tell the truth, she will have a great deal to say about it. And, this is the important point, what she has to say will be much more informed than the person who has grown up to be a habitual liar.

The honest person will have the benefit of being able to compare the life she has, which includes quality, trusting relationships, with an imagined life that does not have such relationships. But the habitual liar cannot adequately compare the life she has with the one she doesn't. She would have to be able to imagine what it is like to have a genuine, deep-seated friendship built on mutual trust, and that is something she has observed only from the outside, as it were; she has no experience of what it is really like to live such a life. So the habitual liar cannot compare the life of honesty to the life of dishonesty; instead she compares the life of lying to a life without lying—that is, she imagines what it would be like to give up all the short-term advantages that come from telling lies. She is likely to come to the conclusion that dishonesty is better than honesty, because the dishonest person can choose when she wants to tell the truth and when she wants to tell a lie, but the honest person always

45. See Miles Burnyeat, "Aristotle on Learning to Be Good," in *Essays on Aristotle's Ethics*, ed. Amelie Oksenberg Rorty (Berkeley: University of California Press, 1980), 69–92.

tells the truth. The dishonest person, she will conclude, has more freedom, more power, more control over her life, than the honest person. That conclusion will be mistaken, but she will have a hard time understanding why.

Applying the virtues to cases can also prove difficult because character traits do not function as reasons for doing something. For example, in deciding to give money to a charity, a person may refer to ways in which it will help others. He is providing a reason for his behavior in term of consequences. But one can also think of such a person as being motivated by love of others. Having the virtue explains why he perceives others as deserving of his compassion; but he himself explains his behavior by using consequentialist reasoning.

Thus, character is not a competing way of thinking about ethics as much as a complementary way of thinking. A person may act courageously ("character") because it is what he would want others to do for him if he were in a similar situation ("fairness"). A person may be described as wise ("character") because she pays careful attention to what is happening in complex situations ("truth"). A person may live a temperate life ("character") because he is concerned about the effects of using too many resources ("consequences").

The story of Andre Trocme, a Protestant pastor in France during World War II, provides a good example. Trocme led the people in the village of Le Chambon in an effort to help thousands of Jews escape Nazi persecution. They offered food, shelter, and medical care, and they falsified documents and escorted the refugees to the Swiss border. Years later, when asked why he risked his life in that way, he replied simply that God commands his followers to help those in need.[46] That, of course, was Trocme's *reason* for acting. He had in mind passages such as Matthew 7:12, which state the basic principle of fairness: "So in everything, do to others as you would have them do to you." That doesn't explain why Trocme felt compelled to pay attention to God's command when so many others in Europe did not. To answer that, one has to look at his character. Philip Hallie, Trocme's biographer, describes an incident that occurred when Andre was young. He and his brother were playing ball one fall day within

---

46. Philip Hallie, *Lest Innocent Blood Be Shed* (New York: Harper and Row, 1979), 160–161.

214 AN ETHICAL LIFE

the walls of the family estate. The gardener had left the gate open, and "a bony, pale man" who was passing by paused at the entrance:

> He looked at the two upper-class boys for what seemed to be a long time, in silence. Then he started shaking his head, and a glance of bitter but detached pity came into his eyes as he said "*Tas de cons*" ("Bastards"). Then he left, closing the postern gate behind him.
>
> For the rest of his life Trocme remembered that *pale voyou* (pale guy), and for the rest of his life he would have to bear the burden of those looks and that judgment. From then on, he knew that *others*, not the "Trocme people" but the poor, the excluded, the bitter ones of the earth were watching him and judging him.[47]

Because character traits consist of how people perceive and respond to situations, they function not as reasons why people act as they do, but rather as explanations of why people find certain kinds of reasons motivating. In short, the just person does not save the life of the refugee simply because it is the just thing to do; rather, she recognizes that she *must* save the refugee's life in those particular circumstances *because* she is just.

Another example of how character is complementary to the other ways of ethical thinking is in cases dealing with those who some consider to be on the periphery of personhood: those who have suffered devastating brain injury and are in a permanent vegetative state, human embryos, those born with Down Syndrome, or those suffering from late stages of dementia. Applying consequentialist or deontological thinking to these issues is often frustrating, because such thinking focuses primarily on the nature of actions rather than the quality of relationships, and these and issues like them require a decision about the moral status of others *before* ethical deliberation begins. (For example, some consequentialists would say that if a human embryo can feel pain, then what one does to it matters; if it cannot feel pain, then what one does to it does not matter. The deontologist says that if an embryo is a person, one must treat it

---

47. Ibid., 50–51.

with respect; if it is not a person, then the category of respect doesn't apply.) But virtue ethics doesn't work in this way.

Such an answer will not satisfy many people; it may seem too arbitrary or too subjective (in other words, too dependent on a particular person's perspective). But such questions are, simply put, very difficult, regardless of which way of thinking we bring to bear. There are different ways of being in right relationship that the just person seeks to discover and live according to. Figuring that out requires examining what becomes of people who see their relationships to others in different ways. What happens to their lives? Do they become better people, happier, more fulfilled? Are they somehow more enriched or else diminished by the character traits developed through their actions?

Several years ago one of my students submitted an essay in which she provided a touching and eloquent testimony to this way of thinking about difficult cases:[48]

> My husband, Brian, was a retired Gunnery Sergeant of the United States Marine Corps. He was a veteran of Desert Storm. Brian had dignity and pride that extended far beyond him; it enhanced and touched the lives of all who knew him. In May of 2002, my husband suffered a massive stroke which left him in a vegetative state.
>
> My husband was referred to by the physicians as he, the patient, or a thirty-eight-year-old white male. They were concerned with the cure. Brian was broken and it was their job to fix him. The doctors had been trained to concentrate on the body, not on the mind or soul.
>
> As the days merged steadily into a fog, Brian lay in the critical care ward, hooked to machines that sustained as well as studied him. I was told to avoid touching him because of the possibility of disconnecting a tube or wire.
>
> One night, a new nurse came on duty. As I was sitting alone in the family room, she came in to speak to me. She sat beside me and held my hand. As she looked me in the

48. I have taken the liberty of changing the names and a few minor details in this story, which is otherwise in the student's own words.

eyes, she said, "Mrs. M, I am so sorry for what has happened to your husband. I hope you don't mind, but I took the liberty of trimming Brian's hair and shaving off his beard. I don't know why, I guess I just know that he always prides himself on his appearance. Knowing that he was a Marine, I understand that he is a very proud and dignified man."

With the nurse's actions and words, I clearly saw the difference between curing and caring. That haircut and shave did not stop the swelling of Brian's brain; nor did it allow him to breathe unassisted. What it did do was allow my husband to retain his pride and dignity during his last days of life. The nurse cared. She saw Brian as a human being, deserving of respect and compassion.

When using virtue ethics to answer ethical questions, the relevant question to ask in a situation such as this is not, "Did the nurse do the right thing?" Rather, the relevant question is, "What kind of a person acts in the way nurse did? Is her way of perceiving patients just? Does she demonstrate an understanding of right relationship to others? Is she the sort of person who finds fulfillment in her work, in her relationships? Is she the sort of person you would want to have as a friend?"

CONCLUSION

Without the virtues, it is impossible to engage successfully in the other ways of thinking. Without a degree of wisdom among disputants, people cannot hope to agree about what the truth is in a particular situation, particularly when the people in question are personally affected in conflicting ways. Without justice, it is difficult to consider the effects of a situation on all people, as consequentialist thinking requires, because the unjust person is not in the habit of fully imagining the real significance of others. Without temperance or courage, it is difficult for a person to perceive what is fair in a situation where strong desires or violent emotions are at work, for thinking about fairness requires a degree of impartiality, which the intemperate or cowardly person may not be able to attain.

Thus, the four ways of thinking are not really separate and competing approaches to solving ethical problems. Rather, they comprise different ways of looking at situations and yet are interdependent, because the virtues underlie them all.

SUGGESTIONS FOR FURTHER READING ON CHARACTER

Aristotle. *Nicomachean Ethics*. Trans. Terence Irwin. Indianapolis, IN: Hackett, 1985.

This is the definitive work on the virtues. It can be difficult to read, but the effort is always repaid by the amount one can learn from Aristotle's close observation of human character. In addition, Aristotle provides a compelling explanation of how the virtues and vices develop through imitation and practice.

Pieper, Josef. *A Brief Reader on the Virtues of the Human Heart*. San Francisco: Ignatius Press, 1991.

This short book is easy to read but not superficial. If contains brief, insightful reflections on the virtues from an author who is steeped in the medieval Catholic tradition.

Plato. *Republic*. Trans. G.M.A. Grube. Rev. C.D.C. Reeve. Indianapolis, IN: Hackett, 1992.

There is much more going on in Plato's *Republic* than just a discussion of the virtues, but that is a key part of the work, and it contains the first articulation of what became known later as the "cardinal virtues." It also explores at length the relationship of character in an individual and character in a society.

Woodruff, Paul. *Reverence: Renewing a Forgotten Virtue*. New York: Oxford University Press, 2001.

Although this book focuses on a single virtue, it also provides one of the best available contemporary explanations of the nature of virtue. Woodruff also demonstrates how relevant classical literature can be in helping one to gain insight into today's issues.

Using the Four-Way Method

SOMETIMES ETHICAL DECISION MAKING is used simply to make up one's mind on a difficult topic. Ethical issues are by their nature difficult to think about clearly, and it is not unusual for one to change one's mind on issues like abortion, stem-cell research, gun control, or capital punishment. Cases where one is personally involved may be even harder to decide, because so much may depend on what one decides to do. Throughout the course of one's life, situations arise requiring decisive action, and sometimes a close friendship is at stake, or personal finances, or even one's career. The Four-Way Method can be a useful process to help a person think through a complex issue or case deliberately rather than impulsively. When making crucial decisions, it is important to know not only what one is doing but why one is doing it.

Personal reflection, however, is not the sole, or even the primary, function of ethical decision making. On some occasions—where one either participates in or leads a group—the aim is to reach consensus or, at least, a peacefully negotiated agreement. On other occasions one may be responsible for communicating a controversial decision to fellow employees, to family, or to the media. Sometimes one must prepare some kind of formal assessment—a report or a recommendation—about what to do in a controversial case or what position to take on an issue. In any of these situations, the Four-Way Method may prove helpful.

GROUP DECISION MAKING

When using the Four-Way Method to discuss a controversial matter in a group setting, it is important to have one person whom all participants trust serve as facilitator. The facilitator makes sure all the participants play by the same rules. He or she will help define the issue under discussion and then lead participants step-by-step through each of the four ways of thinking. The facilitator will have to be able to recognize when one of the participants tries to skip over steps; it will be her task to get everybody back on track. For example, while discussing the consequences of a particular situation, somebody may object that a certain action would be dishonest. The facilitator would then have to say something like, "Please hold that thought. That will be an important part of our discussion when we get to talking about fairness, but right now we are only looking at the consequences of the various solutions." This kind of refereeing will keep everybody using the same kind of reasoning at the same time and also ensure that everybody knows they will get a chance to share their observations and concerns at the appropriate time. The importance of this cannot be emphasized enough. If participants in a group discussion do not trust the facilitator to guide the discussion through each of the four ways of thinking in an orderly and respectful fashion, then the dominant personalities in the group will tend to take over the discussion and attempt to manipulate other members of the group into agreeing with their favored solution.

Sometimes, simply guiding a group through the discussion of a complex problem using the Four-Way Method will result in agreement by the end of the process. This happens most often when it becomes clear that the different ways of thinking all point toward the same solution. Often, however, disagreements about how to resolve the issue will remain, especially when the participants in the discussion have competing personal interests involved in the outcome.

There is no foolproof way of getting everybody to agree on controversial issues. But using the Four-Way Method will at least allow reasonable participants in the process to see clearly where the difficulties lie and often lead to follow-up steps the group can agree on that, if taken, would move them toward agreement. Is there, for example, uncertainty about how the law applies to a situation? Is there disagreement about what the likely effects of a proposed solution would be? Is there an expert or a scientific study that could be consulted to resolve the disagreement about effects?

In many scenarios, disagreements may persist. In such cases the goal is a shared understanding of why a disagreement remains so that participants can see a way forward to eventually reaching agreement. In cases where it is clear that even eventual agreement is unlikely, participants should be able to acknowledge the ethical basis for their opponents' position.

COMMUNICATING

People often do a poor job of communicating controversial decisions to others persuasively because, in part, most people do not like criticism, and communication (especially public communication) frequently invites criticism. People also tend to take positions on issues without thoroughly examining the reasons that might be relevant to the situation at hand. If convinced that the reasons they have for taking the position have ethical merit, they are likely to get defensive when challenged. As discussed in chapter 2, one could have reasons with ethical merit but still be challenged by others who also cite reasons with ethical merit. That happens because there are different kinds of reasons, and sometimes the different ways of thinking can lead to different, and incompatible, conclusions.

When communicating one's reasons for a controversial decision, it is important to address all four types of reasoning, both for one's own sake—to understand clearly the grounds for one's decision—and for the sake of others, so they clearly understand the reasons. If an organization announces a controversial decision and refers to only some of the four ways of ethical reasoning in supporting its position, it will often be criticized on the basis of the types of reasoning it neglected. This does not mean the position was indefensible; rather, the position was not adequately defended by anticipating possible objections.

Consider the example of a government organization that took extraordinary steps to get public input for a major decision, only to invite resistance because the organization failed to take into account the four ways of ethical thinking.

In 2006 the U.S. Fish and Wildlife Service (FWS) announced that it was developing a new environmental management plan (EMP) for the Upper Mississippi Wildlife Refuge, the largest national wildlife refuge in the United States. The plan would create new rules and regulations for recreational use, commercial use, and wildlife management in the refuge. To garner public support, the FWS published a document that addressed the scientific, historical, and political context for the EMP, and it outlined four different proposed plans, each supported by research detailing the positive and negative consequences that the proposed plans would most likely have for taxpayers, refuge users, and wildlife. The document effectively addressed two of the four ways of ethical reasoning—truth and consequences—but nothing in the document addressed either fairness or character.

The FWS then scheduled a series of listening sessions in communities along the upper Mississippi River to answer questions about the proposed plans and gather responses from interested members of the public. The responses would be taken into account before selecting one of the four plans for implementation. The listening sessions turned out to be a public relations disaster. The majority of the people attending the listening sessions shared two chief concerns: they didn't trust the FWS leadership (character), and they didn't think the process for soliciting public input would have any significant influence on which plan was ultimately selected (fairness). In fact, the impressive detail of the document developed by the FWS describing the four proposed plans served to arouse suspicion in the minds of many members of the public. It looked like the FWS had completed its decision-making process and was holding listening sessions just to persuade the public to accept the plan it had already decided was the best one.

In cases such as this, it is easy for an individual or a group to use only one or two ways of ethical reasoning and then in the face of criticism to persist in the preferred way or ways of reasoning without fully appreciating the ethical merit of the criticisms. Thus, in communicating a controversial decision or proposal, it is nearly always a good idea to look not only at whether one is addressing possible objections but whether one is addressing the ways of thinking from which those objections might proceed.

WRITING CASE STUDIES AND ISSUE ANALYSES

Another important consideration in using the Four-Way Method is being clear on whether one is examining a case or an issue. A case refers to an event or situation involving particular people or organizations at a point in time. An issue, by contrast, is more abstract. Capital punishment is an issue. Tom Jones being executed by lethal injection by the state of Tennessee on February 26 is a case.

When analyzing cases it is important to be as specific as possible, particularly in defining whose actions are under consideration. For example, in the Mathy Construction case (presented in chapter 2), many people could have had a significant effect on how things turned out: the voters, the owners of the company, the city council, and the homeowners. Each group had a different role to play in the situation and therefore had a different set of possible actions they could have taken in response to it. If the goal of examining such a case is to recommend a course of action, it is crucial to identify whose actions one has in mind. Otherwise, one's analysis will lack focus, and the recommendation will not be persuasive.

A case study may be based on personal experience, interviews, news reports, or other sources. Whatever the source of information, it is important to discover as much relevant information as possible and leave out the irrelevant. Everything included in a case study should be relevant to consideration of the recommended action. However, it is rarely possible to include all the relevant information. There is nearly always more information that could be gathered—some key eyewitness to events, some expert opinion, some technical analysis—that would be helpful, or even decisive, in reaching a justified conclusion. That is just the way case studies are. They do not include everything, but they should include everything that is reasonably accessible and relevant.

One may think of a case study as a map. A map should be sufficiently detailed to meet one's needs, but not so complicated that one cannot readily figure out where one is and how to get where one wants to go. A completely accurate map would also be completely useless. For one thing, it would be as large as the world, and it would take just as much effort to find your way with the map as without it.[1]

A good case study helps the reader find his way, that is, to think through a situation clearly and coherently. If the case study concerns an ethically controversial situation, it should help the reader know what is happening (or what happened), what kinds of solutions are reasonably possible, what the consequences of various solutions would be, whether the possible solutions would be fair, and whether the possible solutions could be performed with good character.

An issue analysis has a broader focus than a case study. Its aim is not to guide the reader toward a certain action but rather to shape general opinions or attitudes about a topic. More selectivity must be employed in choosing how much information to include in an issue analysis, because the amount of potentially relevant information is generally much greater than with a case study. Thus, an issue analysis could range in length from one page to several thousand pages. It all depends on how in-depth the writer wants to go on the topic. A case study is generally (though not always) shorter.

The following examples demonstrate how to use the Four-Way Method to write an analysis of an issue or a case study. Each example has four parts with a concluding recommendation. Either example could easily be expanded to include more information and to consider a wider range of possibilities.

The first example, a case study of a bear killed by police in a city park, follows the Four-Way Method closely and demonstrates how the method may be used to review a case that has occurred in the past to determine whether the action was ethically justified or whether another course of action would have been preferable. The second example looks at the issue of capital punishment. It also follows the Four-Way Method but uses it as a general framework to develop a short, persuasive essay arguing against capital punishment. (One could, of course, use the Four-Way Method to write an essay in support of capital punishment instead.) The examples are provided here as illustrations in the use of the method, not as the final word on the topics under discussion.

---

1. The idea of a precisely exact map of the world is proposed by the American philosopher Josiah Royce in a supplementary essay to *The World and the Individual* (New York: Macmillan, 1916), 503.

Case Study: The Bear in the Park

Question: Did police officers act appropriately when they shot and killed a black bear in a city park?

Truth

On the morning of June 27, 2009, a three-hundred-pound black bear wandered into Myrick Park in La Crosse, Wisconsin, a city of approximately fifty thousand residents. Visitors to the park notified police, who arrived in squad cars and chased the bear into a section of the park away from the playgrounds. The frightened bear climbed a tree. As a crowd of onlookers gathered to see the bear, police officers consulted with officers from the Wisconsin Department of Natural Resources (DNR). The crowd of onlookers was growing, and many children were present. Many of the people in the crowd did not seem to realize that a wild bear could be dangerous. The police department had no policy for dealing with wild animals in public areas. They examined their options. The nearest tranquilizer gun that could be used on a bear was about three hours away. There was no obvious escape route for the bear to return safely to a wooded area away from people. They decided the best way to ensure public safety would be to shoot the bear. They fired three rounds into the bear and it fell to the ground. A DNR pickup truck removed the dead bear from the park.[2]

Consequences

Among the many possible actions the police officers could have taken, three stand out as most likely, and they were the three actually considered by those at the scene.

1. Use a tranquilizer to subdue the bear and transport it to a remote area.
2. Kill the bear.
3. Allow the bear to leave the park on its own.

2. Anne Jungen, "Bear Shot in Myrick Park," *La Crosse Tribune*, June 28, 2009; Anne Jungen, "DNR Warden Defends Shooting of Bear at Myrick," *La Crosse Tribune*, June 30, 2009; Anne Jungen, "Local Officials Defend Shooting Black Bear in Myrick Park," *La Crosse Tribune*, July 9, 2009.

Each of the three possible solutions could have affected those involved, including the police officers themselves, the DNR officers, the immediate bystanders, residents of the neighborhoods surrounding the park, and the bear.

Option 1 would have positive consequences for everyone if it could be accomplished successfully. However, the nearest tranquilizer gun was in the city of Eau Claire, Wisconsin. No one on the police force was trained in the use of tranquilizers, and the DNR staff had only a few individuals with such training, none of them in the immediate area. If, while waiting for the tranquilizer and trained professional to arrive, the bear climbed down from the tree, it could pose a danger to bystanders. The bear itself would likely survive being tranquilized; however, that could not be guaranteed. There would be a significant risk of injury to the bear from falling out of the tree or from a negative reaction to the tranquilizer. There would be the risk that whatever lured the bear into the city in the first place would lure it there again in the coming months, possibly posing a risk to residents of the surrounding neighborhoods.

Option 2 would best ensure the safety of the immediate bystanders and residents of the neighborhoods surrounding the park. Police were able to position themselves to shoot the bear from an angle that posed no risk to bystanders. However, some visitors to the park were outraged that the bear was killed in front of them, causing emotional trauma to their children. Of course, the bear itself was killed.

Option 3 would be most likely to save the life of the bear; however, it would put the immediate bystanders and the police and DNR officers at most risk of injury. The police officers would have to evacuate the park, posing an inconvenience to the visitors, especially to those who had traveled long distances or planned special events like birthday parties at the park. It is possible that the park would have to be closed for most of the day. It would also require blocking off several streets and notifying residents along those streets to create a safe escape route for the bear. That could incur significant financial cost to the police department and the DNR, especially if the bear did not respond in a predictable fashion. There remained the possibility that the bear would return in the future.

In reviewing the potential consequences for each of the three options, one factor stands out: the only significant and certain negative consequence in any of the three options is to the bear. Other options, especially options 1 and 3, involved risks to people, but those risks could be minimized if proper precautions were taken to evacuate the park and notify residents in the surrounding areas. Everything thus depended on how seriously to take the harm to the bear. If injuring or killing the bear is regarded as a significant negative consequence, then option 3 appears to pose the greatest likelihood of a positive outcome with minimal negative consequence. If injuring or killing the bear is regarded as a negligible consequence, then option 2 would be preferable (with the condition that the park should be evacuated first to keep children from witnessing the shooting). Option 1 is the least advantageous solution, because it alone carries risks to both the bear and the bystanders.

Fairness

Which of the three possible solutions would be most respectful to others? Which of the three solutions treats others as autonomous, that is, as having a right to choose for themselves? For the visitors to the park and the neighboring residents, options 1 and 3 could be done in a way that would be respectful and give them the opportunity to know about and freely respond to the actions. What actually took place—shooting the bear without evacuating the park and without notifying bystanders—was not respectful because it did not allow parents an opportunity to remove their children from the area. Police officers should not have allowed children to witness the shooting of the bear without their parents' consent.

Another way of thinking about this question is to ask, if one of the police officers had been visiting the park with her family, what would she have wanted done? It is most likely that any parent, in such a circumstance, would want the safety of her children to be ensured, even if that meant being inconvenienced by being forced to leave the park. She would also want to be informed about what was taking place, so she could explain what was happening to her children as she saw fit. Again, options 1 and 3 appear to be most respectful.

The remaining question is what would be most respectful toward the bear. It is not clear whether the bear's wishes in this matter should be treated with the same weight as the wishes of the visitors to the park; however, it is inarguable that the three possible solutions have a greater and more lasting effect on the bear than on anyone else. Only option 3 appears to be fair to the bear. The bear had not acted aggressively toward anyone. According to observers, when he first wandered into the city he seemed to be hungry and looking for food; as he entered into the park he was confused and frightened. Option 1 could perhaps save the bear's life, though there would be considerable risk. Option 2 would kill the bear.

Character

Which virtues and vices are relevant to the possible solutions in this case? First, it seems that any of the three solutions requires a degree of courage, especially among the police and DNR officers. Black bears are wild animals and potentially dangerous. Courage is especially required for options 1 and 3, because they pose greater risk. There is the risk of physical harm to bystanders, for one thing, but courage is also required to do what is right in the face of public criticism. In a circumstance such as this, it is important not to let fear of criticism determine the solution, because that makes it more likely that future decisions will also be influenced by fear.

Wisdom is also required in this case. The decision to shoot the bear may reflect the vice of ignorance, especially if taken in response to unfounded concerns about the bear's threat to public safety. It is not clear from reports of the event whether any expert on bear behavior was on hand to give advice about how the bear was likely to respond if the park was evacuated and the bear was given time and space to come down from the tree. DNR officers were present, but not all employees of the DNR have equal amounts of training and expertise in such areas. A wise course of action would have included consulting with an expert in bear behavior to determine whether the bear could be either tranquilized safely or led out of the park without undue risk to the public.

Conclusion

Because public safety was at stake in this case, the way of thinking that seems most relevant is consequences, because it places a heavy emphasis on choosing the solution with the best outcome. But given that all three options could be undertaken in such a way as to ensure a fairly high level of public safety, it seems that the deciding consideration has more to do with fairness and character. That makes option 3 appear to be the best one, provided, of course, that an expert in wild animal behavior is consulted and agrees that allowing the bear to leave the park on its own may be accomplished safely and effectively.

Issue Analysis: Capital Punishment

Question: Is capital punishment ethically permissible?

Truth

The death penalty is a legally recognized form of punishment in thirty-four states of the United States. Its use has increased steadily from 1980 (when zero prisoners were executed) until 1999 (when ninety-eight prisoners were executed). Since 1999 the use has slowly declined. In 2010 forty-six prisoners were executed. As of January 1, 2010, 3,261 prisoners were awaiting execution on death row. Of the inmates on death row, 44 percent were white, 42 percent were black, 12 percent were Hispanic, and 2 percent were of other races. Since 1973, 138 prisoners have been released from death row after having been found innocent of the crimes for which they were originally sentenced. All thirty-four states use lethal injection as the primary method of execution, though some states still allow the use of other forms of execution as an alternative, including electrocution, gas chamber, and hanging. The most common alternative to punishing serious crimes is life imprisonment without the possibility of parole.[3]

Consequences

Two arguments are commonly cited for using capital punishment rather than the alternative of life imprisonment without the possibility of parole: the comparative financial costs of the two forms of punishment and the deterrent effect of the death penalty.

---

3. Statistics in this section were compiled from the Death Penalty Information Center, *http://www.deathpenaltyinfo.org.*

Despite widespread popular belief that the death penalty is less expensive than life imprisonment, in fact, the death penalty costs more, sometimes much more, than life in prison. A recent study in the state of Washington found that death penalty cases cost an average of $600,000 more per case than trying similar crimes as non-capital cases.[4] In 2010 the Legislative Services Agency in the state of Indiana compared the cost of capital cases to the cost of life-without-parole cases. The former averaged $449,887; the latter averaged $42,658.[5] In 2008 the state of California issued a report estimating current costs of implementing the death penalty at $137 million per year while changing to a maximum penalty of lifetime incarceration instead of the death penalty would cost $11.5 million annually.[6]

Since 1976, when the U.S. Supreme Court upheld the constitutionality of capital punishment in *Gregg v. Georgia*, numerous studies have been conducted on the possible deterrent effect of the death penalty, but the results are uncertain. Individual studies appear to contradict one another. A thorough review of such studies by John J. Donahue and Justin Wolfers in 2005 concludes that "our key insight is that the death penalty . . . is applied so rarely that the number of homicides it can plausibly have caused or deterred cannot be reliably disentangled from the large year-to-year changes in the homicide rate caused by other factors."[7] Since no convincing evidence exists that the death penalty has a deterrent effect, one cannot reasonably defend the practice on that basis.

Thus, in comparing the costs and benefits of the two forms of punishment, life imprisonment costs less and has not been shown to have any less deterrent effect than the death penalty.

---

4. "Final Report of the Death Penalty Subcommittee of the Committee on Public Defense," Washington State Bar Association, December 2006, *http://ulv.web.officelive.com/Documents/dpxWash.pdf.*

5. "The Cost of Seeking the Death Penalty in Indiana," July 1, 2010, a report by the Indiana Legislative Services Agency, *http://www.in.gov/ipdc/general/DP-COST.pdf.*

6. "Report and Recommendations on the Administration of the Death Penalty in California," California Commission on the Fair Administration of Justice, June 30, 2008, *http://www.ccfaj.org/documents/reports/dp/official/FINAL%20REPORT%20DEATH%20PENALTY.pdf.*

7. John J. Donahue and Justin Wolfers "Uses and Abuses of Empirical Evidence in the Death Penalty Debate," *Stanford Law Review*, vol. 58, no. 3 (2005).

Fairness

In the United States, approximately 2 percent of convicted murderers are sentenced to death, but the nature of the crime committed is not the only factor determining who receives the death penalty. One charge that gets raised repeatedly is that systematic racism in the criminal justice system prevents capital punishment from being implemented fairly. And, in fact, several studies over the years have demonstrated that those who kill a white person are more likely to be executed than those who kill people of other races.[8] Another concern about fairness is that so many people who end up on death row are poor and have subsequently received incompetent legal representation. In 2001 Supreme Court Justice Ruth Bader Ginsburg observed: "I have yet to see a death case among the dozens coming to the Supreme Court on eve-of-execution stay applications in which the defendant was well represented at trial."[9]

Even a cursory glance at the evidence reveals that, whatever the merits of the death penalty, it is being implemented arbitrarily. Perhaps steps could be made at the state level to address that unfairness, but it would require a systematic effort to greatly reduce the institutionalized racism in the criminal justice system and a major investment in resources for public defenders.

Character

What happens to the character of people who witness and carry out the executions? It is interesting to note that at one time executions were done in the public square, but there was a significant moral reaction to such events becoming spectacles. Today executions are carried out behind closed and locked doors and at times deliberately chosen to reduce public visibility. But if executions are carried out

8. Raymond Paternoster, Robert Brame, et al., "An Empirical Analysis of Maryland's Death Sentencing System with Respect to the Influence of Race and Legal Jurisdiction," *http://www.newsdesk.umd.edu/pdf/finalrep.pdf*; Michael L. Radelet and Glenn L. Pierce, "Race and Death Sentencing in North Carolina: 1980–2007," *North Carolina Law Review*, vol. 89, no. 6 (2011).

9. Ruth Bader Ginsberg, "In Pursuit of the Public Good: Lawyers Who Care," University of the District of Columbia, David A. Clarke School of Law, Joseph L. Rauh Lecture, April 9, 2001, *http://www.supremecourt.gov/publicinfo/speeches/viewspeeches. aspx?Filename=sp_04-09-01a.html*.

behind closed doors because the emotions they arouse are shameful, or the effects on witnesses are detrimental, then shouldn't we be concerned about those whose job it is to carry out the executions?[10]

An additional character concern is the motivation for capital punishment. Some people of course are sincerely concerned to see justice done, and are convinced that capital punishment is the only punishment appropriate to certain kinds of violent crimes. However, it is also evident that many people support capital punishment out of a desire for vengeance. That is understandable. Anyone who imagines himself in the position of the victim's family would want to see the perpetrator punished severely. But the state is not a person. The obligation of the state is not to see that vengeance is satisfied but that justice is carried out. It has to ensure that both the investigation and the prosecution of a crime are conducted dispassionately, reliably, and fairly. The state has no business pursuing vengeance, and when it allows itself to become the agent of vengeance it loses its integrity.

Conclusion

Capital punishment is widely used in the United States, and yet it bears considerable financial costs to taxpayers without offering any benefit in terms of increased public safety. In addition, the application of the death penalty is at best arbitrary and at worst racist; either one violates the basic principle of fairness to which the criminal justice system ought to be committed. Finally, capital punishment is motivated at least in part by the desire for vengeance, a sentiment that is understandable yet incompatible with the integrity citizens expect of their government.

FINAL REMARKS

The Four-Way Method is not a foolproof method for determining what is right and what is wrong. There is no such method. Like any tool, the Four-Way Method can be used well or it can be used poorly.

---

10. For an insight into this question see "Witness to an Execution: A Day in the Life of a Death Row Employee," National Public Radio, *http://www.npr.org/ programs/atc/witness/*.

Used well, it can serve to make one's reasoning clearer, more coherent, and more engaging than it might otherwise be. Used to facilitate group discussion, it may help people better appreciate one another's points of view, especially in cases of serious disagreement. At the very least, it provides people with a common framework for discussing ethical problems, and well-intentioned, civil discussion is at the heart of an ethical life.

Recommended Reading

Anscombe, G.E.M. "Mr. Truman's Degree." In *The Collected Philosophical Papers of G.E.M. Anscombe*. Vol. III, *Ethics, Religion and Politics*. Oxford: Blackwell, 1981.

Aquinas, Thomas. *Treatise on the Virtues*. Translated by John A. Oesterle. Notre Dame, IN: Notre Dame University Press, 1984.

Arendt, Hannah. *Eichmann in Jerusalem: A Report on the Banality of Evil*. New York: Penguin, 1963.

Aristotle. *Nicomachean Ethics*. Translated by Terence Irwin. Indianapolis, IN: Hackett, 1985.

Augustine. *Confessions*. Translated by F. J. Sheed. Indianapolis, IN: Hackett, 1993.

Austen, Jane. *Pride and Prejudice*. In *The Complete Novels*. New York: Penguin Classics, 2006.

Bennett, Jonathan. "The Conscience of Huckleberry Finn." *Philosophy* 49 (1974): 123–134.

Bentham, Jeremy. *The Principles of Morals and Legislation*. Amherst, NY: Prometheus Books, 1988.

Booth, Wayne C. *The Company We Keep: An Ethics of Fiction*. Berkeley: University of California Press, 1988.

Brandt, Richard. *Hopi Ethics: A Theoretical Analysis*. Chicago: University of Chicago Press, 1974.

Burnyeat, Miles. "Aristotle on Learning to Be Good." In *Essays on Aristotle's Ethics*, edited by Amelie Oksenberg Rorty. Berkeley: University of California Press, 1980.

Carson, Thomas L. "Lying, Deception, and Related Concepts." In *The Philosophy of Deception*, edited by Clancy Martin. New York: Oxford University Press, 2009.

Cavell, Stanley. "Othello and the Stake of the Other." In *Disowning Knowledge in Six Plays of Shakespeare*. New York: Cambridge University Press, 1987.

Chesterton, G. K. "The Ethics of Elfland." In *Orthodoxy*. Grand Rapids, MI: Christian Classics Ethereal Library, 2011.

Confucius. *Analects.* Translated by Edward Slingerland. Indianapolis, IN: Hackett, 2003.

Dawkins, Richard. *The God Delusion.* Boston: Houghton Mifflin, 2006.

de Tocqueville, Alexis. *Democracy in America.* Translated by Arthur Goldhammer. New York: Library of America, 2004.

DeYoung, Rebecca Konyndyk. *Glittering Vices.* Grand Rapids, MI: Brazos, 2009.

Dweck, Carol S. *Mindset: The New Psychology of Success.* New York: Random House, 2006.

Echo-Hawk, Walter R. *In the Courts of the Conqueror.* Golden, CO: Fulcrum, 2010.

Emerson, Ralph Waldo. *Essays and Lectures.* New York: Library of America, 1983.

Epictetus. *The Handbook.* Translated by Nicholas P. White. Indianapolis, IN: Hackett, 1983.

Fontenrose, Joseph. *Delphic Oracle: Its Responses and Operations, with a Catalogue of Responses.* Berkeley: University of California Press, 1978.

Foot, Philippa. *Virtues and Vices.* London: Blackwell, 1978.

Forster, E. M. *A Passage to India.* New York: Harcourt, 1942.

Franklin, Benjamin. *Autobiography and Other Writings.* New York: Oxford University Press, 2009.

Freud, Sigmund. *Group Psychology and the Analysis of the Ego.* Edited by James Strachey. New York: Norton, 1959.

Gawande, Atul. *The Checklist Manifesto.* New York: Metropolitan Books, 2009.

Gilbert, Daniel. *Stumbling on Happiness.* New York: Random House, 2006.

Greenfield, Patricia M. "Technology and Informal Education: What Is Taught, What Is Learned." *Science.* Vol. 323, no. 5910 (2009): 69–71.

Greenleaf, Robert K. *My Life with Father.* Indianapolis, IN: Greenleaf Center for Servant Leadership, 1988.

———. "Seeing Things Whole." In *Seeker and Servant: Reflections on Religious Leadership*, edited by Anne T. Fraker and Larry C. Spears. San Francisco: Jossey-Bass, 1996.

Gruenfeld, Deborah H., M. Ena Inesi, Joe C. Magee, and Adam D. Galinsky. "Power and the Objectification of Social Targets." *Journal of Personality and Social Psychology.* Vol. 95, no. 1 (2008): 111–127.

———. "Power and Perspectives Not Taken." *Psychological Science.* Vol 17, no. 12 (2009): 1068–1074.

Hallie, Philip. *Lest Innocent Blood Be Shed.* New York: Harper and Row, 1979.

Hare, John. *Why Bother Being Good? The Place of God in the Moral Life.* Downers Grove, IL: InterVarsity Press, 2002.

Hearne, Vicki. *Animal Happiness: A Moving Exploration of Animals and Their Emotions.* New York: Skyhorse, 1994.

Hellwig, Monika K. *Public Dimensions of a Believer's Life: Rediscovering the Cardinal Virtues.* Lanham, MD: Rowman & Littlefield, 2005.

Herodotus. *The Histories.* Translated by Andrea L. Purvis. In *The Landmark Herodotus,* edited by Robert B. Strassler. New York: Anchor Books, 2007.

Hitchens, Christopher. *God Is Not Great: How Religion Poisons Everything.* New York: Twelve Books, 2007.

Hobbes, Thomas. *Leviathan.* Indianapolis, IN: Bobbs-Merrill, 1958.

Homer. *The Iliad of Homer.* Translated by Richmond Lattimore. Chicago: University of Chicago Press, 1951.

James, William. *The Principles of Psychology.* Vol. 1. New York: Holt, 1890.

John Paul II. *On the Hundredth Anniversary of Rerum Novarum* [*Centesimus Annus*]. 1991. Available online at *http://www.vatican.va/holy_father/john_paul_ii/encyclicals/documents/hf_jp-ii_enc_01051991_centesimus-annus_en.html.*

Jones, James. *Bad Blood: The Tuskegee Syphilis Experiment: A Tragedy of Race and Medicine.* New York: The Free Press, 1981.

Jonsen, Albert R., Mark Siegler, and William J. Winslade. *Clinical Ethics,* 5th ed. New York: McGraw-Hill, 2002.

Kant, Immanuel. *Grounding for the Metaphysics of Morals.* Translated by James W. Ellington. 3rd ed. Indianapolis, IN: Hackett, 1993.

Kohlberg, Lawrence. *Essays on Moral Development.* Vol. 1: *The Philosophy of Moral Development.* San Francisco: Harper and Row, 1981.

Krueger, Katie. *Give with Gratitude: Lessons Learned Listening to West Africa.* Madison, WI: Gratice Press, 2009.

Leopold, Aldo. *A Sand County Almanac, and Sketches Here and There.* New York: Oxford University Press, 1949.

Lipstadt, Deborah E. *Denying the Holocaust: The Growing Assault on Truth and Memory.* New York: Macmillan, 1995.

Louv, Richard. *Last Child in the Woods: Saving Our Children from Nature-deficit Disorder.* Chapel Hill, NC: Algonquin Books of Chapel Hill, 2008.

Machiavelli, Niccolò. *The Chief Works and Others.* Translated by Allan Gilbert. Durham, NC: Duke University Press, 1965.

MacIntyre, Alasdair. *A Short History of Ethics.* New York: Macmillan, 1966.

———. *After Virtue.* Notre Dame, IN: Notre Dame University Press, 1981.

Marcus Aurelius. *Meditations.* Translated by G.M.A. Grube. Indianapolis: Hackett, 1983.

Milgram, Stanley. *Obedience to Authority: An Experimental View.* New York: HarperCollins, 1974.

Mill, John Stuart. *Utilitarianism.* 2nd ed. Indianapolis, IN: Hackett, 2002.

Nagel, Thomas. "What Is It Like to Be a Bat?" In *Mortal Questions.* New York: Cambridge University Press, 1979.

Nell, Onora. *Acting on Principle: An Essay on Kantian Ethics.* New York: Columbia University Press, 1975.

Nickerson, Raymond S. "Confirmation Bias: A Ubiquitous Phenomenon in *Many Guises.*" *Review of General Psychology. Vol. 2, no. 2 (1998): 175–220.*

Nussbaum, Martha C. *Love's Knowledge: Essays on Philosophy and Literature.* New York: Oxford University Press, 1990.

Oden, Amy G. *And You Welcomed Me: A Sourcebook on Hospitality in Early Christianity.* Nashville: Abingdon, 2001.

Ophir, Eyal, Clifford Nass, and Anthony D. Wagner. "Cognitive Control in Media Multitaskers." *Proceedings of the National Academy of Sciences.* Vol. 106, no. 37 (2009): 15583–15587.

Piaget, Jean. *The Moral Judgment of the Child.* New York: The Free Press, 1965.

Pieper, Josef. *The Four Cardinal Virtues.* Notre Dame, IN: Notre Dame University Press, 1966.

———. *A Brief Reader on the Virtues of the Human Heart.* San Francisco: Ignatius Press, 1991.

Plato. *Apology.* In *The Trial and Death of Socrates.* Translated by G.M.A. Grube. Indianapolis, IN: Hackett, 1975.

———. *Euthyphro.* In *The Trial and Death of Socrates.* Translated by G.M.A. Grube. Indianapolis, IN: Hackett, 1975.

———. *Republic.* Translated by G.M.A. Grube. Rev. C.D.C. Reeve. Indianapolis, IN: Hackett, 1992.

Rawls, John. *A Theory of Justice.* Cambridge, MA: Harvard University Press, 1971.

Richardson, Robert D. *First We Read, Then We Write: Emerson on the Creative Process.* Iowa City: University of Iowa Press, 2009.

Royce, Josiah. *The World and the Individual.* New York: Macmillan, 1916.

Sandel, Michael J. *Justice: What's the Right Thing to Do?* New York: Farrar, Straus, and Giroux, 2009.

Scarre, Geoffrey. *On Courage.* New York: Routledge, 2010.

Schmitt, Hans A. *Quakers* and *Nazis: Inner Light in Outer Darkness.* Columbia: University of Missouri Press, 1997.

Scully, Matthew. *Dominion: The Power of Man, the Suffering of Animals, and the Call to Mercy.* New York: St. Martin's Press, 2002.

Sherman, Nancy. *The Fabric of Character: Aristotle's Theory of Virtue.* Oxford: Clarendon Press, 1989.

Singer, Peter. *Practical Ethics.* 2nd ed. New York: Cambridge University Press, 1993.

Sinnott-Armstrong, Walter. *Morality without God.* New York: Oxford University Press, 2009.

Thoreau, Henry David. *Walden; or, Life in the Woods.* New York: Library of America, 1985.

Thucydides. *On Justice, Power and Human Nature: Selections from the History of the Peloponnesian War.* Translated by Paul Woodruff. Indianapolis, IN: Hackett, 1993.

Twain, Mark. *The Adventures of Huckleberry Finn.* Edited by Sculley Bradley, Richmond Croom Beatty, E. Hudson Long, and Thomas Cooley. 2nd ed. New York: W. W. Norton, 1977.

———. *Life on the Mississippi.* New York: Library of America, 1982.

Wattles, Jeffrey. *The Golden Rule.* New York: Oxford University Press, 1996.

Wegner, Gregory P. *Anti-Semitism and Schooling under the Third Reich.* New York: Routledge, 2002.

Weil, Simone. *The Iliad, or The Poem of Force.* Wallingford, PA: Pendle Hill, 1956.

———. Miles, Sian, ed. *Simone Weil: An Anthology.* Edited by Sian Miles. London: Virago, 1986.

Winch, Peter. "Who Is My Neighbour?" In *Trying to Make Sense.* Oxford: Blackwell, 1987.

———. *Simone Weil: "The Just Balance."* New York: Cambridge University Press, 1989.

Wood, Denis, and Robert J. Beck. *Home Rules.* Baltimore: Johns Hopkins University Press, 1994.

Woodruff, Paul. *Reverence: Renewing a Forgotten Virtue.* New York: Oxford University Press, 2001.

Index

lying, 21
Lying, Deception, and Related
    Concepts, 22n4

M

Machiavelli, Niccolò, 141n19–42
Magee, Joe C., 86n17
Mahabharata, 135n1
Malvern, Jack, 90n23
Mamet, David, 159n
Mandela, Nelson, 40
manipulation, 154, 157–60, 162, 165
Marlock, Dennis, 89
Marshall, John, Chief Justice, 124
Martin, Clancy, 22
mass murder, 132
Master of Deception, 89n
Mathy Construction, 61–62, 223
McAlpine, Linda, 64n
McPhee, S.J., 90n24
Melians, 138–40
Melos, 138–39
meta-analysis, 102
might makes right, 39
Milgram Experiments, 164
    significance of, 165
Milgram, Stanley, 164n–65
Mill, James, 113
Mill, John Stuart, 112–14
Miller, D.T., 90n25
*Mindset: The New Psychology of
    Success*, 180n
Minneapolis Star Tribune, 161n
Miracle on the Hudson, 184
misconceptions
    about ethics, 50
    common, 15
misperception
    of social norms, 91
moderation, 185
moral absolute, 25
Moral Judgment of the Child, The, 13n

moral responsibility, 79
Moral Responsibility (chart), 75–76
morality, 16
Morality without God, 45n24
mores, 16
Morning Edition, 83n12
Mortal Questions, 153n
Mr. Truman's Degree, 132n29
MSN Money, 120n11
Mueller, Robert, 80n
Mufson, Steve, 77n
multitasking, 181
My Life with Father, 179n12
Myrick Park, 225
mythology, Greek, 28

N

Nagasaki, 132
Nagel, Thomas, 153n
narcissism, 206
Nass, Clifford, 181n17
Nathan, 85
National Aeronautics and Space
    Administration, 78n8
National Enquirer, The, 96n
National Public Radio,
    82–83n12n13, 232n
National Social Norms Institute, 91n
nature, 170
    essential, 146
Nature, 102n37
Nazis, 123–24
New Stadium, The (chart), 109–10
New York Times, The, 96, 97n33,
    139n17
Newton, Sir Isaac, 113
Nickerson, Raymond S., 87n18n19
Nicomachean Ethics, 50, 172n3, 187n
Nixon, Richard, President, 139
nonmaleficence, 54
norms, cultural, 39
North Carolina Law Review, 231n8